More praise for Benjamin Franklin

"For an introduction to the mind of Franklin—one of the most inquisitive, productive, and engaging minds of his or any other day—readers can't do better than this incisive volume." H. W. BRANDS, *Los Angeles Times Book Review*

"This wonderful biography of an extraordinary man results from a perfect marriage of subject and scholar. . . . Morgan proves himself still at the height of his powers. . . . The author probably comes as close to understanding him as anyone can. . . . It's hard to imagine a better life study of a man we've all heard about but who is barely known." *Publishers Weekly*

"So much has been written about Benjamin Franklin in the 212 years since his death that you might imagine there's nothing left to say. But there always is. Now comes another biography of the man, a fairly short one, and in my opinion it's one of the best." MAX HALL, *Boston Globe*

"The distinguished historian Edmund S. Morgan . . . distill[s] the singularly eventful life of . . . Franklin . . . [to] give the great man, in every important sense, his due. . . . Morgan carefully documents and elucidates with scarcely a wasted word." JONATHAN YARDLEY, *Washington Post Book World*

"Morgan's concise biography reminds us of who [Franklin] was and—importantly—who he wasn't. . . . Morgan's book . . . is a quiet, wise and revealing perspective on that man many of us thought we knew well." WILLIAM W. STARR, *The State* (Columbia, S.C.)

"A superb introduction to Franklin's wide-ranging intellect, shrewdness, common-sense, good will, and his 'innate affinity for people of all kinds.'" WILLIAM F. GAVIN, *Washington Times*

Benjamin

Franklin

EDMUND S. MORGAN

Yale Nota Bene

YALE UNIVERSITY PRESS   NEW HAVEN AND LONDON

A Note on the Type

This book was set in Monotype Fournier, a typeface named for the innovative French type designer Pierre-Simon Fournier le jeune (1712–68), scion of a distinguished family of type-founders. A prolific designer of typefaces and typographic ornaments, Fournier is the author of *Manuel Typographique* (1764–66), the seminal work on typefounding. There he set out a system of standardizing type measurement in points, a system still used throughout the world. Franklin obtained some of the type for his press at Passy from Fournier's son Simon-Pierre Fournier le jeune, who carried on the family business.

In 1925 Fournier's type was revived by the Monotype Cor-poration of London, to popular acclaim. The version used to-day is a contemporary adaptation of Monotype Fournier for composition in a Postscript environment.

First published as a Yale Nota Bene book in 2003.
First published by Yale University Press in 2002.

Designed by Nancy Ovedovitz and set in Monotype Fournier type by The Composing Room of Michigan, Inc. Printed in the United States of America by R.R. Donnelley & Sons.

Library of Congress Control Number: 2003106761
ISBN 0-300-10162-7 (pbk.)

A catalogue record for this book is available from the British Library.

10 9 8 7 6 5 4 3 2 1

For Marie

Contents

Preface

Entranced by the scientific discoveries of his day, Benjamin Franklin sometimes regretted having been born too soon. He missed "the Happiness of knowing what will be known 100 Years hence." By then there would be "Discoveries made of which we have at present no Conception." He was right about that. But we may be permitted a small regret of our own for having been born too late to enjoy his company. We can never catch the warmth of his smile, the tone of his voice, the little gestures, the radiant presence that drew people to him wherever he went.

Fortunately he has made it possible for us to know the man behind that presence better than most of those who enjoyed it could have. Franklin can reach us in writing that speaks with a clarity given to few in any language at any time, and writing was his favored mode of communication. We can read his mail. And we can read an astonishing amount of everything else he wrote. He has helped us by saving many of the letters he received, and people liked him enough to save many of the letters he wrote to them. He left us an autobiography that recounts his first fifty-two years of public and private life; and in his remaining thirty-two years he was so closely involved in the great events of the time that the public archives of England, France, and the United States are full of papers from his pen. He began life as a printer, first as an apprentice to his brother James, who ran a newspaper in Boston, and then on his own in Philadelphia, where he filled his newspaper with many of his own writings and every year published an almanac (*Poor Richard's Almanack*), which he enlivened with the homespun proverbs for which he is still remembered. Later, when he was too busy with public affairs to publish his own things, he kept writing books and pamphlets and newspaper articles for others to publish. So there is a lot of paper still around with Franklin's name on it. For the past fifty years scholars have been collecting every surviving scrap of it from all over the world, and it will eventually fill forty-six or more printed volumes of the *Papers of Benjamin Franklin*. Meanwhile, it is all available on one small disk, a product of those inconceivable discoveries he dreamt of. This book exists because of that disk, which enabled me to write it—no, compelled me to. And the disk itself exists because of the vision of David W. Packard at the Packard Humanities Institute, to whom I am deeply indebted for an advance copy of it.

Although Franklin was born nearly three hundred years ago, in 1706, few people past or present are as accessible as he is on this disk and in these volumes. Is he worth the trouble? Obviously some of us think so. Otherwise the disk and volumes would not be here. Nor would the hundreds of volumes about Franklin that have been written since his death in 1790. The one before you is purposely short. It is meant only to say enough about the man to show that he is worth the trouble. It is the result of reading everything on the disk and in the volumes but not much else, and therefore pretty one-sided, a letter of introduction to a man worth knowing, worth spending time with.

For myself one of the pleasures of getting to know Franklin has come from sharing the experience with the person to whom this book is dedicated. Her understanding of the man has sharpened and shaped my own. The book is as much hers as mine.

As every author knows, it is a long way from the writing desk (and I still write on a desk with a pen) to the published book. Ellen Cohn, editor of the Franklin *Papers*, read the manuscript at the outset and saved it from several egregious errors. The staff of Yale University Press under the direction of John Ryden brought their collective skills to transforming it into what you have in your hands. They made the process a pleasure for the author by involving him in their work at every stage. I wish to thank them all: Lara Heimert, Keith Condon, John Long, Nancy Ovedovitz, and especially Susan Laity.

E.S.M.

I An Exciting World

The first thing to do is to overcome the image of a man perpetually at his desk, scribbling out the mountain of words that confronts us. Because Franklin wrote so well and so much it is natural to think of him with pen in hand. But the man we will find in his writings likes to be in the open air, walking the city streets, walking the countryside, walking the deck of a ship. Indoors, he likes to be with people, sipping tea with young women, raising a glass with other men, playing chess, telling jokes, singing songs.

Don't start with his first surviving writings, the labored compositions of a precocious teenager, which he slyly introduced into his brother's newspaper under the facetious name of Silence Dogood. Instead, meet an athletic young man on a sailing ship, headed back to America from his first trip to England. He had gone there in 1724 with glowing promises of support from the then governor of Pennsylvania, who turned out to be something of a con man. When the governor's promises failed him, Franklin had used his skills as a printer to make his living in London for a year and a half, enjoying the sights and sampling the temptations of the big city. Now, with this behind him and still only twenty years old, he has boarded ship for the voyage back to Philadelphia, ready for whatever comes his way.

The ship has stopped at the Isle of Wight, trapped there by contrary winds for several days. So young Franklin and some other passengers go ashore for a walk. Most of them stop for refreshment at a convenient tavern, but Franklin and two others keep going and make a hike of it. Overtaken by night they find they have to cross a tidal inlet to get back, and the owner of the only available boat refuses to stir from his bed to ferry them across. They decide to commandeer his boat, but it is moored to a stake that the incoming tide has surrounded, leaving the boat fifty yards from shore. Franklin strips to his shirt and wades out in the water and mud up to his waist but finds the boat chained and locked to a staple in the stake. He tries to wrench out the staple. No go. He tries to pull up the stake. No go. Back to shore, and the three start looking for a farmer's haystack to sleep in. But one of them has found a horseshoe. Maybe they can use it to pry the staple loose. Franklin is back in the water again, and this time he succeeds. He brings the boat ashore and they all climb aboard, but halfway across in the dark they stick in mud shallows. After breaking an oar and climbing out into the mud up to their necks, they finally drag the boat loose and use the remaining oar to paddle it to the opposite shore and tie it down. Muddy and wet, and perhaps a little shamefaced, they make their way back to their friends.

It was probably no accident that Franklin was elected to go into the water for the boat. This is a muscular young man, about

The Thames near Chelsea where Franklin went swimming in 1725–26

five feet nine or ten, full of the energies—physical, intellectual, and sexual—of youth. In the London print shop he keeps in shape by carrying a double weight of type forms up and down stairs. In his leisure hours he enjoys a form of exercise that few people of his time dared to try: he swims, and he is good at it. He makes the Thames his playground and shows off to friends on a boating excursion by jumping in and swimming from near Chelsea to Blackfriars, a distance of at least two miles, "performing on the Way many Feats of Activity, both upon and under water." Like many athletes, he put on weight when his life became more sedentary, and the multitude of Franklin portraits were all painted after he turned plump and middle-aged. By then his physical energy had flagged, his sexual energy remained alive but a little frustrated or at least constrained, while his intellect, never slowing down, had made him the figure that the whole world wanted to immortalize in paint and marble. But think of him first in his twenties and thirties, on his feet and ready to go. On this voyage home, when they finally got a favorable wind and put to sea, Franklin amused himself by diving off and swimming around the ship. He never gave up his enjoyment of swimming and was still teaching timid friends how to do it when he was in his seventies. He even experimented with attaching paddles to his hands and feet, like modern skin divers, to step up his speed.

People at the time were under the illusion, as many still are, that getting cold and wet (swimming, walking in the rain, wearing damp clothes) was the way to "catch cold." There was not yet a germ theory of disease, but Franklin proved, to his own satisfaction at least, that people caught cold from one another and from "*too full Living* with too *little Exercise*," not from being chilled. He found that he could spend two or three hours in the water with no ill effects. So get out of the house and enjoy the fresh air, let it rain. Even when he had to be indoors Franklin wanted fresh air and dismayed everyone by opening his window at night. On a political mission with future president John Adams, when they had to share a room for the night, the two quarreled (as they did about a great many things) over opening the window. Adams ungraciously fell asleep while Franklin continued to lecture him about the virtues of fresh air.

An Insatiable Curiosity

If we watch Franklin in the fresh air for a while, we quickly become aware of his most conspicuous virtue, the thing that would earn him world-wide fame in his own lifetime: his insatiable curiosity. There was more to see outdoors than in, and Franklin could not see anything without asking himself what it was, how it got that way, what made it tick. He had that rare capacity for surprise that has made possible so many advances in human knowledge, the habit of not taking things for granted, the ability to look at some everyday occurrence and wonder why. See him still on that voyage from London back to America. He watches everything that happens, including the sharks that keep him from swimming for a while, and he hooks up some seaweed and notices little heart-shaped yellowish lumps. He counts forty of them on a single strand of the weed. Examining them he finds that some have an opening "thrusting out a set of unformed claws, not unlike those of a crab, but the inner part was still a kind of soft jelly." Then he notices a tiny crab walking around and conjectures that all the lumps are embryo crabs. By keeping the seaweed in salt water and finding another smaller crab in it the next day, he convinces himself "that at least this sort of crabs are generated in this manner."

He did not pursue his study of pelagic crabs, and since he was more often on land than at sea he found more things to wonder about there, but his travels kept him fascinated with water and its behavior, not only in the ocean but in rivers and lakes, even in jars and bottles. As we get to know him we find that his curiosity, once aroused, keeps him ever on the lookout. On another sea voyage he made himself an oil lamp to read by from a glass in which he floated the oil and a wick on water, hanging the glass from the ceiling of his cabin. Quickly he became more interested in the water and oil than in his book. As the ship rocked he noticed that the water was "in great commotion" compared to the oil. And after the oil burned away during the night to a thin film the water too stopped moving. Franklin as usual wondered why, and when he came ashore kept trying out the effects of differing amounts of oil on water. He could not explain what he found, and neither could learned friends he showed it to, who promised him that they would "consider it." They doubtless went home and quickly forgot what they had seen. But Franklin in a letter to a more sympathetic friend set down in a few words the attitude that made him what we would call a scientist. "I think it is worth considering," he said, "For a new appearance, if it cannot be explain'd by our old principles, may afford us new ones, of use perhaps in explaining some other obscure parts of natural knowledge."

Franklin never stopped considering things he could not explain. He could not drink a cup of tea without wondering why tea leaves gathered in one configuration rather than another at the bottom. He was always devising experiments to help him understand what he saw around him, but he made the whole world his laboratory. From pouring oil on water in a glass, he turned to pouring it on the surface of ponds and lakes and watched a tiny amount of it flatten out the ripples. He carried a bamboo cane with a vial of oil in its hollows to make experiments at every stream or lake he passed in his walks. He compared the way a drop of oil on a piece of glass stayed put, while on water it instantly spread out in an iridescent film too thin to measure. Why?

At age sixty-seven we find him organizing an expedition on a windy day near Portsmouth, on the English Channel, to see whether oil would flattten the surf a quarter of a mile offshore. Pitching up and down in a small boat he could see that the oil poured from a bottle flattened the white caps but had little effect on the size of the waves. No matter. He was careful to record the details "even of an Experiment that does not succeed, since they may give Hints of Amendment in future Trials." And the experiment prompted him to new conjectures about the nature of the repulsion between oil and water and how it operated.

For Franklin the world was so full of strange things that it is hard to keep up with his efforts to understand them. The ocean continued to furnish surprises for him throughout his life. When he learned that the ocean voyage between England and America generally took two weeks longer going west than it did going east, he conjectured that the rotation of the earth was slowing down the westward movement. But then he discovered the Gulf Stream. A Nantucket whaler roughed out the location of it for him on a map, which he then had engraved for the benefit of ship captains, because he calculated that the eastern flow of the current slowed down ships traveling westward in it by as much as seventy miles a day and speeded up those headed east. He also found that he could help chart the course of the stream himself by keeping track of the ocean's temperature on his transatlantic voyages. The water in the Gulf Stream was warmer than the surrounding sea. Thereafter when he crossed the ocean he could be found on deck taking daily temperature readings to plot the course of the stream himself as the vessel crossed and recrossed it.

When he was seventy-eight years old, Franklin set down in a remarkable letter to a friend some of the ideas about ships and the sea that had come to him in the seven times he had crossed the Atlantic. The letter is full of suggestions that were never carried out and a few that were: new ways to rig a ship to reduce wind resistance, new designs for the hull to make it steadier and roomier, and new ways to propel it through the water or to stop or slow it down. Franklin's designs all assumed that the only power available besides wind would be human power, but even so he could propose not only new ways to use oars but also propellers operated by hand both in the air and the water as well as jet propulsion activated by hand pumps.

The fact that Franklin thought about doing things better with nothing but hand power tells us something both about him and about his time. He liked doing things himself. He was continually designing experiments and constructing apparatus to carry them out, but mostly they were things he could do by himself or that he could get some craftsman to do according to his directions. He must have been very good with his hands, and the world he knew was a world in which nearly everything was done by hand. That world was changing, even in his own lifetime, but in order to recapture his sense of wonder at the things he found in it, we have to keep in mind what he did not wonder about, what was not even there to wonder about, and the things even he took for granted.

We get a hint of the difference between his world and ours when he remarks in passing to a friend that "No Species or Genus of Plants was ever lost, or ever will be while the World continues." Franklin assumed, with most other people of the time, that God had created the world and all the creatures in it, and God would not be likely to create something and then change His mind and let it perish. Nor was He thought to have kept on creating new things. Charles Darwin had not yet turned the plants and animals Franklin knew into an unstable collection of organisms all in the process of becoming something else over immense expanses of time. The crabs Franklin found in the seaweed had a peculiar method of propagating themselves, but it was the way God had ordained for them on the day of Creation. The things that Franklin touched or felt, the water he swam in, the air he breathed, were made up of what he called particles. He assumed that they were too small to be seen by the naked eye, but he could have had no hint of the alarming forces hidden inside them. Water was water, oil was oil. Our world has grown more mysterious than his in a thousand ways, and the more mysterious the more we examine it. While the things we see and feel do look and feel to our senses much as they did to Franklin, we know in a way he could not that they are not what they seem and that with the proper instruments we would find them to be well beyond our everyday comprehension. Scientists have probed deeper and deeper into the dynamic structure of matter and its infinite explosion in what we still call the universe. As a result we cannot look meaningfully at anything in quite the way Franklin did.

But it is also easy to exaggerate the differences. Franklin had the same curiosity about the world that drives today's scientists. He was one of the succession of probers who have transformed our vision of what we see. And watching his probing brings us back to a time when the world could reveal profound secrets to an ordinary man armed only with the imagination to ask why familiar things happened the way they did. But of course ordinary men cease to be ordinary when they not only ask such questions but exert themselves to find the answers. And that is what Franklin continually did.

On the evening of October 21, 1743, in Philadelphia, Franklin was preparing to watch the eclipse of the moon (checking out his own almanac) scheduled for nine o'clock, but by eight a northeast storm had covered the skies, and he had to give up. The storm was a bad one and lasted for two more days, the way nor'easters often do. In the coming week in the newspapers from other colonies, which he regularly exchanged with other publishers, he read of the damage inflicted by the storm up and down the coast from Virginia to New England. Then came a letter from his brother in Boston who had observed the lunar eclipse there. How could his brother have seen the eclipse before the storm hit, when Boston was well to the northeast of Philadelphia? Since it blew from the northeast, it should have come from there. Had the storm already passed in Boston? Anyone with less curiosity than Franklin might well have wondered a little about that and then forgotten it. But Franklin began stopping travelers passing through Philadelphia to ask when the storm first struck in different places. It soon became clear that the storm that blew from the northeast had come from the opposite direction. Subsequent simple observations showed him that all "N East Storms begin to Leeward and are often more violent there than farther to Windward." And he characteristically went on to try to account for the fact by speculations about warm air rising in the southwest and drawing in colder air from the northeast to produce storms and make them more violent the closer they were to the point where they originated. He did not have the apparatus of modern meteorology to check his conclusions or he would doubtless have done so and found them to be a little off the mark, but not far.

The movement of air interested him as much as that of water.

(Waterspouts combined the two, and he was fascinated by them.) Everybody knew that hot air (heated by fire) rises and escapes through a chimney, some of it as smoke. But Franklin became an authority on stoves and chimneys because he stopped to ask where the air came from that went up the chimney with the smoke. It had to come from somewhere, from open doors or windows or from cracks in the walls. Once you recognized that fact, you could heat your house most efficiently by providing a direct access from the fireplace to the outside air and also by recirculating warm air within the house. He tried various ways of achieving that effect, not all of which worked, but neither do all of those that are still being tried.

It can scarcely come as a surprise to anyone who has ever heard of Franklin to learn that his probing of the world's wonders extended to electricity. The image of him flying a kite in a thunderstorm is as familiar as the one of George Washington confessing to the destruction of his father's cherry tree, the difference being that Franklin really did fly the kite. In getting to know him, we need not dwell on his electrical experiments to demonstrate the consuming curiosity that we have already seen to be so much a part of him. But we cannot know him the way people of his time did without recognizing how much those experiments affected the way they looked at him, nor can we place him in his time without recognizing how little people knew about electricity before he explained it to them.

Franklin began those experiments when he was forty. Ten years later they had made him famous throughout the world, so that wherever he went his reputation had preceded him, and many approached him with a respect bordering on awe. Franklin always took pains to dispel any such awe. He never traded on his reputation or acted condescendingly. He took people at face value and had a knack for meeting kings and beggars, children and adults, politicians and scientists all on equal terms. Perhaps it was because his curiosity reached toward every person as well as every thing he encountered. But we have to look a little at his achievements in electricity, if only to remind us of a world that hitherto had gotten along without knowing the first thing about it.

The only kind of electricity known when Franklin began to study it was what we call static electricity, the kind that produces a shock when we shuffle across a rug on a cold dry day and touch something. In 1740 scientists at the University of Leyden had just found a way of producing and storing static electricity by rotating a glass bottle coated with foil against a piece of felt. An English friend sent one to Franklin, and he immediately began testing to see what would attract sparks from it and what objects (for example, corks suspended from a thread) it would repel. One of his earliest discoveries was that a pointed metal rod would attract a spark from a greater distance than a blunt one. Franklin and his friends in Philadelphia conducted various ingenious experiments in shocking one another and using electric force to whirl pinwheels and perform other parlor tricks but also to test and record what the "electric fluid" could or could not do. Almost at once Franklin was able to distinguish between positive and negative charges of electricity, between conductors and nonconductors (terms he originated), and within a few years he had persuaded himself that lightning was nothing but powerful electric sparks passing between oppositely charged clouds and between clouds and the earth. In November 1749 he made a list of a dozen ways in which lightning resembled the "electric fluid" he had experimented with (crooked direction, swift motion,

A collection of Leyden jars for storing static electricity

crack or noise in exploding) and asked himself, "since they agree in all the particulars wherein we can already compare them, is it not probable they agree likewise in this [in both being electric]?" And he added, "Let the experiment be made." Franklin offered an elaboration of his views in a volume published in London in 1751, which was immediately translated into French and published in Paris the next year. In it he suggested an experiment that would place a long pointed iron rod from the top of a tower or steeple ending at the bottom near a charged glass tube. If a spark passed to the tube during a thunderstorm it would prove that lightning was electric. French scientists, following his instructions, tried the experiment successfully about a month before Franklin conceived the simpler experiment with the kite. Suddenly he was famous. His experiments, confirmed in good scientific fashion by replication, not only gave the world a new understanding of electricity but also furnished the way to protect buildings and ships from it: lightning rods. Thereafter he was as much sought after for advice about lightning protection as he was for smoking chimneys. He later planned and supervised the lightning rods to guard the Royal Arsenal at Purfleet. The pointed rods were an application of his first simple discovery that points both drew sparks most effectively from an oppositely charged tube and repelled one of the same charge. Pointed lightning rods, he discovered, would actually charge "out of a cloud silently, before it could come near enough to strike."

It was not merely these practical applications but his theoretical basis for them that won him such respect among the learned. The conclusions Franklin drew from his experiments laid the foundations for all subsequent electrical research. Yet the Franklin we are trying to know may himself have placed the highest value on the practical applications. We have approached him first through his wide-ranging curiosity and its fruitful results because they were a conspicuous, enduring, and essential part of him. He kept on with experiments of all kinds throughout his life, even while heavily engaged in pressing public business. But this was a complex man. His own values located his scientific speculations and discoveries somewhere to one side of his main purpose in life. There is a hint of this in his refusal to engage in controversy with people who challenged his scientific theories. When another scientist wrote a long argument to the effect that lightning rods should be blunt rather than pointed and denounced Franklin for the opposite view, Franklin was expected to answer, but he never did because of his "extreme Aversion" to public altercation on philosophic matters. Experiments would demonstrate in time whether he was right or wrong. Meanwhile, to engage in a public defense of his theories would demonstrate only a vanity that he might feel but preferred to conceal, even from himself.

Virtue

Franklin's aversion to public altercation did not prevent him from playing a leading role in the political controversies of his time (so conspicuously that Europeans often credited him with starting the American Revolution). And while he saw no point in fighting over scientific theories or opinions that could be proved or disproved by observation or experiment, he could not be quite so detached about religious opinions, which could be neither proved nor disproved but which, perhaps for that very reason, have usually been affirmed and defended as absolute truths. People feel a need to know who they are, and in finding out they usually reach very decided opionions about a god who made them.

Franklin was no exception. His curiosity about the world he lived in led him continually back to its Creator and to whatever rules He might have prescribed, not only for the behavior of the water and air and earth of His creation but also for the people He placed in it. As a young man Franklin did a lot of thinking about that and more than once changed his mind. After he finally settled on what he believed, he did not talk much about it, but that belief gave direction to everything he did and to what he thought he ought to do. In order to know him well, we have to watch what he did—he always said that actions speak louder than words—but we can better understand what he did in a long and active life if we first follow his efforts to make up his mind about what God wanted him to do.

Franklin seems never to have doubted the existence of God or of His creation of the world—how else did everything get here?—but he hesitated to accept any of the conflicting opinions about Him propagated with such certainty by every established religious sect and church. As a boy growing up in Boston, Franklin had been exposed to the sermons of a variety of ministers, all of whom explained the details of God's place for man with an assurance they professed to get from His direct revelation of Himself in the Bible. Boston was the headquarters of New England Puritanism, embodied in its Congregational churches. By the time Franklin left in 1723, at the age of seventeen, there were six of them in Boston, many with two ministers, to serve about 1,500 families. There were also an Anglican (episcopal) and a Baptist church and a small Quaker meeting. But these attracted only small numbers and certainly not the Franklin family.

At the Old South Church, where Franklin's father was an active member, Franklin learned of a God who had divided His human beings into those He intended to bring eventually to His side in heaven and those He intended to consign to eternal punishment in Hell. They all deserved Hell because their ancestor, Adam, had sinned, but Christ, the Son of God, had died to save those who had faith in Him. Faith came only to the few whom God arbitrarily visited with an inward experience known as conversion, entailing much inner turmoil and soul-searching before it ended in faith. Faith was all that mattered. Good behavior or "good works," obedience to God's commands in the Bible, could be a result of faith but meant nothing in themselves. They were good because God commanded them, but only Christ had performed them perfectly, and it was only by sharing in His perfection through faith in Him, not by their own feeble efforts, that human beings could be saved.

Franklin listened to these ideas in his own church and in visits to others, including the one where the famous Cotton Mather expounded them. He heard them at home, too, where his father Josiah, a pious candlemaker, did his best to instill them in his eleven children. Josiah originally hoped to see his youngest son in the pulpit. It was only when the cost of schooling proved too great that he started him on a career as a printer by apprenticing him to his brother James, from whose fraternal tyranny Benjamin famously fled to Philadelphia. But it seems doubtful that Franklin could ever have found a place in the ministry, either in New England or anywhere else. He was only fifteen when he began to have doubts about the Christianity he heard preached in church. Reading books that defended it, he discovered the arguments of people who had made a radical attack on it. In England a number of "deists" rejected a god who condemned most of mankind to eternal torment because of what a supposed ancestor had supposedly done. Their God was an infinitely benevolent being, and He revealed Himself to human beings only by what He visibly did in His visible universe, not through any direct revelation in the Bible and not through any incarnation in a son named Jesus.

In reading the arguments of outraged Christians against these views, Franklin found what was refuted more persuasive than the refutation. By the time he left for Philadelphia and then for England he was a convinced deist. It would have been folly to announce the fact in Boston or even in Philadelphia, but he continued to pursue his thoughts on God and the universe, uninhibited by any reliance on the Bible that his ministers so confidently took to be the word of God. When he arrived in England, where deists and "free thinkers" abounded, he was ready to give the public his own daring conclusions, which carried the deistic premises to a staggering result. Full of the confidence of youth—he was not yet twenty—he composed and printed a short pamphlet in which he proved all too easily that God left no room in His creation for religion or for any difference between right and wrong, between good works and bad. Since He was omnipotent and benevolent, He must have constructed His world and everything and everybody in it with the capacity to act only as He wanted them to. It was therefore useless to debate the right or wrong of anything. By definition anything that anybody did or had done to them was right. Otherwise God would not have allowed it to happen.

Although the pamphlet won him the attention of other deists in London, Franklin soon regretted his smart-aleck dismissal of morality. As he told it with comic self-deprecation in his autobiography forty-six years later, his regret was prompted by the behavior of two friends whom he had convinced of his views. They demonstrated their conviction by refusing to pay back money he had lent them (why should they, since whatever they did was right?). Their betrayal made him suspect that his reasoning, "tho' it might be true was not very useful." After that admission he went on to conclude that it was probably not true either, that some logical error had crept into his reasoning, "so as to infect all that follow'd, as is common in metaphysical Reasonings," reasonings not subject to proof or disproof by observed fact.

In repudiating his own erroneous "metaphysical reasoning" Franklin did not turn back to the religious dogmas that the ministers of Boston had tried to pound into him in their Sunday sermons. He never came to accept the Bible as a divine revelation or Jesus as the son of God. But he characteristically discovered a new basis for Christian morality in the usefulness that was so unhappily missing from what he had earlier taught his friends about the rightness of everything. His new view was "that tho' certain Actions might not be bad *because* they they were forbidden by it [the Bible], or good *because* it commanded them, yet probably those Actions might be forbidden *because* they were bad for us, or commanded *because* they were beneficial to us."

That is how Franklin remembered his change of heart and change of mind in the autobiography, and it seems to have been an accurate description. He enunciated the same view of morals in *Poor Richard's Almanack* for 1739, in slightly different form: "Sin is not hurtful because it is forbidden but it is forbidden because it's hurtful. . . . Nor is a Duty beneficial because it is commanded, but it is commanded, because it's beneficial." Franklin arrived at this formula for reading the biblical Commandments only after a great deal of thinking on his own about what was hurtful and what was beneficial to himself and to the rest of God's creation. In the years after he repudiated his youthful rejection of all morality, he made several attempts to formulate his own religious beliefs, and probably made several more besides those that have survived. At one point he expressed a belief in a single supreme God who supervised a number of lesser gods, one of whom had created our world; and he dreamed up an elaborate ritual for a private deistic religious service of his own to take the place of what went on in churches. He also formulated different definitions of the virtues he thought God commanded as beneficial, and as early as 1731 planned a book that he still thought about completing fifty years later. It was to be about the art of virtue, practical advice about achieving virtue that would become a kind of manifesto for an international party dedicated to promoting virtue. It is impossible to follow the exact sequence of Franklin's thinking in these early years. Clearly he had decided by the time he returned from England to Philadelphia that, far from being meaningless, virtue, that is, morality, was the essence of all true religion, Christianity included. He may have hoped to influence Christian churches to adopt such a view. At any rate he made the attempt with the Presbyterian church in Philadelphia.

By the 1730s Presbyterians had become the most numerous denomination in Philadelphia, outnumbering even the Quakers, who had founded the city fifty years earlier. Presbyterians taught the same doctrines that Franklin had heard so often in Boston, but in 1734 the Philadelphia church installed a preacher from Ireland, Samuel Hemphill, as associate to the aging pastor Jedidiah Andrews (a Harvard-educated New Englander). Hemphill, unbeknownst to Andrews, had ideas about the importance of morals that resembled Franklin's, and Franklin began attending church, delighted by this reinforcement of his own beliefs. A livelier preacher than Andrews, Hemphill quickly achieved a popularity that made his heretical views on morality the more threatening to orthodox Presbyterians. Presbyterians differed from Congregationalists in subjecting individual congregations to supervision by a synod composed of all the ministers in a region, and this body promptly haled Hemphill before them on charges of heresy. Franklin came to his rescue in newspaper articles and pamphlets that actually confirmed the synod's suspicions of what Hemphill was teaching. On top of that Franklin denied the synod's right to dictate what Hemphill or any other minister taught in church.

Franklin's articles are the clearest statement he ever made about Christianity as he thought it ought to be. Where his Boston preachers had made faith the ultimate goal of man and mere morality worthless except as a possible sign of faith, Franklin declared flatly that "Morality or Virtue is the End, Faith only a Means to obtain that End: And if the End be obtained, it is no matter by what Means." He ridiculed the idea that either Adam's sin or the righteousness of Christ could be inherited or "imputed" to Adam's posterity. People who were brought up to do right had no need of the "spiritual *Pangs* and Convulsions" accompanying the conversions that were supposed to end in faith. The heathen might be converted to Christianity, but people brought up in Christian morality had no need of any kind of conversion. Nor could they expect to be saved by the righteousness of Christ. They had to earn their own salvation by their own righteousness.

Franklin's defense of these views as Hemphill's (which they may have been) would have been enough to condemn Hemphill, but the synod had no need to consider them, for they discovered that Hemphill's eloquent sermons had been cribbed from those of acknowledged English deists (Arians). That was sufficient reason to suspend him from office. In disgrace he left town, and Franklin left the church, never to return and never again to engage in public disputes about religion.

All the American colonies were at this time on the verge of a religious revival that brought to thousands the pangs and convulsions of the conversions Franklin abhorred. But far from denouncing the revival, he reported its triumphs in his newspaper and made a good friend of the man who did the most to promote it, the itinerant English minister George Whitefield. The emotional excesses of the revival provoked a split in American churches between those who saw it as a work of God and those who condemned it as enthusiastic nonsense, but Franklin did not enter the contest—let others pursue their useless quarrel over a meaningless experience. He had more important things to think about.

If his memory in the autobiography was correct, it was shortly before the Hemphill trial that he formulated his most lasting definition of the virtues he sought to attain in his own life, without the aid of any church or minister. We have to look carefully at Franklin's list of virtues, through which he says he sought to achieve "moral perfection," because it presents a puzzle to anyone trying to know him. Here it is, as he presents it in the autobiography, part 2:

I. TEMPERANCE.
Eat not to Dulness
Drink not to Elevation.

2. SILENCE.
Speak not but what may benefit others or your self. Avoid trifling Conversation.

3. ORDER.
Let all your Things have their Places. Let each Part of your Business have its Time.

4. RESOLUTION.
Resolve to perform what you ought. Perform without fail what you resolve.

5. FRUGALITY.
Make no Expence but to do good to others or yourself: i.e. Waste nothing.

6. INDUSTRY.

Lose no Time.—Be always employ'd in something useful.—Cut off all unnecessary Actions.—

7. SINCERITY.

Use no hurtful Deceit.

Think innocently and justly; and, if you speak; speak accordingly.

8. JUSTICE.

Wrong none, by doing Injuries or omitting the Benefits that are your Duty.

9. MODERATION.

Avoid Extreams. Forbear resenting Injuries so much as you think they deserve.

10. CLEANLINESS.

Tolerate no Uncleanness in Body, Cloaths or Habitation.—

11. TRANQUILITY.

Be not disturbed at Trifles, or at Accidents common or unavoidable.

12. CHASTITY.

Rarely use Venery but for Health or Offpsring; Never to Dulness, Weakness, or the Injury of your own or another's Peace or Reputation.—

13. HUMILITY.

Imitate Jesus and Socrates.—

The list is as interesting for what it leaves out as for what it includes. His virtues would all pass the test of usefulness that he had assigned as the reason for their being commanded, presumably by God. And it will be seen that his own conception of usefulness included being useful to others. All his surviving papers testify to his lifelong wish to be useful to his friends, to his countrymen, and to mankind in general. Franklin devoted most of his life to public service. But his list of virtues is focused on habits of behavior that would be useful to him personally and would not usually be considered essential ingredients of moral rectitude: temperance, silence, order, resolution, frugality, industry, moderation, cleanliness, and tranquillity would make for a happy life, but neglect of them would not usually be regarded as morally evil except as it might indirectly affect other people. The remaining four—sincerity, justice, chastity, and humility—would affect his relations with others, but even so, Franklin's definition of chastity would not have excluded extramarital affairs if they were not injurious to the well-being or reputation of his partners. These four are framed not as a positive duty to others but rather as ways of not doing them any harm.

What is totally missing from the list is charity, love of one's fellow man. And charity, it will become evident, was actually the guiding principle of Franklin's life. It is tempting to conclude that he left it out because it was a virtue that Christians so often failed to exhibit while professing to hold it above all others. By exhibiting it conspicuously in his own life while making no pretension to it, he was perhaps affirming to himself the superiority of a "moral perfection" that had nothing to do with Christianity.

Franklin placed temperance at the top of his list, and Poor Richard enjoins it again and again in different guises: Eat to live, and not live to eat; To lengthen thy Life, lessen thy Meals; Take counsel in wine, but resolve afterwards in water; He that drinks fast, pays slow; Nothing more like a Fool, than a drunken Man. All these were in the first almanac in 1733, and in subsequent years he found a hundred different ways to say the same thing. The most frequent admonitions, for which Poor Richard became famous, were those to industry and frugality. There were so many of them that in his last almanac, for 1758, he collected them in a speech he attributed to one Father Abraham. It was immediately reprinted separately and continued to be, usually under the title "The Way to Wealth." There were over a hundred editions in more than a dozen languages over the next fifty years.

Because of the popularity of this tract and the title given it by publishers (not by Franklin), his name has been associated ever since its publication with industry and frugality, as though these were the guiding principles of his life, with wealth as his objective. Franklin certainly did value industry and frugality, along with the other virtues on his list, and they did bring him wealth, enough so that he could retire at the age of forty-two, when he placed the running of his business in the hands of his partner David Hall. He was still a young man, and if wealth had been his objective he could probably have had it in as large a measure as anyone in America. But Franklin had never thought of industry and frugality as the way to wealth but as a way to contentment, and Poor Richard warned that "Content and Riches seldom meet together." Franklin was struck by "the general Foible of Mankind, in the Pursuit of Wealth to no end." Poor Richard phrased the thought for him: "If your riches are yours, why don't you take them with you to the t'other World," for "the use of Money is all the Advantage there is in having Money." And in a letter to a friend Franklin gave his view that "what we have above what we can use, is not properly *ours,* tho' we possess it."

Living Usefully

Obviously the man we want to know had something other than riches in mind when he retired from business. Given his interest in science—he was just beginning his electrical experiments— he could have devoted the rest of his life to it. But we have already noted that he did not, nor did he consider his scientific work as important as the rest of the world did. His refusal to defend his views against criticism reflected not only an aversion to public controversy about them but also a conviction that scientific inquiry was not itself as worthy of anyone's time and effort, not as useful, as public service.

He stated his priorities in 1750 in a letter to Cadwallader Colden, later lieutenant-governor of New York. Colden shared his interest in science, and the two had often exchanged views and reports of experiments. In a letter no longer extant Colden had apparently expressed a determination to withdraw from public life and devote more time to the scientific experiments that they both designated as "philosophical amusements." Franklin congratulated him on the prospect but then offered a warning that represented the values he had been developing since his own retirement from business: "let not your Love of Philosophical Amusements have more than its due weight with you. Had Newton been Pilot but of a single common Ship, the finest of his Discoveries would scarce have excus'd, or atton'd for his abandoning the Helm one Hour in Time of Danger; how much less if she had carried the Fate of the Commonwealth."

This view is worth pondering in our effort to know Franklin. Twenty-eight years later, Thomas Jefferson expressed an opposite view of the relative merits of science and public service. In a letter to David Rittenhouse, a much lesser scientist than Franklin but widely respected by his contemporaries as an astronomer, Jefferson expressed concern that Rittenhouse was squandering his time in public service in the Pennsylvania legislative assembly. This was in the midst of the American Revolution. Philadelphia was just recovering from occupation by the British, and the city and state certainly needed the best efforts of its citizens. So did the United States, and Franklin was in Paris, winning the alliance that secured American independence. Jefferson was fully cognizant of the situation, but he thought that Rittenhouse (and presumably Franklin too) should be pursuing the scientific experiments that others were less capable of performing. "Tho' I have been aware," he wrote, "of the authority our cause [the Revolution] would acquire with the world from it's being being known that yourself and Doctr. Franklin were zealous friends to it, and am myself duly impressed with a sense of the arduousness of government, and the obligation those are under who are able to conduct it, yet I am also satisfied there is an order of geniusses above that obligation, and therefore exempted from it. No body can conceive that nature ever intended to throw away a Newton upon the occupations of a crown. . . . Are those powers then, which being intended for the erudition of the world, like air and light, the world's common property, to be taken from their proper pursuit to do the commonplace drudgery of governing a single state, a work which may be executed by men of an ordinary stature, such as are always and every where to be found?"

The timing of the two letters accentuates their contrasting views. Jefferson was writing in the midst of a war in which scientific achievements would count for little, Franklin in a period of peace following a war between England and France, concluded in 1748, in which Franklin had been principally responsible for organizing the defense of Philadelphia against French privateers. The coming of peace and his simultaneous retirement from that task and from business had left him with the same leisure to pursue philosophical amusements that Colden envisaged in 1750. Philadelphians wanted him to represent them in the colony's legislative assembly, but he told them he would not serve if elected, and he wrote Colden at this time, September 29, 1748, that "I am in a fair Way of having no other Tasks than such as I shall like to give my self, and of enjoying what I look upon as a great Happiness, Leisure to read, study, make Experiments." And make experiments he did. It was in the next couple of years that he convinced himself and the world that lightning and electricity were identical and that buildings could be protected from it by lightning rods. Yet by 1750 he had also convinced himself that scientific discoveries would count for little beside public service.

It would perhaps not be too much to say that Franklin underwent a new dedication to public service between 1748 and 1750. He had never been without strong feelings about it. In his scientific work he had always had the possibility of public utility in mind. After his earliest electrical experiments, playing with sparks and shocks and making things move about by invisible forces, he reported his chagrin that "We have hitherto been able to discover Nothing in this Way of Use to Mankind." The lightning rod changed that. Earlier, when his experiments with the movement of air enabled him to design the Franklin stove, the governor of Pennsylvania was so impressed with it that he offered to give Franklin a ten-year patent on its manufacture. Franklin declined the offer as he later declined to profit from his lightning rods. It was apparently a matter of principle with him as early as 1744 that "as we enjoy great Advantages from the Inventions of others, we should be glad of an Opportunity to serve others by any Invention of ours, and this we should do freely and generously."

During the first couple of years of his retirement from business he seems to have developed a new commitment to using his talents in behalf of others. Although he had refused service in the Pennsylvania Assembly in 1748, he accepted election from Philadelphia in 1751 (and was reelected every year thereafter until he left for England as the Assembly's agent in 1764). In 1750 he wrote the letter to Colden extolling public service above science. In the same year he wrote his mother that when his life was over, "I would rather have it said, *he lived usefully*, than, *He died rich*." And he obviously meant useful to others. In preparing his almanac for 1752, he filled it with passages from a long poem by Richard Savage, "On Public Spirit in Regard to Public Works," and added some lines of his own in praise of those who dedicate high talents to the public.

> Talents and Will to the same Person giv'n,
> The Man ennobled doth an Hero rise,
> Fame and his Virtues lift him to the Skies.

Franklin was far from claiming such a hero's place for himself, but if his virtues devoted to public service should bring him fame, he would not shrink from it. In a letter to Jared Eliot (another friend devoted to scientific experiments) in 1751, he agreed with him that the love of praise was universal, "tho' we are generally Hypocrites, in that respect, and pretend to disregard Praise."

By now it must be apparent that Franklin is not so easy to know as he sometimes seems to be. He has an insatiable curiosity and applies himself seriously and successfully to scientific discovery, but he discounts its importance. He rejects his Christian upbringing and develops a religion of practical virtue that says nothing about the golden rule of loving one's fellow men, but he dedicates his life to serving them. We see in his letter to Eliot that he was not immune to praise, and throughout his life he earned a lot of it. He earned it in serving the public. But his public service was not simply a duty he imposed on himself. It was deliberate, conscious, contrived, but at the same time natural. He sought it as he sought company, sought friendship. He is so hard to know because it is so hard to distinguish his natural impulses from his principles.

Self-Control

Wherever Franklin went people loved him. Wherever he lived he made friends, close friends, loyal friends, adoring friends. His friends often had no direct connection with his public service— they simply loved the man—but his personal charm lay behind his public success. Even at three centuries' distance, it sometimes fairly leaps from a page. Try reading Franklin's account of his conversation with the Bishop of St. Asaph's eleven-year-old daughter when he was escorting her in a coach from her family's home in London. What fun they both had picking suitable husbands for her three older sisters! Franklin's charm seems effortless, extended freely to everyone around him. And yet it was in some measure conscious and controlled. For all his seemingly spontaneous openness, he kept a kind of inner core of himself intact and unapproachable. One biographer recognized this invisible barrier in an often quoted sentence: "In all of Franklin's dealings with men and affairs, genuine, sincere, loyal as he surely was, one feels that he is nevertheless not wholly committed; some thought remains uncommunicated; some penetrating observation is held in reserve."

That statement may exaggerate a little, and with the benefit of so full a mass of his papers we may penetrate closer to the secret self behind the public man. But we have to admit at the outset that there are things we will never know about Franklin. He talks disarmingly about his early life and career in the autobiography he wrote ostensibly for the benefit of his son William, but nowhere in the autobiography or any surviving papers does he tell us who William's mother was, or anything about her. The boy was born in 1728 or 1729 (Franklin never tells us when), shortly before the father married Deborah Read Rogers (without a ceremony, for it was not yet clear that her absconded husband was dead). William became at once a part of the family, and his father doted on him (until he chose the wrong side in the Revolution), but he was not Deborah's child, and it is unlikely that we will ever know anything about his mother or Franklin's relations with her.

Franklin's marriage to Deborah was loving and happy. She bore him two children. But something in their relationship eludes us. He spent the last ten years of her life away from her in London. He wrote her affectionate letters, and she wrote as many to him. But meanwhile he enjoyed the company of many other women of all ages. He obviously delighted them, and they delighted him. His letters to them are quite different from his letters to Debby, full of flirtation and fun, as are his much later letters to the ladies of Paris, who showered the old man with kisses and extravagant expressions of love and devotion. Was more than flirtation involved? Franklin leaves us guessing. In other matters too Franklin often keeps us wondering what he was really like. The autobiography, like most autobiographies, is a work of art, but it conveys the image of a man who is partly real

Deborah Read Franklin, 1758–59

and partly someone that Franklin would like his son (and perhaps others) to admire and imitate. It is difficult to tell which is which.

But if Franklin holds something back, he does not deceive us. He knew how to keep his mouth shut, but when he spoke, he generally meant what he said and generally practiced what he preached. We can learn something about what made him so widely liked in private life and so successful in public by reading the morsels of advice he handed out in *Poor Richard's Almanack,* in between the encomiums to industry and thrift. *Poor Richard,* among other things, is a manual of etiquette and of the virtues that led to moral perfection. Its advice about how to behave often sounds like a description of Franklin's own well-controlled behavior. First of all, he would not discount his own worth or try to keep himself entirely in the background in any company. "Tho Modesty is a Virtue, Bashfulness is a Vice." Therefore, "Hide not your Talents they for use were made / what's a Sun-Dial in the Shade!" Withdrawal from the world in solitude, despite what monks and nuns might think, was not the way to promote virtue: "Lot was upright in the City, wicked in the Mountain." But mingling in the world did not mean showing off. Without discounting his own talents, he took care not to be an open book: "Let all Men know thee, but no man know thee thoroughly"—and as we have already suggested, no man ever did. He would use his talents to help anyone he could, but he recognized any display of vanity, whether in himself or others, as a weakness that could destroy his effectiveness. His autobiography described how his efforts to suppress pride were overcome by taking pride in not being proud. In actuality he was pretty successful in hiding any kind of pride. He put his objective succcinctly, if a little cryptically, in Poor Richard's "Deny Self for Self's sake." Therein lies his refusal to defend his scientific hypotheses. The way to advance oneself was to show no interest in advancing it. He was, in a sense, too vain to allow a show of vanity to diminish his reputation.

Reputation lay in other people's high opinion of you. And the surest way to lower that opinion was to present yourself too forwardly. Therefore, "Visits should be short, like a winter's day / Lest you're too troublesom hasten away." And don't make visits too often: "Friendship increases by visiting Friends, but by visiting seldom." Franklin was a sociable creature and fond of being with others, but he took pains not only to limit his visits but also to listen more than he spoke. "You may talk too much on the best of subjects," and a sure way to bore people was to "say things merely 'cause they're good" if they did not fit what people were talking about. What was even worse was to disparage others, whether of the company or not, by witty remarks about their faults. "He makes a Foe who makes a jest."

It did not follow that he thought everything he heard from others was necessarily worth listening to. Too many other people were ready to talk when they had nothing to say: "Halfwits talk much but say little"; "Here comes the Orator! With his Flood of Words, and his lack of Reason." But the way to get along with other people was to suffer such fools gladly. "Speak with contempt of none, from slave to king, / The meanest Bee hath, and will use, a sting." Franklin never offended people except intentionally. He was capable of denouncing the folly of others, but only if it served a purpose. Otherwise he made a point of restraining his passions, for "He that cannot bear with other People's Passions, cannot govern his own," and "He is not well-bred, that cannot bear Ill-Breeding in others." Franklin was so successful in restraining his passions that the image of him which has come down to us is one of dull placidity, a comfortable old gentleman staring out at the world over his half-glasses with benevolent comprehension of everything in it. But when Franklin devoted himself to public service, he brought plenty of passion with him. By the time he turned fifty, though he called himself "a fat old Fellow," one of his political opponents, who acknowledged Franklin's "virtue and uncorrupted honesty," was appalled by the fact that his "face at Times turns white as the driven Snow with the Extreams of Wrath." In a conference with Thomas Penn, the proprietor who controlled the government of Pennsylvania and owned the public lands there, Franklin's wrath was silent but evident. In a letter he reported that he came away with "a more cordial and thorough Contempt for him than I ever before felt for any Man living—A Contempt that I cannot express in Words, but I believe my Countenance expressed it strongly."

If Franklin curbed his passion in personal encounters like this, he had no trouble putting it into words designed to influence public opinion. We will see his wrath turned loose in the many bitter satires he composed during his public career, like the one arguing that the British practice of shipping convicts to the American colonies should be matched by a regular export of rattlesnakes from the colonies to Britain, or, as the quarrel with England grew toward outright war, his suggestion in the newspapers that the British army be assigned to castrate all American males in order to reduce the growing and ungovernable American population. Franklin usually directed his barbs against policies rather than persons, but sometimes a policy became so closely associated with an individual that he could not resist naming names—but only in such a way as to gain public support. One of his most effective attacks on British taxation of the colonies came in dedicating to Lord Hillsborough (secretary of state for the colonies) his pamphlet entitled *Rules by Which a*

Great Empire May Be Reduced to a Small One (a summary of the policies England was following). Occasionally he composed angry letters to people he regarded as public enemies, but after letting off steam this way, he seems generally to have left the letters unsent.

In this self-denial, as in the overall direction of the Poor Richard aphorisms, we get a picture of a man who deeply valued self-control. What is perhaps less obvious is how big a self Franklin had to bring under control. Franklin occasionally reproached himself for his indolence, but the reproaches are about as convincing as the habit of zealous saints in bemoaning their sinfulness. Franklin had always to be doing something. If he had to sit still, say at a meeting where the proceedings bored him, even his doodling on a sheet of paper became an intellectual exercise of extraordinary complexity: constructing parallel columns of numbers known as magic squares or circles, in which the figures all added up to the same number in every direction. His exuberant intellectual energy needed more control than most people's to keep him from making himself obnoxious by upstaging everyone around him. And his energy was combined with a sense of humor that needed reining in too, in order to keep him from bursting into unseemly laughter at the folly of the world in which he found himself. His quick perception of the comic weaknesses of human nature might have turned a lesser man into a cynical snob, but Franklin never considered himself exempt from the weaknesses he found in others. He took pains to conceal his recognition of other people's harmless errors: "He's a Fool that cannot conceal his Wisdom" and "There's a time to wink as well as to see." Only when men in power acted foolishly, adopting policies harmful to others, did he lift the restraints on

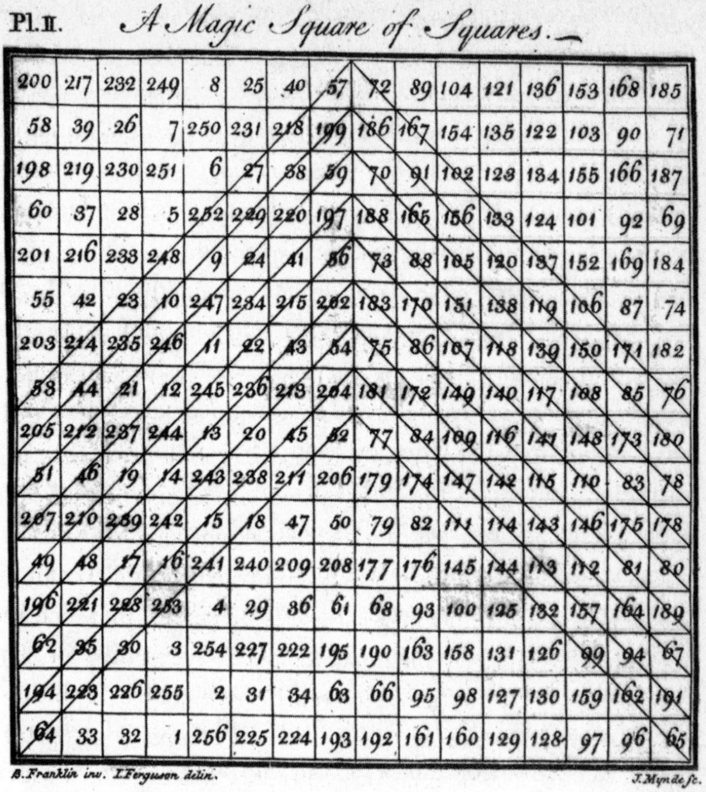

Pl. II.

A Magic Square of Squares. Franklin crafted this puzzle some time before 1752. The numbers in each column, horizontal or vertical or within the double diagonals, all add up to the same amount, 2,056, and so do the sixteen numbers in any four-by-four square.

both his passions and his wit. Otherwise, just as he gave his excess of passion an outlet in angry letters never sent, he gave his wit and humor an anonymous outlet in outrageous essays like his letter (not made public until the next century) on the choice of a mistress and in literary hoaxes mocking social conventions.

The hoaxes began early, when he contributed the essays by Silence Dogood to his brother's newspaper, showing (to himself at least) how easy it was for a clever teenager to write the fashionable moralizing drivel that filled the presses of the time. His most successful hoax, which he never acknowledged writing, was the speech of one Polly Baker, allegedly addressed to the judges of a court in New England that was ready to punish her for having her fifth illegitimate child. Polly argued eloquently that she was doing God and society a service in obeying the command to "increase and multiply." The argument was so plausible and so persuasive that it not only convinced the imagined judges to release her but captured the fancy of newspaper editors all over the world for a hundred years and even convinced a number of European philosophers that Polly's plea had actually been delivered and had resulted in one of the judges marrying her.

Although Franklin's hoaxes, like this one, were playful outbursts of his irrepressible amusement at the absurdities of human conventions, he could use them for serious public purposes. Many human institutions invite ridicule, and some invite reform or destruction by people like Franklin who take public service seriously. When public policy and public law support practices too entrenched to be moved by rational argument, ridicule may be the most powerful weapon that can be deployed against them. Franklin used it against British colonial policy and he used it against United States policy in allowing the continuation of slavery and the slave trade. At one time he held household slaves himself, but three weeks before his death, while supporting a petition to Congress against the slave trade, he wrote one of his most appealing hoaxes. In a letter to the *Federal Gazette* he offered a letter purportedly written a hundred years earlier by one Sidi Mehemet Ibrahim, a fictitious Muslim statesman, in answer to a petition proposing to halt the practice of enslaving Christians and to free those already enslaved. In it Franklin turned the tables on every agument offered then or later against the immediate abolition of slavery: Christians would not work unless forced to; they would not return to their native countries but stay and pillage their former masters; they were better off as slaves than free people in Christian countries for they had security and the benefit of true religion instead of the infidelity to which they were subjected at home. They could never be assimilated because Muslims could not pollute themselves by intermarrying with them, and so on. Every sentence hit home, and many still do. Franklin's countrymen had not yet caught up with him on this subject, nor did they follow his lead on many other matters. But we can perhaps find in this quiet derision of human weakness and wickedness a suggestion of the lively wit that made him such good company. If he kept passion and wit under control, he did not keep them hidden. They were always there, ready for use, not simply against conventional follies but in support of love, friendship, and fun.

"I Find I Love Company"

We have been looking at why people liked Franklin and the way he conducted himself to make them like him. It took some practice. It was deliberate. But it was not a way of manipulating people for his own benefit except in the enjoyment of their company. Eventually his self-control became a great political asset, but by the time Franklin entered politics it had become second nature to him, no longer something he had to keep reminding himself of in the maxims of Poor Richard.

It became second nature, but it grew from first nature, that is, from Franklin's innate affinity for people of all kinds. Franklin wanted people to like him because he liked them. True, in the course of a long life, especially after he entered politics, he made enemies and sometimes returned their enmity. But he made far more friends. And he needed them. If it is true that he always held something of himself in reserve, it is also true that he could not get along without company. In the shipboard journal he kept while returning from England in 1726, he described the ostracism of another passenger who was caught cheating at cards. The very thought of what it would be like to be shut out that way horrified him. "I have read abundance of fine things," he wrote, "on the subject of solitude, and I know 'tis a common boast in the mouths of those that affect to be thought wise, *that they are never less alone than when alone*. I acknowledge solitude an agreeable refreshment to a busy mind; but were these thinking people obliged to be always alone, I am apt to think they would quickly find their very being insupportable to them." Franklin's consuming curiosity about the world and what made it tick extended to the people in it, accompanied by a delight in being one of them. As he enjoyed watching the ways of the world, he enjoyed simply being with its people, sharing thoughts with them, feeling affection for them, laughing with them, and finding out who they were and who he was. As he grew older, he confessed to an old friend—they were both in their fifties—"I find I love Company, Chat, a Laugh, a Glass, and even a Song, as well as ever." He was writing from England to Hugh Roberts, a Philadelphia merchant, recalling their times together in a club Franklin had started thirty-four years before, when they were both just starting out. He called it the Junto, and it is a good place to watch his second nature growing out of his first and to begin following the career that shaped his life and the lives of so many others.

Franklin has returned from England on the voyage where he rejected the supposed joys of solitude. Now he is working for Samuel Keimer, a Philadelphia printer who acts the petty tyrant over his employees. The Junto includes the three young men besides Franklin who work for Keimer. The others are friends he has made outside the shop: a glazier, a shoemaker, a surveyor, and a woodworker. They are mostly young men on the make, only two of them out of their twenties, one of them only eighteen. Apart from their youth they have little in common other than Franklin's choice of them, but most of them will stick together for many long years. From time to time they admit others to their group and a few drop out, but they keep the size to no more than a dozen so they can all meet in one room once a week on Friday evenings, first at an alehouse, later in a room they rent for the purpose. Yes, as Franklin remembered, they are there to chat, laugh, drink, and sing, but these are very serious young men, out to enjoy one another's company but eager to improve their minds and their fortunes while they do it. At every meeting they discuss a number of questions proposed by the members or listen to a paper written by one of them, pausing long enough for a friendly glass between bouts of earnest talk. Some of the discussions are directed at public policy: "Does the Importation of Servants increase or advance the Wealth of our Country?" Some are spiritual: "Can a Man arrive at Perfection in this Life as some Believe; or is it impossible as others believe?" Some are political:

"If the Sovereign Power attempts to deprive a Subject of his Right, (or which is the same Thing, of what he thinks his Right) is it justifiable in him to resist if he is able?"

In addition to debating such grave matters—much as college students of the time were required to do in their senior year—the members of the Junto, if they followed the rules they adopted, were also on the lookout to help one another in practical ways. Franklin devised twenty-four separate queries for each person to answer at every meeting, such as, "Have you lately heard of any citizen's thriving well, and by what means" or "Have you lately heard how any present rich man, here or elsewhere, got his estate?" Franklin and his friends were all interested in getting rich, or at least in prospering, and a whole series of questions was directed toward promoting that end for all the members:

> Hath any body attacked your reputation lately? And what can the Junto do towards securing it?
> Have you lately heard any member's character attacked, and how have you defended it?
> Hath any man injured you, from whom it is in the power of the Junto to procure redress?

There were several more like this, but some addressed the possibility of affecting public policy to benefit others as well as themselves: "Have you lately observed any defect in the laws of your *country* of which it would be proper to move the legislature for an amendment? Or do you know of any beneficial law that is wanting?" Ominously for the future, this one was followed by "Have you observed any encroachment on the just liberties of the people?" It seems unlikely that every member could have responded to every question every week. The fragmentary records that have survived tell us little about the actual meetings, but in his autobiography Franklin recalled that the discussions were conducted according to his own later prescriptions for making conversation pleasant and productive: "Our debates were . . . to be conducted in the sincere Spirit of Enquiry after Truth, without fondness for Dispute, or Desire of Victory; and to prevent Warmth, all Expressions of Positiveness in Opinion, or of direct Contradiction, were after some time made contraband and prohibited under small pecuniary Penalties." The Junto was a school of good manners and good works. It is hard to see how there could have been much song and laughter accompanying its sober discussions, but the members enjoyed themselves enough to continue for forty years. It might even have continued much longer if Franklin had not been called away from it for so long in public service after 1754. But, as we shall see, the Junto itself was where his public service began.

Of course the large questions he discussed there on Friday nights could not occupy much of his attention during the rest of the week. He was only twenty-one when he started the club. He had to earn a living, and the only way he knew how was as a printer. He quickly saw that there was no future in working for Keimer. He and Keimer's other employees, free to talk about the man in their Friday meetings, must have agreed that he was hard to work for. At any rate one of them, Hugh Meredith, quit along with Franklin, and the two of them set up their own printing business, with help from Meredith's father. When Meredith shortly decided that he had neither the talent nor the taste for being a printer, two other Junto members lent Franklin the money to buy him out; and Meredith headed out happily for a farm in

Carolina. Within two years of leaving Keimer, Franklin had not only become the sole proprietor of a thriving printing business but had won all the official printing for the colony, bought the newspaper Keimer had just started (they were right about Keimer, he was a born loser), and opened a stationery and book shop. In those two years he had also fathered a son with the woman he never identified for us and married Deborah Read, whom he had courted unsuccessfully six years before, when he first arrived in Philadelphia from Boston. So by the time he was twenty-five Franklin had already found his place in the local community: he was a printer, a businessman, a father, and a husband.

He took all these roles seriously. As a printer and business-man, he was so successful that in the years ahead he set up other printers in business in other cities in return for a share of their profits. At the age of thirty he won the postmastership of Phila-delphia. By the time he was forty-two his income from printing partnerships, other investments, and the post office was enough to enable him to retire from business. Meanwhile he had fathered another son, Francis (who died young), and a daughter, Sarah. He kept in close touch with his family and with his brothers and sisters throughout his life. His younger sister Jane remained his favorite sibling, and he easily shrugged off her disapproval of his free and easy religion. Within his own family he was most ob-viously and most demonstrably fond of his son William, who be-came his closest confidant until William chose the wrong side in 1776. For that Franklin never forgave him. Jane took the right side, and her then-famous brother did everything he could to make life comfortable for her as she suffered from the British in-vasion of Boston and from a succession of family disasters. Deb-orah never faltered in her love and trust; and he never lost a deep affection for her, though we will never know whether he remained sexually faithful during his long absences.

Franklin was clearly an astute businessman and an averagely good family man. But neither his business dealings nor his family relations tell us much about him as a person distinct from a thousand others. The honesty and fairness that marked his business dealings and which he enshrined in the sayings of Poor Richard were certainly admirable and worthy of imitation, but success in business was for him only a means to an end. And his affection for his family, while obviously genuine, was much like that of any good father or husband. We have already noticed the extraordinary intellectual curiosity that distinguished him from most other people. It is certainly one of the traits that strikes us first in getting to know him, as it struck so many people who first encountered him in his quest for answers to the questions that kept popping up in his restless mind. But we have to accept his own view that the pursuit of scientific knowledge was not his goal in life and that public service was more important. It was evidently more important than the business he gave up, and more important than family, as his long absences from home and his ultimate rejection of his beloved son William suggest. If we want to know him the way he knew himself, we have to follow him outside his family, outside his business.

Which means learning to know just what this public was that he wanted to serve. It was a public that grew and changed as Franklin grew and changed. The Franklin we want to know is recognizably the same man in 1770 or 1780 that he was in 1730, but the public he served, the larger group that commanded his loyalty beyond his family or business, was not the same. And his own sense of who he was could not be the same either. To know the man as we can, with his whole life completed and laid out before us in the words he left behind, we have to watch him grow, ever the same jovial, friendly, curious person, but one who serves a changing public and himself plays a large role in changing and defining that public even as he changes and defines himself in the process.

2 "A Dangerous Man"

There is an old saying that a man is known by the company he keeps: his reputation depends on what sort of people he is seen with. The saying holds a larger meaning: a man knows himself through the people, the companies, he feels part of. Everyone belongs to a number of them: family, clan, town, country, church, race, class, party. Some we are born into, others we choose for ourselves, but both affect our sense of who we are and the way others identify us. Franklin was a printer, and printers, even though widely separated—few towns in America could support more than two or three—made up a kind of company, joined in their special skills and special problems. Two years after he acquired his own newspaper, the *Pennsylvania Gazette*, Franklin wrote for it "an Apology for Printers," which still furnishes printers and publishers everywhere with a kind of creed, distinguishing and defining them as a guild, separate from the writers who write what printers print. Franklin himself was also

Printing press used by Franklin in London in
1726

a writer and wrote some of the things he printed, but he usually
wrote anonymously and never thought of writers as a company
of people he belonged to. Even in his old age, when he was representing the United States abroad, he still thought of himself as
a printer, made friends with other printers there, and set up a
press in his house in France to print things just for fun. But the
fraternity of other printers was only one of the companies he
kept. He was a joiner. He needed close contacts in the kind of
small group he created in the Junto; and he helped to create many
others, such as a fire insurance company and a company to found

a hospital, whose members he cherished as part of his being. On a brief trip to Boston, he sent back greetings "to all our old Friends of the Junto, Hospital, and Insurance." He also identified himself with other like-minded people he found at hand. He joined the Masons in Philadelphia, the Club of Honest Whigs and the Royal Society in England, the Académie Royale in France—but not, as we have seen, any church, anywhere.

Philadelphian

Belonging to these companies helped tell him and us who he was, but if asked the question by a stranger he would probably not have answered that he was a member of this or that group he had voluntarily joined, like the Masons or the Junto. Besides saying that he was a printer he might have said that he was a Philadelphian or a Pennsylvanian, or an American. If people are known by the company they keep, the company that identifies them in the most basic way is geographic. Franklin was in some sense a citizen of the world. He did many things because he thought they were good for the world at large, not just for any group within it. But as the Junto or the Masons or the Club of Honest Whigs was too small and partial a group to define an identity, the whole world was too large. People are known by where they come from, by the company that occupies a special, recognized place on the globe.

Before he reached his twentieth birthday Franklin had lived in several such places: Boston, Philadelphia, London. When he returned to Philadelphia in 1726, he stayed for thirty-one years and knew himself as a confirmed Philadelphian, a Pennsylvanian, and an American. He remained so ever after, even as he served

Pennsylvania and America during much of his life away from them, in England (1757–62 and 1764–75) and in France (1776–85). He was in England long enough to think at times of making himself into an Englishman, and he occasionally thought also of returning to New England, while his friends in France would gladly have kept him there. Franklin quickly made himself at home wherever he went, but he never lost his attachment to Philadelphia or Pennsylvania or America. And his service to each of them made him who he was and in no small measure made them what in his lifetime they became.

It will be worth considering just what each of them was, what kind of company they amounted to at the time Franklin made his attachment to them and started his commitment to serving them. Perhaps the most conspicuous thing about all three was their growth. When Franklin arrived in Philadelphia from England in 1727, he came at the beginning of a mass movement of people through the city that lasted for the next three decades. Roughly 77,000 people landed at Philadelphia's docks during that time, most of them from what is now Germany, the rest mainly Scots and Irish from northern Ireland. The immigrants fanned out into the interior of Pennsylvania, more than tripling the population. The Germans went mainly to the north, the Scots-Irish to the west. Philadelphia absorbed some of them, growing from about seven thousand inhabitants to around seventeen thousand, but for three decades the city was home to more people in transit than there were residents.

Philadelphia and Pennsylvania were both only forty-six years old when the great influx began, and neither was prepared for it. The government of both had been devised in 1701, twenty years after the first settlements, by an agreement (the Charter of Privileges) between the settlers, most of whom were Quakers from the British Isles, and William Penn, the founder and proprietor, in effect the owner, of Pennsylvania. As thus defined, the government of the colony in 1727 still consisted of a governor named by the proprietors (sons of William Penn) and an Assembly of twenty-six representatives from Philadelphia and the three counties adjoining it. The Quakers still constituted a majority in those counties (though not in the city) and in the Assembly. When the tide of immigration subsided after 1759, five more counties had been added in the west to hold the newcomers, but though these five soon held half the colony's population, they were together given only ten seats in the Assembly, while Philadelphia and the three eastern counties still held twenty-six, occupied mostly by Quakers.

In most of the other British colonies in North America, the same kind of disproportional representation in the legislative assembly developed as settlers moved into the interior, but nowhere was the inequality quite so flagrant. And nowhere did the Assembly have quite so large a share in the government. In other colonies a governor's council as well as the governor himself had to agree to any law that the assembly might propose. In Pennsylvania the governor appointed the Council to advise him, but the Council had no powers of its own, as it did in every other colony, where it constituted the upper house of the legislature. The people of Philadelphia and the three eastern counties constituted a kind of oligarchy, limited only by a governor under orders from a proprietor who lived three thousand miles away.

The city of Philadelphia had its own problems of government. At the time Penn agreed to the Pennsylvania Charter of Privileges, in 1701, he also provided Philadelphia with a city

View of Philadelphia (detail), ca. 1756, drawn "under the direction of
Nicholas Scull, Surveyor General of the Province of Pennsylvania." Scull

government in the form of a self-perpetuating Common Council. The Council elected from their own number a mayor and a
board of aldermen, who served as a court of justice for the city
and adjoining country. Thus during Franklin's residence from
1727 to 1757 Philadelphia was governed by a body with no immediate responsibility to its citizens, and Pennsylvania by an Assembly chosen almost entirely from the three eastern counties
and by proprietors in London who sent instructions to a deputy

was one of the original members of Franklin's Junto in 1727.

in Philadelphia. Legislation to meet the colony's needs required agreement between the proprietors in London (who had been converted from Quaker to Anglican) and the Quakers who dominated the Assembly. Legislation to meet the city's needs required action by a council that never had to consult the people affected by it. The Assembly and the governor found it hard to work out disagreements because the governor's hands were tied by his instructions, leaving him little room for compromise. The Common Council of Philadelphia could act unimpeded by outside pressures, but by the same token it felt no pressure to act at all.

If that government is best that governs least, Philadelphians and Pennsylvanians were well off, and they got along surprisingly well for a time. Franklin would eventually devote himself to reforming the government of Pennsylvania and of the other British colonies in America. But before he undertook that task, he cut his teeth on schemes to improve the quality of life in Philadelphia. The failure of government action to deal with minor local problems as they occurred left room for people to act on their own in voluntary associations formed for particular purposes. In his thirty years of residency, Franklin discovered the ideal outlet for the usefulness he craved in initiating one association after another to meet people's needs as they arose. His trade as a printer gave him a singular advantage. Thomas Jefferson was later to say that if he had to choose between government without newspapers or newspapers without government, he would unhesitatingly choose newspapers. Philadelphia was not without government, but the ineffectiveness of it gave a special importance to newspapers, as Franklin gradually discovered after he began publishing the *Pennsylvania Gazette* in 1729.

In its pages he furnished Philadelphians and other Pennsylvanians with a common fund of knowledge about themselves and about what went on in the rest of the world. The news columns, as in other newspapers of the time, were mostly about the rest of the world, copied from the latest London papers to arrive in America, with occasional items from papers in other colonies. (Franklin eventually held partnerships with the printers of at least six of them.) But Franklin also told people what was happening to them at home—fires, floods, lightning strikes, acci-

dents, marriages, deaths, meetings, celebrations, robberies—
and as time went on he included more and more about politics.
What probably mattered most to Philadelphians in their daily
lives was the advertising: books, clothes, cows, horses, and land
for sale, things lost and found, and yes, runaway servants and
slaves. As a printer and publisher Franklin had his finger on the
pulse of life in Philadelphia, and he was continually bringing
companies of people together in associations to improve it.

Even before his determination to devote his life to usefulness
in public service, Franklin took pleasure in making daily life better for himself and everyone around him. The Junto was a company of like-minded young men joined for companionship, for
help in getting ahead, but also for helping other Philadelphians,
other Pennsylvanians. Philadelphians at this time enjoyed belonging to clubs. There were several besides the Junto: a club of
unmarried men who met at their own Bachelors' Hall, a club of
Welsh immigrants known as the Society of Ancient Britons, a
club of the well-to-do called the Colony in Schuylkill, whose
members built a castle on the banks of that river. When others
heard about the Junto and wanted to join, Franklin arranged for
particular members to start new clubs on the Junto model, as adjuncts to it.

Through the Junto, Franklin saw the opportunity to use
Philadelphians' fondness for clubs as a means of securing the
success, the safety, the health, and the cultural life of the city. His
first venture, apart from multiplying subsidiary juntos, grew out
of an experiment of the Junto members in bringing the books
they owned to their meeting place, where they could all have access to one another's volumes. The total number brought in was
too small to satisfy Franklin, and there was no one to take care of

them between meetings. So Franklin proposed a more ambitious scheme. In 1731 he got fifty people to put up forty shillings each, with a promise of ten shillings more per year, to start a library from which all the subscribers could borrow. The result was the Library Company of Philadelphia, still flourishing today. Only four of the original directors were from outside the Junto: a physician, a merchant, a blacksmith, and a shoemaker.

Conspicuously absent from the list of founding members was one of the most learned men in America, who lived just outside Philadelphia. James Logan had come to Pennsylvania as William Penn's secretary, and he had a library of his own, far larger than the new Library Company could expect to purchase. Logan was an avid reader, not only of books in English but also in Latin, Greek, Hebrew, and Arabic, languages he had taught himself unaided. He had made his fortune in the fur trade and spent it on books. In the years ahead he was to make important contributions to astronomy, botany, and optics that were published in London and Leyden. Though Logan did not join the Library Company, Franklin knew where to go for advice about spending the money subscribed to fill its shelves. Getting Logan's assistance also offered Franklin the opportunity to talk with him, and for the next twenty years, while Logan lived, Franklin never passed up a chance. Logan evidently enjoyed it as much as Franklin. "Our Benjamin Franklin," Logan wrote to a friend in England, "is certainly an Extraordinary Man, . . . one of a singular good Judgment, but of Equal Modesty."

Logan's English friend, to whom he confided this view, was Peter Collinson, a Quaker merchant and scholar who in turn became a friend at long distance of Franklin's and provided the equipment that prompted his first experiments in electricity.

Collinson also helped the Library Company with gifts of books; and just as one friendship leads to another, so the Library Company of Philadelphia led to other such libraries in other places. Forty years after its founding, Franklin took pride in the fact that "This was the Mother of all the N. American Subscription Libraries now so numerous." "These Libraries," he wrote in the midst of the American Revolution, "have improv'd the general Conversation of the Americans, made the common Tradesmen and Farmers as intelligent as most Gentlemen from other Countries, and perhaps have contributed in some degree to the Stand so generally made throughout the Colonies in Defence of their Privileges." Libraries helped to make Philadelphians and Americans what they became.

Founding the Library Company furnished Franklin with a political experience that stood him in good stead in later projects to get Philadelphians to help themselves by helping their neighbors. He found it easiest to gain support for an enterprise if it seemed to arise spontaneously and not as something of his own devising. His procedure was to lay the groundwork in discussion at the Junto and its affiliated clubs and to run articles in his newspaper that would suggest the need for a new institution. In this way he started a volunteer fire company. After writing a piece for the Junto on fire prevention, suggesting a club to fight fires, he ran the piece in the *Gazette* as a letter from someone else addressed to the printer. The club proposed, modeled on one in Boston, would not only fight fires but would carry furniture and other valuable items from burning houses and guard them in the street. Not one club but several were soon formed, and they dramatically reduced the damage from fires in Philadelphia. The clubs' success in protecting property led Franklin after a few years to a more ambitious undertaking, a fire insurance company—the Philadelphia Contributorship, whose members elected Franklin to the board of directors. And of course his shop (now under the direction of his partner, David Hall) printed the forms for policies.

At about the same time he came to the aid of a good friend, Dr. Thomas Bond, who had unsuccessfully attempted to raise funds for a hospital to be open free of charge to the poor of the city, whether inhabitants or strangers. Franklin stepped in by printing an appeal for the hospital in the *Gazette*, and when subscriptions lagged he devised a stratagem for gaining support from Pennsylvania's legislative assembly. He persuaded those who had made contributions to petition the assembly for funds. He knew that the members of the Assembly from rural areas would be reluctant to make the grant because they would assume that it would be mainly beneficial to the city. So Franklin asked for the large sum of £2,000, to be granted only if the petitioners raised an equal amount. The assemblymen discounted the possibility of the petitioners raising that much on their own, so they granted the petition. But the prospect of having contributions matched by the Assembly made it much easier to find donors. Franklin and his friends quickly raised the necessary amount and got the grant. Franklin was promptly chosen manager of the hospital, opened it in temporary quarters in 1752, and three years later moved it to its own building constructed for the purpose.

Franklin was behind virtually every scheme that made the city an attractive place to live. He became expert at getting people to help pay for projects for their own benefit, from paving the streets and making them safe at night to caring for the sick and improving the minds of the healthy. It could all be done by making people see the advantages of virtue, advantages that were "free and easy" if you took the long view. While he stayed away from churches, he made donations to them—they might help some people love their neighbors. He even contributed to building a steeple for the Episcopal church. And in 1740, when the churches closed their doors to George Whitefield and the throngs who wished to hear him, Franklin was doubtless instrumental in arranging for the construction of a huge hall (70 feet by 100 feet) where ministers of all denominations could preach. Franklin says nothing about any role of his in the enterprise, but Whitefield's friendship for this infidel could scarcely have been accidental. Since the building was to be nonsectarian, with the trustees selected from each of the town's religious denominations, when one of them died the others found it appropriate to replace him with Franklin because he was of no sect and thus literally nonsectarian.

When the religious enthusiasm that prompted construction of the building had died away, Franklin was able to use the space to promote nonsectarian virtue in a manner more to his own liking. In 1749 he wrote and published a long pamphlet on education, proposing a school of higher learning and what it should teach, including "an *Inclination* join'd with an *Ability* to serve Mankind, one's Country, Friends and Family; which *Ability* is (with the Blessing of God) to be acquir'd or greatly encreas'd by *true Learning;* and should indeed be the great *Aim* and *End* of all Learning." He distributed the pamphlet gratis among prominent Philadelphians, having taken pains to present it "not as an Act of mine, but of some *publick-spirited Gentlemen;* avoiding as much as I could, according to my usual Rule, the presenting myself to the publick as the Author of any Scheme for their Benefit." His friends then solicited subscriptions to purchase the empty building constructed for Whitefield. The fact that Franklin was by then a trustee both of the building and of the proposed academy made the transfer easy. A substantial space was set aside for the itinerant preaching originally intended and the rest divided into classrooms. The Academy of Philadelphia, which became the University of Pennsylvania, opened its doors on January 7, 1750, and within two years had three hundred students.

Pennsylvanian

By the time he organized the college and the hospital, Franklin's way of doing things had already earned him a reputation that made every project he undertook easier than the one before. People trusted him. And with trust came power, a power he never sought or at least gave no sign of seeking. He may well have enjoyed it. It would have been a little more, or a little less, than human not to enjoy it; and without power he could scarcely have realized the public usefulness he had fixed on as his life's goal. But what won him people's trust and the power that accompanied it was his care to act the part of a foot soldier in campaigns where he was in fact the commanding officer. He made an asset out of an apparent weakness, the fact that he was not a good public speaker. To be known as a gifted speaker would have made him conspicuous and thus have undermined his ability to work for his goals more quietly. At any rate, in an age of great public rhetoric, he never made a memorable public speech—not in any political campaign, not in the Philadelphia Common Council, not in the Pennsylvania Assembly, not in the Continental Congress, not in the great Constitutional Convention of 1787. He was always Poor Richard, never saying too much in any company, especially very large company. His specialty was listening and then making the right suggestions to the right people at the right time.

The power that came to Franklin in Philadelphia, whether sought or unsought, would probably have been his wherever he lived. He later gained it in England (though not enough to save the empire) and in France, where the whole country seemed to lie at his feet. But in the early stages of his public career, the people of Pennsylvania may have been the more ready to thrust power in his hands because the structure of government in the colony left a vacuum that could be filled most readily by the voluntary associations Franklin was so adept at organizing. The extent of his power became evident in 1747 when the people of Philadelphia and Pennsylvania discovered in a new and not quite welcome way that they were part of a larger whole, the British Empire.

In 1747 Franklin had been serving for more than ten years as clerk of the Pennsylvania Assembly. He was not one of the twenty-six members, simply their hired clerk, paid to record what they said and did—or refused to do—an ideal position for the editor and publisher of the colony's foremost newspaper. He sat at every meeting, obliged to write down every motion that was made, though not the speeches for or against its passage. Probably most of the speeches were vapid—he records his boredom with them—but they kept him informed of what was going on in the colony; what the proprietors and their governor wanted, and what the people's representatives wanted or did not want; what was done, and what did not get done. And one thing that did not get done in an assembly dominated by Quakers was anything to defend the colony against outside enemies.

Peace at any price was a fundamental principle for Quakers, and in Pennsylvania they had taken pains from the beginning to avoid warfare with the Indians whose lands they invaded. Penn himself had placed James Logan in charge of Indian relations, and Logan retained the position as the colony's population exploded with the great influx of Scots-Irish and Germans in the 1730s. Logan negotiated a series of treaties with the local Indians and others deep in the interior to keep the relentless westward push of settlement as bloodless as possible. But Logan understood what many Quakers refused to understand, that principled nonviolence is not always compatible with survival. As he confessed to Franklin later, though he continued to be nominally a Quaker, "Ever since I have had the power of thinking, I have clearly seen that government without arms is an inconsistency." Logan could conciliate the Indians for a Pennsylvania government that foreswore the use of arms, but neither he nor anyone else in Pennsylvania could keep England at peace with France and Spain. During most of the first century of Pennsylvania's existence, England engaged in one war after another with France or Spain. During those wars most of the battles took place in Europe, but the American colonies of each side became fair game for the other.

In its formative years Pennsylvania would have been no great prize, but Philadelphians nevertheless got a reminder of their vulnerability as early as 1709, when a French privateer plundered a farm on the banks of the Delaware; and in the same year Quaker pacifism received a serious challenge when the Queen of

England called on Pennsylvania for men to help with an invasion of Canada. The Assembly evaded the queen's demand and got away with it because the military campaign was dropped. Before the war ended in 1713 a debt-ridden William Penn came close to giving his fellow Quakers a more serious challenge by negotiating to sell his province back to the crown. Such a move would have made it impossible to evade future royal demands for help in imperial wars. At the last minute the deal fell through, leaving the Pennsylvania government in the anomalous position that Franklin later encountered.

At the time of William Penn's fruitless negotiations with the queen, Franklin was a boy of seven in Boston; but in the 1740s, when England was again at war with France, Franklin was the clerk of an Assembly sitting in the most prosperous and most defenseless city in the American colonies. Logan was still keeping peace with the Indians, but the Assembly was dominated by Quakers who thought that England's wars were none of theirs. Logan sought another way out of the dilemma by trying to persuade his fellow Quakers at their yearly meeting to give up their seats in the Assembly in favor of people who had no scruples against fighting the French. But he was unsuccessful. King George's War (the War of the Austrian Succession) came close to home in 1745 when Massachusetts mounted an expedition against Louisbourg, the French fortress at the mouth of the St. Lawrence River. The Governor of Massachusetts, William Shirley, wrote to the Governor of Pennsylvania asking for men and money for the campaign. Franklin listened from his clerk's seat as the members of the Assembly dodged the issue. One of them stated the group's position plainly at the outset: "We have often been importun'd to do something in our own Defence, and have always refus'd: Therefore it will not become us to raise Men and Money to go and disturb those that neither meddle nor make with us; People with whom we have nothing to do." This was a fair statement of the Quaker view, but the members knew that it would be impolitic to disclose it so baldly to outsiders, so they cobbled together a reply to the governor declining to take part in the expedition on the grounds that the request had not come directly from England and might not properly represent English policy. "In short," Franklin concluded to himself, "the Governor and Assembly have been only acting a Farce and playing Tricks to amuse the World."

The *Pennsylvania Gazette* did what it could to correct the view that the French in Louisbourg were "People with whom we have nothing to do." In the previous year, Franklin pointed out, they had burned the English town of Canso in Nova Scotia and closer to Philadelphia had captured four ships off the Delaware Capes. "It is therefore in their own NECESSARY DEFENCE as well as that of all the other British Colonies, that the People of New England have undertaken the present Expedition against that Place, to which may the GOD OF HOSTS grant success." Perhaps as a result of this argument, the Assembly in July granted £4,000 to New England for the purchase of provisions, including "Wheat or other grain." The Assembly made no objection when the governor interpreted "other grain" to mean gunpowder, but by the time Pennsylvania acted, Louisbourg had already fallen to the New Englanders. The following year Franklin sent an order to his English friend William Strahan for a map of North America and another one of the world, "they being to be hung, one on each side the Door in the Assembly Room." They would remind members of the Assembly that Pennsylvania was not an island, a fact they were still exasperatingly slow to grasp.

The capture of Louisbourg reduced the danger of raids on the other colonies from that quarter, but in the summer of 1747 French privateers from other bases were at work again in greater numbers on the lower reaches of the Delaware. The Assembly dismissed any French threats as mere bravado. By October, despite reports from the West Indies that French privateers were mounting a campaign to capture Philadelphia the following summer, the Assembly could only "hope there is no Danger." Franklin thought hope a poor defense, and he had convinced himself that the Quaker assemblymen did not speak for the majority of Quakers, let alone for the rest of the colony, in their ostrichlike heedlessness. It was time for him to get the people to do for themselves what their government refused to do.

He began with newspaper articles arguing, with quotations from acknowledged Quaker spokesmen in England, that the Quaker testimony against war was not "absolutely against *Defensive War*." Two weeks later, on November 17, 1747, after consulting with Junto members, he gave Pennsylvanians a wake-up call in a pamphlet which he titled *Plain Truth*, purporting to be written by "A Tradesman of Philadelphia" (which in fact he was). The truth he made plain was that Pennsylvania was a plum ripe for picking. The enemy had discovered its defenselessness and the impotence of its government. Its people were unprepared to do do anything for themselves because everyone was waiting for someone else to do something. Settlers in the interior thought they need not worry about what might happen to the city, and Philadelphians thought that any Indian allies of the

French would attack only the interior. Quakers refused to act because conscience forbade them; others refused because they were willing to wait for disaster in order to blame the Quakers for it. "But are these the Sentiments of true Pennsylvanians," Franklin asked, "of Fellow-Countrymen, or even of Men that have common Sense or Goodness? Is not the whole Province one Body?" It was time to act as one body or face destruction. And there was a way to do it. Franklin estimated that there were sixty thousand men of fighting age in the colony, exclusive of the Quakers, and he concluded with a promise to lay before the public a plan to bring rightminded Pennsylvanians together in a military association to do what government was failing to do. The Association would organize a militia and raise money for arms and fortifications to defend the colony.

The other voluntary associations that Franklin brought into being—the library, fire companies, hospital—offered no challenge to the government whose ineffectual operations he observed from his clerk's seat in its Assembly. Now he was proposing a voluntary association to perform the most basic function of government: the protection of its citizens. He had worked out the details, and he wasted no time putting his plan into action. On November 21, 1747, four days after publishing his pamphlet, he called a meeting of tradesmen and mechanics who had helped in his earlier projects and laid the plan before them. With their approval he organized a larger meeting two days later at the hall built for Whitefield, where "the principal Gentlemen, Merchants and others" of the city endorsed it. The very next day he supplied printed copies of a pledge for people to sign, agreeing to eight articles joining them into military companies. The companies would furnish themselves with arms, elect their own officers, and send representatives from each county to "a General Military Council" whose regulations would "have the Force of LAWS with us." Franklin printed the text in his newspaper, along with explanations justifying each article. The companies, he explained, were to be formed of those living near enough to one another to meet conveniently, and thereby "to mix the Great and Small together. . . . Where Danger and Duty are equal to All, there should be no distinction from Circumstances, but All be on the Level." The election of officers by the men they were to command would avoid the common problem of armed forces where officers were appointed from above, namely, "that Persons absolutely disagreeable to the People are impower'd to command them."

This was Franklin's first exercise in state-making (for that was what it amounted to), and it shows already the commonsense, democratic principles he would display nearly thirty years later. Now the people of Pennsylvania jumped at the chance to form a militia with officers of their own choosing. Immediately a thousand signed up in Philadelphia alone, and as the word spread into the country there were soon ten thousand men under arms, organized in more than a hundred companies. Franklin provided manuals of arms for their training at the printing office. James Logan sent words of encouragement and derided his Quaker friends who "spare no pains to get and accumulate estates, and are yet against defending them, though these estates are in a great measure the sole cause of their being invaded."

The Association gave Pennsylvania an effective armed force, but if the colony was to fend off an invasion it needed fortifications and heavy armament. And Franklin knew that money to pay for them would be more difficult to raise than men, so he proposed a lottery and printed ten thousand tickets to be sold at £2 apiece, with £3,000 to go to the Association, the rest in prizes to the purchasers. The tickets quickly sold out, and the Association was soon constructing batteries on the banks of the Delaware, ordering cannon from London, and begging more from New York. (In the autobiography Franklin recounts how Governor George Clinton was persuaded to lend them by a liberal quantity of madeira wine at dinner.) When the £3,000 proved insufficient, Franklin was able to raise £3,500 more in another lottery.

There is no doubt that Franklin was behind the whole defense effort. Two years later Logan wrote to Thomas Penn, William's son, who had assumed from his brother Richard all the powers of the proprietor: "He it was that by publishing a small piece in the year 1747 with his further private contrivances, occasioned the raising of ten Companies of near one hundred men each in Philadelphia and above one hundred companies in the Province and Counties, of which I have a List. He it was who set on foot two Lotteries for Erecting of Batteries, purchasing great guns and to dispatch which he went himself to New York and borrowed there 14."

Although Logan and doubtless most other people recognized that Franklin was behind the whole business, Franklin stuck to his policy of keeping as much as possible out of sight. When one of the Philadelphia companies elected him their colonel, he declined the honor in order to serve as a private soldier. In that capacity he took his turn in the nightly watch at one of the batteries until the war ended in 1749. Franklin would doubtless have been gratified by Logan's noticing his self-effacement, as Logan did in concluding his letter to Penn: "and all this without much appearing in any part of it himself, unless in his going to New York himself in Company with others of whose going he was the occasion, for he is the principal Mover and very Soul of the Whole."

Franklin recognized that his military organization of the colony posed a direct challenge to the authority of a government that had refused to use its power to achieve what his voluntary association had done. His association had the look of the social contract that eighteenth-century thinkers envisaged as the origin of all government. So Franklin was careful not only to keep his place in the back seat but also to keep the militia from appearing to rival the existing government. By the terms of the Association the elected officers confirmed their position by obtaining commissions from the Governor's Council. When elections for the Assembly were held in October 1748, it would have been a simple matter to organize the militia to vote the obstructionist Quakers out of office. But nothing of the kind was done. And Franklin himself discouraged those who wanted to elect him to the Assembly, assuring them in the later fashion of General Sherman that if elected he would not serve. At this time Franklin had not yet acquired his contempt for the principal proprietor, Thomas Penn. Penn had contributed electrical apparatus to the Library Company and would later donate books and a telescope. The Association hoped for his help and approval now in getting done what his governors had tried unsuccessfully to do in appeals to the Assembly. But Penn saw the Association for what it potentially was and Franklin for what he might become.

As soon as he heard of it in a favorable letter from the secretary of the colony, Richard Peters, Penn saw it at once as "a Military Common Wealth," the creation of which was "little less than Treason." If the people could act "independant of this

Thomas Penn, date unknown

Government, why should they not Act against it"? And Penn's
sentiments toward the man who had brought together this seditious organization were anything but grateful: "He is a dangerous Man and I should be very Glad he inhabited any other Country, as I believe him of a very uneasy Spirit. However as he is a
sort of Tribune of the People, he must be treated with regard."

3 An Empire of Englishmen

Penn's assessment of Franklin, though needlessly hostile, was not far off the mark. At the time Franklin certainly appeared to be "of a very uneasy Spirit" if by that is meant that he seldom took his ease. During the years of the Association and those immediately following the peace of 1748, Franklin's mind was so active in so many different ways that we have to stand back and wonder how one man could be doing so much and thinking about so many things. This was the time when he was winding up his business affairs and turning over the running of his print shop to his partner. This was the time when he was designing and conducting his most crucial experiments in electricity, identifying lightning as electrical, differentiating conductors and nonconductors as well as positive and negative charges, and inventing the lightning rod, for all of which the Royal Society honored him in 1753 with its first Copley Medal for the advancement of scientific knowledge. This was the time when he ascertained that northeast storms come from the southwest. This was the time when he was deciding to devote his life to public service and considering how to do it, the time when he organized the hospital, the academy, the insurance company, and the time when he accepted membership in the Philadelphia Common Council, became an alderman, and finally agreed (in August 1751) to be elected to the Assembly. Despite his efforts to keep himself in the background he had become the best-known and most popular man in Philadelphia and, indeed, a tribune of the people.

Whose America?

Franklin would have been uncomfortable with that title, but in the year or two before he entered the Assembly as an official representative of Philadelphia and thus part of the governing body of Pennsylvania, he did a lot of thinking about the people to whose service he was deciding to dedicate himself. In the summer of 1749, as he watched the ships deposit some twelve thousand new arrivals, mostly German, on the Philadelphia docks, he had to wonder what the people of Pennsylvania were becoming. The immigrants in a single year amounted to almost as much as the city's resident population. They came with goodwill, recruited by Quaker merchants in Rotterdam who had developed a flourishing trade in transporting them to the land of religious liberty and economic opportunity. Most of them spread out into the back country, but they were coming in such numbers as to make Franklin think that "This will in a few Years become a German Colony: Instead of their Learning our Language, we must learn their's, or live as in a foreign Country."

The prospect did not please him. Like most of us, Franklin

identified himself not only by the company he kept but by the company he did not keep. He had long since decided that he belonged to no church. It went without saying that he was not a German. He was, as he saw it, an Englishman, though not living in England itself, and he wondered whether the English in Pennsylvania could assimilate so many Germans. In his recent experience with the Association, he had appealed to the Germans' previous history as warriors, but comparatively few had joined his militia. "How good Subjects they may make, and how faithful to the British Interest," he thought, was "a Question worth considering." He noticed that in neighborhoods where Germans settled, the English moved out. He was clearly upset by what was going on, and it started him thinking about the whole process of colonization, of population growth, of the effect immigration and emigration had on a country's population and what governments should do about it.

What the British were doing was not to his liking. Their laws in England imposed capital punishment for a host of felonies that did not seem quite to deserve it, but to alleviate such cruelty Parliament in 1718 had passed an act providing for transportation to the colonies as an alternative to hanging for convicted felons. Many were sent to Pennsylvania's neighboring colonies of Virginia and Maryland, where they could serve out their time (some seven years, some fourteen) in a kind of slavery to tobacco planters. The result of their presence was a plague of crimes committed by hardened criminals. When the colonies passed laws forbidding importation of convicts, the authorities in England vetoed them on the grounds that such laws would prevent the peopling of the colonies. It was a way of peopling that Franklin would gladly have prevented. To discourage it, the

Pennsylvania Assembly in 1749 had levied a duty on convicts landed at the colony's docks. Franklin learned in 1751 that this too had been derailed in England.

That England saw its colonies as a place to dump convicts made Franklin face a fact that would trouble him for the next twenty-five years: Americans had virtually no control over what England chose to do to them. He wanted to serve the public, and he was ready to spend his days as a legislator writing laws and making policies to benefit the people of Pennsylvania. But any policies he and his colleagues in the Assembly might devise, using their intimate knowledge of what their people needed, could be arbitrarily thwarted by officials three thousand miles away who knew next to nothing about them. Franklin's first response to this fact was an anger that he only gradually learned to master. He had thrown himself spontaneously and wholeheartedly into preparing Pennsylvanians to defend themselves against the enemies of England. He was proud to be English. But he was also proud to be a man and expected to be treated like a man. For England to treat the English in America as inferior to the English in England was not only unfair, it was unwise, not to say totally mad. And while his anger was hot, he took the only way open to him to rebuke those he could not control—he dashed off the most biting satirical piece he ever penned. There would be many more to come on England's folly in treating Americans as not quite English but none so angry as his proposal to round up rattlesnakes and ship them to England in thanks for England's gift of thieves and cutthroats. The *Pennsylvania Gazette* was still his newspaper, and in it he printed the proposal to release shiploads of rattlesnakes in the gardens of England's nobility and gentry and especially "in the Gardens of the *Prime Ministers*, the *Lords of Trade* and *Members of Parliament*." There they could teach the makers of English policy "to *creep,* and to *insinuate,* and to *slaver,* and to *wriggle* into Place (and perhaps to *poison* such as stand in their Way) Qualities of no small Advantage to Courtiers." Rattlesnakes, he concluded, would be "the most *suitable Returns* for the *Human Serpents* sent us by our *Mother* Country."

Franklin's anger was so bitter because he felt betrayed by his own kind, by the very people he felt himself part of. He did not want to become a German. Clearly, Germans were preferable to convicts, but he would rather have kept company with people like himself. In examining the population statistics, he could envision an American continent filled with good, law-abiding Englishmen and their descendants, and it could be done without any diminution of England's own population. Late in 1749, while preparing *Poor Richard's Almanack* for 1750, he had noted that the colonies were thought to be doubling in population every thirty years and that the increase was attributed to immigration. His own opinion, however, was that "People increase faster by Generation in those Colonies, where all can have full Employ, and there is Room and Business for Millions yet unborn," while old settled countries like England already had as large a population as their existing economies could sustain. In 1751, as he entered the Pennsylvania Assembly, he wrote out his "Observations Concerning the Increase of Mankind," with some hints about the way he would prefer to see the increase take place in America. Americans, he calculated, were doubling in number, not every thirty years but more like every twenty, while the population of old countries like England remained relatively stable. Where warfare, persecution, emigration, or other causes reduced a country's population, the vacancy would open up opportunities, and people would marry younger, have more children, and quickly make up the difference. In America the opportunies had been endless from the beginning; some eighty thousand people from England had multiplied to a million, "and yet perhaps there is not one the fewer in Britain, but rather many more, on Account of the Employment the Colonies afford to Manufacturers at Home."

For a man who saw himself as an Englishman living in America, the multiplication of American Englishmen prompted thoughts about a glorious future for both Britain and America. Even without any further immigration the Americans, doubling at least every twenty-five years, "will in another Century be more than the People of England, and the greatest Number of Englishmen will be on this Side the Water." That thought might have given pause to Englishmen in England. Did Franklin recognize that he was making an unspoken threat, that if there were more English in America than in England, power could move across the ocean and there would be no more senseless regulation of Americans by officials who knew nothing about them? He gave no hint that he thought so, but he must have seen deeper implications than he specified when he went on to rhapsodize, "What an Accession of Power to the British Empire by Sea as well as Land! What increase of Trade and Navigation! What Numbers of Ships and Seamen! We have been here but little more than 100 Years, and yet the Force of our Privateers in the late War, united, was greater, both in Men and Guns, than that of the whole British Navy in Queen Elizabeth's Time." Privateers were privately owned warships sailing under royal commissions, designed to prey upon enemy commerce, but they could easily be gathered into a regular navy.

Franklin did not spell out what kind of naval force the colonies might mount or how they might use it in another hundred years of growth. He wanted nothing more than for Englishmen to keep multiplying in America. These were the people he wanted to serve. If more English came over, so much the better. Why allow anyone else to come? "And since Detachments of English from Britain sent to America, will have their Places at Home so soon supply'd and increase so largely here; why should the Palatine Boors [that is, Boers, peasant farmers] be suffered to swarm into our Settlements, and by herding together establish their Language and Manners to the Exclusion of ours? Why should Pennsylvania, founded by the English, become a Colony of *Aliens*, who will shortly be so numerous as to Germanize us instead of our Anglifying them, and will never adopt our Language or Customs, any more than they can acquire our Complexion."

Franklin's view was as politically incorrect in 1751 as it would be today, and he lived to regret it when the Germans came to play a decisive role in Pennsylvania politics. His words did not find their way into print until 1754, but they were there to embarrass him in the 1760s, when political opponents made good use of them against him. In 1751 he went all the way in what would now be called ethnocentrism: he wanted to keep out not only Germans but everyone else except the English. Most of the world was peopled by men and women of darker skin than the English: Africa by blacks, Asia and America (before the English came) by the "tawny" colored. Even most Europeans were "generally of what we call a swarthy Complexion," including most Germans, except for the Saxons from whom the English were descended. Keep them all out. Keep America white. It is perhaps no coincidence that Franklin, living in the colony with the greatest ethnic diversity, should become the first spokesman for a lily-white America. In the last sentence of his paper he offered a wistful apology: "But perhaps I am partial to the Complexion of my Country, for such Kind of Partiality is natural to Mankind."

Franklin did not stop yearning for an American continent peopled by the British until 1775. But he was always a realist. The Germans were in Pennsylvania to stay, and it would be best to pursue measures that would keep them happy with the existing government and make them as English as possible. He corresponded with his friend Collinson about it, urging that "Methods of great tenderness should be used." Collinson suggested, among other things, intermarriage, but Franklin doubted that Englishmen would find German women attractive and vice versa. The most important problem was language, as it so often is in ethnic divisions, and Franklin became a trustee for a charitable society to pay for schools to teach English in the German settlements. There was a good deal of resistance and resentment by Germans who felt both patronized and threatened by this attempt to Anglicize them. Franklin had to admit that "Their fondness for their own Language and Manners is natural: It is not a Crime." What made their attitude disturbing was not simply the affront Franklin felt to his own ethnic pride in having this crowd of strangers invade his particular colony. What troubled him was the larger question of how their presence would affect the future of his continent, his America.

When he wrote his reflections on population in 1751, the question of who would ultimately control the continent was an open one. The Spanish were firmly settled in the south and the southwest, and the French were moving aggressively from Canada into the backcountry of New York, Pennsylvania, and Virginia. Although Germans were not yet united as a major European power, the fact that Pennsylvania was filling up with them had to be seen in relation to the international struggle into which Americans had already been drawn, none more than Franklin himself in his organization of a Pennsylvania militia. No one expected the peace that England and France had made in 1748 to last. Franklin heard rumors (fortunately unfounded) in 1753 that the French were planning a colony of Germans in the Illinois country, and this sounded ominous in view of the refusal of Pennsylvania's Germans to join his militia in 1747.

As the French threat grew, the Germans became a minor factor in it. The imminent contest for the continent, perhaps more evident to Europeans than to the Americans themselves, put a halt to the flow of immigrants: why settle in a battlefield? And the Germans already present posed a less immediate problem than the French and the Indians whom they courted as allies throughout the backcountry from New England to Virginia and the Carolinas. The French in Canada were planting forts and fortifications in the very backyards of the English, a menace that each of the colonies confronted without much help from the others. While James Logan lived, he had kept Pennsylvania secure from Indian attack by cultivating friendship with the Iroquois, who dominated the other tribes in the western parts of the colony. His successor as secretary of the Governor's Council, Richard Peters, continued the policy, and Franklin in his new prominence in the Assembly was soon drawn into the negotiations, where he could see for himself the solidity of the French presence and the weakness of the English in their piecemeal efforts to deal with it.

Indian diplomacy consisted largely of highly formal speeches of friendship accompanied by equally formal presentations of gifts to compensate for the inevitable outrages that marked the westward advance of settlement. As the conflict with France approached, the governments of New York, Virginia, and Pennsylvania separately courted as allies not only the Iroquois but the lesser tribes as well and even the tribes from the Ohio and Mississippi regions. Franklin became involved in the process at the so-called Treaty of Carlisle in 1753, in which the Pennsylvanians demonstrated their desire for the Indians' friendship with more than £800 worth of gifts and promises to rein in the greediness of the private fur traders (whose diplomacy rested on getting the Indians drunk before doing business with them). But as he listened to the Indians' response to the treaty negotiations, it was apparent to Franklin that no single colony could deal effectively with them in a contest with the French. The Indians who met the Pennsylvania commissioners at Carlisle had just come from a meeting at Winchester to collect similar gifts and promises from the Virginians. In both cases the conferences were overshadowed by the Indians' reports of French troops marching into their territories, building forts, and openly boasting of their intention to control everything and everybody.

The Albany Plan

As early as March 1751, Franklin had become convinced of the need for a union of the colonies to deal consistently and fairly with the Indians. Acting together, the colonies could "form a Strength that the Indians may depend on for Protection, in case of a rupture with the French; or apprehend great Danger from, if they should break with us." Hitherto each colony had acted on its own, and when one of them was threatened, the others always found some reason to look the other way. If the Iroquois could form a powerful union that had lasted from time immemorial, some kind of union ought not to be beyond the capacity of a dozen English colonies "to whom it is more necessary, and must be more advantageous." Franklin thought it might be done if a few "Men of good Understanding" drew up a reasonable plan and went "in the Nature of Ambassadors" to the several colonies to meet with other men of influence and through them get the various assemblies to agree.

Franklin had been thinking for a long time about what men of good understanding could do for one another and for their neighbors. Each of his projects for improving life in Philadelphia had been a matter of assembling people in organizations for mutual assistance, whether in a fire company or a library, a hospital or an academy. And the investigations prompted by his fruitful curiosity about the natural world carried him beyond Philadelphia and Pennsylvania to men in other colonies who could help one another search out the mysteries of electricity, of wind and waves, of ocean currents and waterspouts and a thousand other things. By the 1750s he had been corresponding for many years with men of understanding in all the colonies: Dr. John Mitchell of Virginia, a physician who was at work on what became for its time the definitive map of the American colonies; Cadwallader Colden, later governor of New York, with whom he continually exchanged views on electricity and gravitation; Jared Eliot of Connecticut, who was devising new schemes of crop rotation and diversification on his farm in Killingworth; John Perkins of Boston, with whom he argued about whether waterspouts ascended from the water or descended from the skies. There were many such men scattered throughout the colonies, and Franklin had already tried in 1743 to bring them together in a society for "promoting useful knowledge."

That project lay dormant while England grappled with France, but Franklin knew that in the large minds of men like these lay the possibility of bringing the colonies together in mutual help against France. He may have thought of mounting a mission for the purpose himself, but if so he must have been given pause when the Pennsylvania Assembly demonstrated that its customary blindness to danger would stand in the way of any agreement of the kind he hoped for. In the spring of 1754, when the Governor of Virginia appealed for assistance against French intrusion near what is now Pittsburgh, Franklin was appointed to a committee to determine whether the area in question was within Pennsylvania's boundaries. When the committee, after careful investigation, reported that it was, the Assembly voted that it was not and adjourned without taking any action to aid the Virginians. When the group reassembled in April (1754) it again ignored the Virginians' plea but attended to an earlier request from the governor of New York and the Board of Trade in England to send delegates to a meeting with the Indians, particularly the Iroquois, at Albany in June. The Assembly agreed to pay for commissioners to attend the meeting and for a small present to the Indians.

In May, when the Governor of Pennsylvania asked the Assembly's advice on instructions for the commissioners and explicitly about "a Union of the several Colonies in Indian Affairs," all it would offer was that "no Propositions for an Union of the Colonies, in Indian Affairs, can effectually answer the good Purposes, or be binding, further than are confirmed by Laws, enacted under the several Governments, comprized in that Union." Consequently, when Franklin and three other Pennsylvanians set out for Albany in June, they carried instructions from the governor that merely authorized them to hold an "interview" with the Iroquois "to renew, ratify and confirm the Leagues of Amity, subsisting between Us and the said Nations of Indians, and to make them the Presents that have been provided for them." They were empowered to do whatever else "shall appear necessary for the engaging them heartily in Our Interest and for frustrating any Attempts which have been made to withdraw them from it."

Franklin had continued to think about a defensive union, but the recalcitrance of the Pennsylvania Assembly was greater than he had anticipated, despite his long familiarity with its ways. On the way to Albany, he stopped at New York City, where at the prompting of his friends there he spelled out thoughts he had sketched earlier about the structure of such a union of the colonies. The heart of the plan was a Grand Council to be chosen by the representative assemblies of each colony. As a representative body (that is, representatives of representatives) it would have the power not only to make laws for all relations with the Indians, including warfare, and to levy taxes for the purpose; the Grand Council would also be in charge of purchasing Indian lands and establishing new colonies in the west beyond the existing settlements. To preside over this "General Government" and enforce its laws, the king would appoint a "President General," empowered, like the royal governors of the separate colonies, with a veto over all acts of the Grand Council. The powers of the General Government would be limited to the external affairs of the member colonies and would not otherwise affect their existing governments.

In 1751 Franklin had thought that influential men from different colonies might come together to adopt a plan like this and then persuade their respective assemblies to agree to it. The Albany meeting would be just such an opportunity. But he could now see that getting the various assemblies to go along was a remote possibility. He was as influential a man as anyone could be in any colony, and he had just been shown that his influence was not enough to get the Pennsylvania Assembly even to consider a plan of union. So he decided to bypass the assemblies and proposed instead that the union be established by act of Parliament.

At Albany the other delegations quickly embraced Franklin's plan with only minor additions of detail. Franklin had been right about "Men of good Understanding" being able to agree on a plan of union. The Board of Trade had asked only that the delegates hold an interview with the Indians. Most of them had not been empowered by their assemblies, any more than Franklin had, to consider a general union. Virginia, a crucial colony, had not even sent a delegation. But the men at Albany in 1754 (like those who met at Philadelphia in 1787 to revise the Articles of Confederation) had no hesitation in exceeding their instructions by proposing a genuine union; and, again like those later in Philadelphia, they saw the need to thwart the shortsightedness of the assemblies that appointed them by an appeal to a higher force (in 1754 the Parliament of England, in 1787 the people). If they required further proof of the need for union, they could find it in the attitude of the small number of Indians who showed up at Albany. The Indians accepted the English presents and promises but did not attempt to disguise their greater respect for the activities of the French in the interior. Without a union, the English in America faced encirclement and conquest by England's enemy, to whom the Indians could easily shift their allegiance. The men of understanding at Albany needed no instruction from their assemblies or from the authorities in England to see the danger. And they also concurred that their assemblies would not consent willingly to the union that seemed to them imperative. It would have to be imposed, as Franklin had decided, by act of Parliament.

Did Franklin realize how momentous a step this appeal to the power of Parliament represented in his own thinking? He had long been troubled by the operation of Parliamentary power in America, and his previous reactions to it had ranged from the anger of his rattlesnake satire to the implied threat of shifting power across the ocean in his observations on American population growth. It must have cost him something to invoke the dominance of Parliament, elected only by Englishmen in England, to overcome the blind obstinacy of representative assemblies elected by Englishmen in America. He still thought of himself as both English and American, that the two terms designated one people. And he still hated the unequal treatment of the English in America by the government of the English in England. But for the moment it was more important to him not to become French. In 1747 that meant enlisting Pennsylvanians in a militia. In 1754 it meant union in treating with Indian allies. If Parliamentary dominance was the only way to achieve union, the equal treatment of equal people would have to wait, but the issue was never far from his mind.

Franklin had some ideas about how to achieve equal treatment eventually. He did not have them fully worked out, but in the week before he set out for Albany he had given a hint of them to Peter Collinson, who had become one of his favorite correspondents. In a letter mostly concerned with scientific matters he deplored the failure of the colonial assemblies to help one another against the French, and then added, "May I presume to whisper my Sentiments in a private Letter? Britain and her Colonies should be considered as one Whole, and not as different States with separate Interests." It seems likely that he thought of a colonial union as a stepping-stone to a larger union in which Britain and the colonies would somehow be joined on equal terms. Though he had abandoned hope of getting the colonial assemblies to agree to any kind of union at the outset, he designed his plan to preserve the element of popular consent in the governing body. His Grand Council would represent the assemblies and through them the people of the several colonies. The president general would represent the king. Thus the entire structure would resemble the government of existing royal colonies except for the absence of a governor's council. While it would require an act of Parliament to get it started, Parliament would have no part in its operation.

At Albany, Franklin fought off efforts to give the proposed president general a share in choosing the delegates to the Grand Council. He had always seen voluntary consent as the way to make things work. The Grand Council was to be an instrument of popular consent so that "a house of commons or the house of representatives, and the grand council, are thus alike in their nature and intention." And as he had given his earlier militia the power to elect its own officers, he here provided that the commissions of military officers in any force raised by the union should be approved by the Grand Council. This would attach a greater degree of popular consent to them than was the case with the militia officers of most colonies (other than those in Franklin's "Association" of 1747), where it was the governor's prerogative to appoint and commission them. As Franklin told Cadwallader Colden, "I am of Opinion, that when Troops are to be rais'd in America, the Officers appointed must be Men they know and approve, or the Levies will be made with more Difficulty, and at much greater Expence."

As he awaited the outcome of the Albany Plan, Franklin made a visit to Boston, where he talked at length about union with the royal governor, William Shirley. Shirley apparently proposed that the colonial assemblies be bypassed, not only in the union's establishment but in its administration by a "Board of Governors and Council," royally appointed. After talking with Shirley, Franklin wrote him three letters, on December 3, 4, and 22. In them we can see how rapidly Franklin's thoughts about the British-American empire were maturing.

Franklin admitted to Shirley that conceivably a "general Government might be as well and faithfully administer'd without the people as with them" but then reminded him gently of what every good politician knows (but which British statesmen never learned in their treatment of the colonies), that when dealing with any people "where heavy burdens are to be laid on them, it has been found useful to make it, as much as possible, their own act." He went on to suggest, not quite so gently, without any apology of "present company excepted," that royal governors of a General Government would be subject to the same corruption as royal governors of particular colonies, "That Governors often come to the Colonies meerly to make Fortunes, with which they intend to return to Britain, [that they] are not always Men of the best Abilities and Integrity, have no Estates here, nor any natural Connections with us, that should make them heartily concern'd for our Welfare; and might possibly be sometimes fond of raising and keeping up more Forces than necessary, from the Profits accruing to themselves, and to make Provision for their Friends and Dependents."

From a General Government invested in royal appointees, with powers like those which the Albany Congress would place in a Grand Council representing, at least indirectly, the people, Franklin foresaw the conflict that would erupt ten years later when the government of England began to impose burdens directly on the colonies. On December 4 he warned Shirley that "it is suppos'd an undoubted Right of Englishmen not to be taxed but by their own Consent given thro' their Representatives" and that "compelling the Colonies to pay Money without their Consent would be rather like raising Contributions in an Enemy's Country, than taxing of Englishmen for their own publick benefit." He did not need to add that treating the colonies like an enemy country might make them one.

Shirley apparently responded with a suggestion that the colonies be given representatives in Parliament. Franklin welcomed the idea, because he hoped "that by such an union, the people of Great Britain and the people of the Colonies would learn to consider themselves, not as belonging to different Communities with different Interests, but to one Community with one Interest, which I imagine would contribute to strengthen the whole, and greatly lessen the danger of future separations." But Franklin had already pointed out to Shirley that laws of Parliament restricting colonial trade for the benefit of English merchants did not treat English and Americans as one community with one interest. He thought that Americans would be happy to form a new union not just with one another but with the English in England, by electing representatives to a new Parliament. But that would require that "they had a reasonable number of Representatives allowed them; and that all the old Acts of Parliament restraining the trade or cramping the manufactures of the Colonies, be at the same time repealed, and the British Subjects on this side the water put, in those respects, on the same footing with those in Great Britain, 'till the new Parliament, representing the whole, shall think it for the interest of the whole to re-enact some or all of them."

Franklin's letters to Shirley show how far he had come in thinking about what it meant to him to be both English and American. They also show how far ahead of other Englishmen and other Americans he had grown. While he and Shirley talked, the colonial assemblies acted, and so did the British government in England. He had been right in despairing of the colonial assemblies. They rejected the plan with a depressing unanimity. Its fate in England was equally hopeless but more complicated than Franklin could have realized. As he remembered it in his autobiography, the assemblies had rejected the plan because they thought "there was too much *Prerogative* in it [the president general's veto power]; and in England it was judg'd to have too much of the Democratic: The Board of Trade therefore did not approve of it or recommend it for the Approbation of his Majesty." By "the approbation of his Majesty" Franklin must have meant acceptance first by the king's Privy Council, which would have received it from the Board of Trade, the Council's advisory body on all colonial legislation. If the Board of Trade had approved the plan and the Privy Council had then presented it to Parliament, and Parliament had passed it into law, then the king (who had long since lost the power to veto acts of Parliament) would have given it official approval, and it would have become law. What the colonial assemblies would have done about a law enacting what they had already rejected is another question, which they were spared the problem of facing. And Franklin himself was spared the problem of deciding what to do in a contest between American representative assemblies and the English Parliament.

What had happened to his Albany Plan in England, had he known about it, might have given him cause to rethink the implications of his appeal for parliamentary enactment. As it happened, while the other members of the congress at Albany had concurred in the appeal, they had taken no steps to secure the plan's presentation to Parliament. There were, in fact, no precedents for such a presentation. But the Governor of New York, who had sent out the Board of Trade's call for the congress, did send a copy of the plan to the board. It arrived after a series of events in the corridors of power in London that reflected the complications awaiting Franklin's dream of an empire of equals. During the summer of 1754, after calling for the Albany meeting, the Board of Trade continued to consider the need for colonial union against the French. Without waiting for the results of the Albany meeting, the board had drafted a plan of its own. The prime minister, the Duke of Newcastle, had encouraged the board to move ahead with it. As finally presented to Newcastle, the board's plan called for a commander-in-chief to take charge of constructing forts and mounting a force to defend any colony under attack. The colonial assemblies were to appoint commissioners whose main function would be to allocate military expenses among the several colonies. But these would be subject to review and revision by the colonial assemblies. It was a much less ambitious plan than Franklin's, though more cumbersome in its details.

Newcastle had the board's plan in hand when word arrived in London on September 8 that the preceding July (at the very moment when the Albany Congress was discussing Franklin's plan) one George Washington had surrendered a force of Virginia militia to the French in the backcountry of what happened to be Franklin's own colony, Pennsylvania. On hearing the news, Newcastle immediately approached the Speaker of the House of Commons, with a view to introducing legislation to adopt the Board of Trade's plan of union. The Board of Trade and the prime minister understood the danger that the French presented, just as the commissioners at Albany understood it. The House of Commons, however, if the Speaker represented them correctly, harbored a foreboding of American independence that outweighed any fear of the French. According to Newcastle's own memorandum of this conversation, the Speaker warned him of the "ill consequence to be apprehended from uniting too closely the northern colonies with each other, an Independency upon this country to be feared from such an union." Newcastle accordingly dropped the proposal. When the Board of Trade in the following month presented him with Franklin's Albany Plan, calling for a much more powerful colonial union, he could scarcely have given it a second thought.

Presumably Franklin never learned of these transactions. He continued to think of himself as no less an Englishmen than an American. It was a common supposition in England from the time the first colonies were founded that they might some day become independent. But Franklin, probably like most other Americans, did not think of independence as something imminent in his own time and saw no reason why it should ever occur so long as England treated the colonies as equals. But here, before he knew about it, the expectation of an American bid for independence was affecting British policy in what would become in only twenty years' time a self-fulfilling prophecy.

A Union of Equals

Franklin was good at wishing for good things—good for others as well as himself—and good at making his wishes come true. He was also realist enough to recognize that he could not make them all come true: he could not fill America with Englishmen to the exclusion of Germans and Africans. He could not get colonial assemblies to see what he and the men at Albany could see, that a union was in their best interests. The methods he had devised for getting Philadelphians to do what was good for them by keeping himself in the background did not work well on a large scale. The wish he had expressed to Collinson in 1754 about a British Empire conceived and organized as one people was a wish, like his others, for something that would benefit the great majority of the people concerned. But it was a wish on a scale that exceeded every other he had ever had. He recognized it as a long-term goal, not to be achieved by organizing an association for the purpose. It would require persuading people gradually to abandon familiar institutions in favor of untried ways of working together. And it would require overcoming the opposition of people who profited from control of the existing institutions at the expense of the larger numbers under their control.

This long-term goal of an Anglo-American empire of equals directed Franklin's public service until he was obliged to give it up in 1775. We can watch him pursue it, working to win the consent of high and low to measures that would move his English-American countrymen toward it. It was a noble goal, and his pursuit of it brought him the fame as a public figure that he already enjoyed as a scientist. But he did not succeed, even in the preliminary stages, and he made a number of enemies in the attempt. He also allowed himself some wishful thinking, in supposing others would see as quickly as himself the desirability of what he was sure would be good for them.

Franklin's confidence that people could be enticed into doing what was best for them had grown with his success in getting Philadelphians to do so; but it rested at bottom on his earlier decision that the difference between right and wrong, good and bad, coincided with the difference between what was beneficial to human beings and what was harmful to them. His projected party of virtue would be the party of the "free and easy." And when he talked of what was right or translated it into *rights*, he continued to think of right or rights as beneficial, or more specifically as "useful," and therefore easy. Usefulness and right were almost synonymous for him. When he told Shirley that it had been found useful to get people to shoulder burdens voluntarily (and thus more *easily*), he went on to remind him that active popular consent was not only useful but right and among Englishmen, his favorite people, was *a right* ensconced in their history, the "undoubted Right of Englishmen not to be taxed but by their own Consent given thro' their Representatives."

Franklin was the least doctrinaire of men. He believed that an active popular consent to acts of government was useful and right, but what made it so was not the consent itself, which could not practicably be given in person by a whole people, but rather the belief that it had been given, through representatives. The wheels of government moved more smoothly when people "*think* they have some share in the direction" (emphasis added). It mattered less that they had such a share than that they thought they had. Remember the question he posed for the Junto back in 1732: "If the Sovereign Power attempts to deprive a Subject of his Right (or which is the same thing, of what he thinks his Right) is it justifiable in him to resist if he is able?" Neither consent nor resistance was an absolute for Franklin: a right was something you thought you had. If you could not exercise it, maybe you should resist but only if you could do so successfully. Don't die in a lost cause.

David Hume, whom Franklin later met and liked, had pointed out in 1741 that all governments, even the most despotic, had to rest on opinion, and thus on a kind of consent, whether obtained through fear or favor. Franklin was saying to Shirley that Englishmen were more easily governed if they believed—in Hume's terms, if they had the opinion—that taxes were levied on them only with their own consent and that they gave that consent through representatives. As he contemplated a union of England and its American colonies in one community, he knew that people in both places would have to maintain the belief that they shared in their own government by consenting through representatives to the taxes it levied and to the laws it passed. Americans currently shared in most government acts affecting them, through representatives in their several colonial assemblies; and they submitted (not very easily) to a few laws restricting their commerce passed by the British Parliament, in which they had no share. If they were to become one community with Britain under the general direction of a newly constituted Parliament, that new Parliament would not only have to have American representatives, but it would have to discard any existing laws that the old Parliament had made for Americans without their consent. Both conditions would be necessary, Franklin maintained, before Americans could believe that they gave their consent to what Parliament did to them.

That they would actually be consenting was not necessary, but they must believe that they were, and the belief could not be sustained if it did not bear some resemblance to fact. A stretch of the imagination was already needed to regard the consent of a representative as the consent of the people who chose him. He was not an attorney, subject to their dictates. He was entitled to use his own judgment in voting for or against any measure that came before the legislative body to which he was elected. That large a distance from actual consent was almost by definition acceptable, but a much larger distance was everywhere the fact for most of the people subject to every existing government, whether in England or America. All representatives were in some sense representatives of representatives. Women, and everyone under the age of about twenty-one, were seen as represented by the men who elected representatives. And the men excluded from voting by property qualifications or servitude were seen as represented by the men who did vote. Moreover, men who voted against a representative who then won the election were still seen as represented by him.

The idea that people could give consent through representatives thus rested at best on some big assumptions. Eventually people would reject some of them, for example that women could be represented by men without any woman ever casting a vote, or that men who did not have property could be represented by men who did. In Franklin's time, people had scarcely begun to question these assumptions. But they were likely to reject another assumption on which consent through representation was sometimes claimed. It would have been impossible to persuade people in, say, Pennsylvania that they were represented by persons elected in Massachusetts. As people were known by where they came from, they could not be brought to believe that they were represented by people chosen from a totally different place—another state, another government. Franklin, for one, could not have taken seriously the idea (advanced later) that he as a Pennsylvanian or as an American was represented in the British House of Commons by men elected in England. He told Shirley as a simple matter of fact, requiring no demonstration, that "the Colonies have no Representatives in Parliament." Because no one living in the colonies, no one who "came from" Pennsylvania or Virginia or any other colony, had a vote in choosing representatives in Parliament, it went almost without saying that no one from the colonies would think he was represented there. A representative could give consent only for the people of the place where he was chosen.

The colonial representative assemblies themselves posed threats to the opinion or belief that all the places they governed were represented in them. In every colony settlers moved west into new places more rapidly than units of representation— counties or townships—were organized. In the New England colonies, where the people who moved west were mainly the children of those who stayed in the East—there were few immigrants to New England—representation was extended to new settlements pretty rapidly. In Pennsylvania and the colonies to the south of it, the people of the backcountry, who were often ethnically different (many German and Scots-Irish) from those of the East, had few or no representatives in their respective assemblies and had to accept the consent of easterners as their own. This geographical inequality did not at first generate an opinion among westerners that they were deprived of rights. In some cases they elected easterners to the few seats allotted them in order to avoid the cost of sending someone to the seat of government, which was always in the East. But by the 1760s and 1770s westerners were beginning to complain of government's inattentiveness to their needs and to question the supposition that they shared in it through the meager representation allotted them. As Franklin could have postulated, they became less easy to govern. In any new British-American union it would have been necessary to bring consent through representation closer to fact geographically, as indeed was done in 1776 and afterward in the exclusively American union.

Franklin would be a member of the convention that altered the government of Pennsylvania in 1776 to assign representation strictly according to the geographic distribution of population and to keep it that way by a new enumeration of the "taxable" inhabitants in each county every seven years. He would also be a member of the Constitutional Convention in 1787 that drafted a similar principle of consent to determine representation in the United States Congress. But before 1776 he was less interested in adjusting the allocation of representatives within American colonial assemblies than he was in the grosser inequity that denied all Americans any share in choosing the members of the Parliament that imposed restrictions on what they could make and on what and where they could buy and sell. He would become equally troubled by the fact that no American had the slightest influence on the veto power that officials in England, responsible to Parliament, could exercise over the laws that colonial assemblies of representatives might have already consented to. Indeed, the representatives in most American colonial assemblies faced a double veto over their actions, first from governors appointed in England and then, if the governors had accepted their acts, from the king, or rather, the king's ministers (who were really the leaders of the majority in Parliament). Rhode Island and Connecticut were exceptions: they elected their own governors and allowed them no veto power, but their acts could still be vetoed in England if they came under surveillance there. Maryland and Pennsylvania also differed from other colonies in that their governors were appointed not by the king's ministers but by the proprietors to whose family an earlier king had assigned the power of government along with the original ownership of the colony itself. In those two colonies the acts of representatives could thus be thwarted before they reached the king's ministers, not by a royally appointed governor but by a governor appointed and instructed by a private English citizen. There would have to be some changes in the colonies as well as in England if the two were to become a single people, united in the opinion that they shared in their own government. The changes in England, as Franklin was to discover, would be more difficult to achieve than those in the colonies. But you had to begin somewhere. Franklin was a Pennsylvanian. He began in Pennsylvania and soon found how difficult it was to take even the smallest steps toward his goal.

Patriotic Frustration

Before the Albany meeting the stubbornness of the colonial assemblies had been the stumbling block in the way of colonial union and of expenditures for defense. In Pennsylvania, Quaker pacifism had been part of the problem, but when the final great war (the French and Indian War) began in 1754, the Quakers gave way, and many who could not overcome their scruples against violence surrendered their seats in the Assembly to Anglicans and Presbyterians. By the time the English dispatched General Edward Braddock and two regiments of British regulars to engage the French in the backcountry, Franklin had already convinced the Assembly to appropriate funds for provisions and other expenses of the expedition. When the general was unable to rent carts and horses to carry the expedition's equipment, Franklin personally persuaded Pennsylvania farmers to supply them. And when the expedition was disastrously defeated, leaving the Pennsylvania frontier open to invasion by the enemy, Franklin persuaded the Assembly to pass a law creating a militia. This time he accepted a colonelcy in it and organized troops and fortifications in the west (until England vetoed the Pennsylvania law creating the militia, another example of English fear of American autonomy).

Franklin's efforts earned him and the Assembly abundant praise and thanks from the general and his staff, thus rescuing Pennsylvania from any charge of irresponsible conduct in the face of the enemy. But meanwhile, as a leading member of the Assembly, Franklin had encountered a special local obstacle to the equal treatment of all Englishmen. In theory the supremacy of the king over all his subjects placed them all on the same footing, even though the king's decrees might in fact be the decrees of a Parliamentary majority. But the king's delegation of a part of his authority to Thomas Penn elevated one of his subjects above those who actually lived in Pennsylvania. And the efforts of his subjects in Pennsylvania to serve him by supplying his troops met with resistance from this overmighty subject. When they levied taxes on their lands to raise the necessary funds, the governor, on instructions from Penn, vetoed every bill that did not exempt the proprietor's own lands, not only the public lands of the colony but those which he had kept as his personal domain. Since all the lands in the colony would suffer from a French invasion, it was only fair that all should share alike in the costs of protecting them, but Penn steadfastly refused.

The governor and the Assembly dueled with each other in increasingly rancorous messages, through two years during which one governor was replaced, with no better results, by another. Franklin was always on the committee assigned to prepare answers to the governor's vetoes, and it was generally he who drafted them. Colonial governors, even when appointed by the king, often quarreled with their assemblies; but in Pennsylvania, since the governor did not enjoy the vicarious majesty of appointment by the king, Franklin allowed himself to use language that he might have hesitated to employ against an agent of the king. In May 1755 he was telling the governor, for the Assembly, that that body "cannot look upon him as a Friend to this Country"; in August, that they had, "if this Bill is still refused, very little farther Hopes of any Good from our present Governor."

The Assembly never gained any further hopes. What rankled most, at least to Franklin, was the interposition of proprietary power between King George II and his Pennsylvanian subjects. The Assembly, he said, "do not propose to tax the Proprietary as Governor, but as a Fellow Subject." Whatever privileges King Charles may have granted the first proprietor, he could not have authorized "the Proprietaries claiming that invidious and odious Distinction, of being exempted from the common Burdens of their Fellow Subjects." What Franklin had stated to Shirley as "useful" and then as "the undoubted Right of Englishmen" became in the Assembly's arguments with the proprietary governor, a "natural Right." More specifically the Assembly denied the power of the proprietor or his governor to amend, alter, or veto the bills in which they levied taxes for the king's service (which was the same thing as the public service). "To dispose of their own Money," they declared, "by themselves or their Representatives, is, in our Opinion, a natural Right, inherent in every Man or Body of Men, antecedent to all laws." Therefore, "neither the Proprietaries, nor any other Power on Earth, ought to interfere between us and our Sovereign, either to modify or refuse our Free Gifts and Grants for his Majesty's Service."

In becoming the principal spokesman for the Assembly in this quarrel with the proprietor, Franklin allowed himself to become preoccupied with something that had only a tenuous connection with his larger vision of an Anglo-American empire. In his observations on the contrasting dynamics of population growth in England and America, in his plan of colonial union, in his letters to Shirley he had shown extraordinary capacity for defining large public issues. Not that he had ever neglected the smaller, mundane details. While thinking about colonial union or population growth, he was continually occupied in preparing his almanacs, designing a flexible catheter for his brother John, writing instructions for his employees about running the post office. When the Albany Plan failed to bring about united action against the French, he did not waste time trying to rescue it. Instead, he turned to doing what could be done without a union. But in the Pennsylvania Assembly's quarrel with the governor, he seems to have lost his perspective, his sense not only of what could be done or of what was useful but also of what was worth devoting his time and energy to.

The proprietor's selfish and shortsighted refusal to allow his lands to be taxed was a detail of no consequence by comparison, say, with the need to get General Braddock's army over the mountains. While it was indeed an obstacle that would have to be surmounted eventually in the kind of Anglo-American union Franklin envisioned, it was a minor obstacle in any large view of the matter. It was out of character for him to wheel out the heavy artillery of "natural right" where the enemy, by his own definition, was the fellow subject of an acknowledged king. His own way of thinking about the most serious social and political issues was in the language of usefulness, of right and wrong, but not of natural right, a phrase loaded with implications of anarchy and revolution. Franklin's preoccupation, not to say obsession, with the proprietary prerogatives not only wasted his immense talents but obscured his vision and his perceptions of what was politically feasible. Did he perhaps feel personally challenged by a man like Thomas Penn, a man of inferior capacities who by virtue of a royal grant to his father could block the patriotic efforts of Pennsylvanians and particularly of the Pennsylvanian who more than any other had directed those efforts? How dare the man stand between him and his king? It is difficult not to see anger distorting Franklin's reasoning in the arguments that he led the Assembly to make in this contest.

To bolster a valid case against an obdurate proprietor and bring pressure on his governor, who was more immediately accessible to their arguments than the proprietor was, the Assembly resorted to another line of attack that was bound to fail. It fastened on a clause in the charter by which the king in 1681 had granted the original proprietor, William Penn, the authority to govern. The grant had empowered Penn to govern through "*Deputies* and *Lieutenants* . . . According unto *their best discretion*, by and with the Advice, Assent, and Approbation of the Freemen of the said Country, their Delegates or Deputies." Franklin and his associates interpreted this clause to mean that the governor, though appointed by the proprietor, was empowered to act according to his own "best discretion," regardless of any instructions from the proprietor. Indeed, any instruction against approving particular bills (notably a bill that taxed proprietary lands) was "in itself void, and a meer Nullity." The proprietor had no power to give binding instructions to his deputy, the governor. Could Franklin not see that this was a farfetched conclusion to draw from the clause in question? It is scarcely surprising that the proprietor took steps to ensure that his deputy did his bidding. He simply required the man he employed as governor, before taking office, to post a £5,000 bond to abide by the instructions given him. There was only one way to counter this move. In 1757 the Assembly took the step that all its arguments had been leading to: it decided to appeal to the king directly to put the proprietor in his proper place as a subject. And there was only one obvious person to carry the appeal to London: Benjamin Franklin.

4 Proprietary Pretensions

We first encountered Franklin on his way back to America from England in 1726, a precocious youngster ready to make his way in the world. We have watched him become a major figure in the life of Philadelphia and Pennsylvania, a major figure among scientists the world over, and we have seen him taking a hand in imperial affairs. We have glimpsed his vision of an English America, in which Pennsylvanians and Virginians and New Englanders would all stand on an equal footing with Englishmen in England. His voyage to England now is in pursuit of that goal, or of a small step toward it, to curb the elevated status of the Penn family over English Americans in their colony.

Old Friends and New

Picture him now, aged fifty-one, settled in the middle of London at 7 Craven Street, near Charing Cross, in four comfortable rooms of a house owned by an agreeable widow, Margaret Stevenson, with a charming daughter, Mary, always called Polly. Deborah is not there. Dead set against crossing the ocean, she remains a Philadelphian, always sympathetic and helpful to her husband but never sharing his expansive participation in a larger world. Franklin writes to her regularly, brings her, at however long range, into his new friendship with the Stevensons, and sends her news of the three traveling companions who share his rooms. One of them is Billy, his son William, now about twenty-six, serving as his father's assistant and almost constantly with him, except when he is studying law at the Middle Temple. Billy has grown up in Philadelphia under his father's watchful eye and political tutelage. When Franklin accepted election to the Assembly in 1751, Billy had taken his place as the Assembly's clerk. He had become close friends with another young man in training for the law, Joseph Galloway, who was himself elected to the Assembly in 1756 and quickly became Franklin's closest ally there. Accompanying his father to London, as he had to Albany, Billy has become a political alter ego for Franklin in the contest with the proprietors.

The other members of Franklin's entourage at Craven Street are something of a surprise, given Franklin's later activities against slavery. They are his own slave Peter, and William's slave King. We learn very little about them from Franklin's surviving letters, other than that Peter was "very diligent and attentive" when Franklin was sick. We only hear of King's existence in 1760, when Deborah had inquired about him, and Franklin answered that he "was of little Use, and often in Mischief." He had run away two years before and was now, with Billy's permission, serving a lady in Suffolk, who was sending him to school.

Peter had stayed with Franklin and behaved "as well as I can expect. . . . So we rub on pretty comfortably." Franklin was able to rub on pretty comfortably with slavery itself for a few more years. Not until late in life did it begin to trouble his conscience.

More immediately in his consciousness for the next five years was London and the people in it. London itself was hard to ignore. With a population of seven hundred thousand, it dwarfed Philadelphia, as it did every other English city. Franklin had not been there long before he started offering proposals for keeping the streets cleaner. They were apparently worse than Philadelphia's: he had to hire a horse-drawn "chariot" to take him through them safely. But worse than the streets was the air. There was no way of avoiding the choking coal smoke inside and out as people lit their fires against the winter cold. Deborah asked in a letter why they did not burn wood, which at least gave off a sweeter smoke, to heat the house at Craven Street, and her husband explained that you would have to get every other house to do it too: "The whole Town is one great smoky House, and every Street a Chimney, the Air full of floating Sea Coal Soot, and you never get a sweet Breath of what is pure, without riding some Miles for it into the Country."

Franklin did a lot of riding into the country. He could not do it in winter, when the smoke was at its worst, because Parliament was sitting then and he had to attend to his negotiations with the government and the Pennsylvania proprietors. He was usually able to escape only in the summer, when he and Billy would take off to see the rest of the country and its people. In 1758 they traveled over "a great part of England" and busied themselves looking up all their distant cousins in Northamptonshire, where Franklin's father had lived before coming to America in 1682.

The next summer they were off to Liverpool and then north to Scotland, where the University of St. Andrews had awarded Franklin an honorary doctor's degree the preceding February. Now he made friends with the luminaries of the Scottish Enlightenment: Sir Alexander Dick, president of the College of Physicians at Edinburgh; David Hume, the great philosopher; and Lord Kames, preeminent jurist and historian. In 1760 Franklin and Billy visited Wales and the following year crossed the Channel to see Flanders and Holland, but it was England and Scotland that had already earned a place in Franklin's heart. They could never displace Pennsylvania and America, but after less than six months in England, he admitted to Deborah that "the regard and friendship I meet with from persons of worth, and the conversation of ingenious men, give me no small pleasure."

Franklin's reputation had preceded him. He had already been elected to the Royal Society, which had given his experiments with electricity worldwide publicity. After he received his honorary degree from St. Andrews, repeated at Oxford, he was always known as Dr. Franklin and accorded a respect he seldom encountered in America outside Philadelphia. But it was more than the respect he met with that drew him to England. He had expressed a deep, inner feeling in his wish to have America filled with Englishmen like himself. His official mission was connected with his desire for Americans to be put on an equal political footing with their brothers and sisters in England. And as always with Franklin there were personal, human ties that mattered. It was no accident that his first summer's travels had taken him in search of his blood relatives. More important, he came to England already on intimate terms with a number of people who

John Fothergill, 1781

had become dear to him, and he to them, without their having ever laid eyes on one another. Franklin had enough human warmth to reach across an ocean.

One of his closest long-distance friends was Peter Collinson, the Quaker merchant and naturalist who had supplied him with the apparatus that started him on his electrical experiments in 1747. It was to Collinson that he wrote accounts of the experiments, and Collinson who reported them to the Royal Society (Collinson's botanical studies had earned him membership in 1728) and who secured his appointment as deputy postmaster for all of America in 1753. Collinson also had helped him gain support in England for both the Library Company and the academy.

Peter Collinson, ca. 1767

In the years before Franklin arrived in England the two had exchanged more than seventy letters on the variety of things that friends talk about. Franklin and Billy spent their first night in London at Collinson's house, and Collinson opened doors for them everywhere.

Collinson seemed to know everybody. When Franklin fell sick shortly after arriving in England, Collinson got his friend Dr. John Fothergill, probably the foremost physician in London, to attend him. Fothergill was already an admirer of Franklin's and in 1751 had supervised the London publication of some of his letters to Collinson on electricity (*Experiments and Observations on Electricity, Made at Philadelphia in America*). Collinson and Fothergill both knew the proprietors of Pennsylvania, Richard and Thomas Penn, and Franklin had already enlisted Collinson's interest in the Pennsylvania Assembly's quarrel with them. His account of its early stages had elicited from Collinson a comment that must have heightened Franklin's confidence. "Can any Man be more wrong headed than your Governor," Collinson asked, "not to pass the most equitable Law in the World[?] Our People at the Helm resent his Conduct." Franklin could take that as a hint that higher authority might share his impatience with proprietary authority. He would be looking to Collinson and Fothergill for advice as he began his negotiations.

Meanwhile, there were other long-distance friends to meet and embrace. Next to Collinson, the person Franklin had become closest to was William Strahan, one of the foremost printers and publishers in England, later a member of Parliament. Franklin had introduced himself to Strahan in 1743 in a letter asking him to recommend a young master printer to take charge of one of the printing businesses that Franklin had started in other colonies. Strahan sent him David Hall. Franklin was so pleased with Hall that instead of dispatching him to start a business elsewhere, he had made him a partner in his own business and in 1747 placed the whole conduct of it in his hands. While few of Strahan's letters survive, Strahan carefully saved Franklin's for us, more than sixty of them from the fourteen years they were writing each other before Franklin's arrival in England. The two even began planning a future match between Strahan's son William and Franklin's daughter Sally when Sally was only twelve. The match never came off but not from any reluctance on the elder Strahan's part. Until the Revolution temporarily estranged them, Strahan pleaded with Franklin to move perma-

William Strahan, 1783

nently to England. To further the cause, Strahan wrote to Deborah, shortly after Franklin's arrival, urging her to join them. "Straney," as Franklin sometimes called him, could not find words enough to express his pleasure in the company of a friend he had hitherto known only on paper. "I never," he wrote, "saw a man who was, in every respect, so perfectly agreeable to me. Some are amiable in one view, some in another, he in all." So come join him, Strahan urged Deborah, and bring your daughter ("I wish I could call her mine").

Deborah could not be moved, then or ever, to make the voyage. We don't have her letter in answer to Strahan. But Strahan evidently showed it to Franklin, and he commended her on it:

"Your Answer to Mr. Strahan was just what it should be; I was much pleas'd with it. He fancy'd his Rhetoric and Art would certainly bring you over." Was Franklin a little too pleased with her refusal? He loved Deborah. But she was the "plain Joan" she had always been, and Franklin was now moving in circles where she would be ill at ease and perhaps make him so. And though there is no hint anywhere in his correspondence that he was unfaithful to her, he did not lack for the feminine companionship he always craved. As Strahan had told Deborah, Mrs. Stevenson had nursed Franklin through the two months' illness that overtook him soon after he moved into her house, "with an assiduity, concern, and tenderness, which perhaps, only yourself could equal."

What Strahan did not add was that Mrs. Stevenson had an eighteen-year-old daughter, Polly, with whom Franklin formed a lifelong, avuncular friendship that lit up both their lives. Polly had to spend much of her time caring for an aunt in Wansted, a village about ten miles from London, with the fortunate result that she and Franklin regularly exchanged letters that reveal the affection they came to feel for each other. Polly had the same curiosity about the natural world that engaged Franklin, and he shared his thoughts with her at such length that he later published some of his letters to her in a new edition of his writings on electricity.

Polly was something special, but London was full of people eager to exchange thoughts with Franklin. Londoners, like Philadelphians, were fond of gathering in clubs, even before the age of the famous London establishments with their own buildings. Coffeehouses and taverns furnished a meeting place where eight or ten or more like-minded men could assemble for food, drink, talk, and fellowship. Social life in London revolved around these informal gatherings. A group that dined regularly together at an inn called the George and Vulture recognized Franklin as a kindred spirit and invited him to join them, and for the rest of his stay in London he could be found there every Monday. This was a gathering of the kind that Franklin had always enjoyed. And he discovered another in the Club of Honest Whigs, meeting on Thursdays at St. Paul's Coffeehouse, where he made enduring friends of Richard Price and Joseph Priestley. With them he could exchange both scientific and political views. It must have been agreeable to him to talk with Whigs, who had ideas about government similar to his own. He was on a political mission, and he needed all the help he could get from people more familiar with the workings of English politics than he could be. One whom he counted on particularly was Richard Jackson, a lawyer famed for his widespread knowledge of practically everything. It was Collinson again who years before had shared Franklin's letters with Jackson, prompting the two to begin exchanging letters themselves. In London, Franklin quickly sought Jackson out for assistance and advice about the best ways of obtaining the freedom from proprietary control he wanted for Pennsylvania.

The advice he got was to negotiate with the proprietors before going over their heads to the Board of Trade or the king's ministers. People on the scene sensed better than Franklin that appealing to higher authority might open a Pandora's Box of rulings and proposals that he would be ill-prepared to deal with. He should have gained some idea of what he was up against when Collinson arranged a meeting with Lord Granville, the presiding officer of the king's Privy Council. Granville had apparently asked for the meeting (Franklin was that well known) in order to question him about the current state of the British military campaign against France in America. In the course of the interview Granville disclosed his own views about the government of the colonies. The king, he informed Franklin, "is the Legislator of the Colonies." The instructions the king gave to governors were "the Law of the Land," regardless of anything the colonial assemblies might do. Franklin attempted to disabuse Granville of this startling opinion, but to no avail.

This was an informal meeting in which the subject of government had come up only incidentally, and Granville obviously knew nothing about what he asserted so confidently. But he was in a position of great power, and his ignorance of American affairs should have confirmed Franklin's suspicion that men in power in England could make decisions for Americans without having the faintest idea of what they were doing. He should have thought twice about the desirability of removing the proprietary obstacle that stood between Pennsylvanians and an ill-informed royal authority.

Franklin did accept Fothergill's intercession in getting the proprietors to meet with him. Unfortunately, face-to-face contacts did not improve either side's opinion of the other. Franklin drew up a statement of the grievances that the Pennsylvania Assembly wished to see corrected, including the proprietors' practice of binding their governors by nonnegotiable instructions. The Penns referred these "Heads of Complaints" to the British solicitor general and attorney general for an opinion on their merits. Thus, despite Franklin's acceptance of his friends' advice about negotiating directly with the proprietors, the matter was placed, though not officially, before the English government.

While the parties waited for an answer, they met several times in discussions that grew more and more heated. It took nearly a year for the attorney general and solicitor general to pronounce on Pennsylvania's list of grievances, and the opinion they gave was not to Franklin's liking. On the basis of it, the proprietors in November 1758 agreed to a limited taxation of their lands but, confident in the support of royal officials, insisted on their right to give binding instructions to their governors. They also informed the Assembly directly that they would negotiate only with "Persons of Candour," meaning not with Benjamin Franklin, whom henceforth they refused to recognize as a legitimate agent of the Assembly.

Outsiders and Insiders

In response to this slap in the face, Franklin wrote to the Assembly in January 1759 offering to resign his agency. But he had already prepared to escalate the quarrel with the proprietors to the point where he might rid the colony of them entirely. While the proprietors were waiting for a legal opinion on his grievances, Franklin was taking soundings from his own legal adviser, Richard Jackson, about the possibilities and consequences of a transfer of the Pennsylvania government directly to the king. The only catch, as he wrote to Isaac Norris in September 1758, would be if some official like Granville should "wish for some Advantage against the People's Privileges as well as the Proprietary Powers." Norris, a good friend who had married James Logan's daughter and was Speaker of the Pennsylvania Assembly during most of Franklin's tenure there, had written him in June 1758 suggesting what Franklin was only too ready to believe. "I should be pleas'd To know," Norris wondered, "What Grounds There are for a Suspicion of my own That the Government wink for a While, at the Irregularities of some Proprietors in order to Resume All such American Grants into their hands at a proper Juncture."

This was a piece of wishful thinking congenial to Franklin. By the time he received Norris's query, Franklin had in hand Jackson's advice about how a transfer of the Pennsylvania government might be achieved and what the consequences would be for the "people's privileges" under the proprietary charter. Jackson knew what his friend wanted to hear and told him that on many of the points at issue with the proprietors, "I intirely agree in my private Opinion with the Assembly of Pennsylvania." But Jackson was careful to state that neither the Privy Council nor the Parliament was likely to side with the Assembly against the proprietors. He did not think it "adviseable to drive any of these Points, much less all at once to a formal Decision at present, if at all." And if circumstances obliged the British government to intervene in the controversy and take over the government of the colony, the consequences might well be disastrous. While he thought Parliament ought not to alter the existing powers of the Assembly, he feared that they would. "We may rest satisfy'd," he warned, "that an Administration will probably for the future always be able to support and carry in Parliament whatever they wish to do so; that they will almost always wish to extend the Power of the Crown and themselves both mediately and immediately." It would require an act of Parliament to take away the proprietors' powers; and if that should happen it was "far from impossible" that Parliament "might think it fit somewhat to new model the present Constitution" of Pennsylvania. Which might mean taking away the powers not only of the proprietors but of the Assembly as well.

Jackson did not suggest that either the administration or the Parliament was contemplating any move against the proprietors. But Franklin somehow persuaded himself that they were and that it would be a good thing. In answer to Norris's query, he wrote in June 1758, with unfounded assurance, "It is certain that the Government here are inclin'd to resume all the Proprietary Powers, and I make no doubt but upon the first Handle they will do so. . . . I believe a Petition from either of the Assemblies [of Pennsylvania or Maryland], expressing their Dislike to the Proprietary Government, and praying the Crown to take the Province under its immediate Government and Protection, would be even now very favourably heard."

Apparently Norris acted on this suggestion. By the time Franklin wrote offering his resignation the following January (1759), the Pennsylvania Assembly had drafted a petition. They then dropped it, for fear that a change of government might operate not only against the proprietors but also, as Jackson had warned, "against the People." That is, they feared that it might result in a reduction of the Assembly's powers instead of an increase. In any case, the Assembly decided that it would be better "to let it lye for Consideration" some other time.

Franklin remained convinced that royal government would be preferable to proprietary. In offering to resign, he asserted that a petition for change "might without much Difficulty be carried, and our own Privileges preserved; and in that I think I could still do Service." Franklin found grounds for optimism in another piece of advice Richard Jackson had given him. In warning about the capacity of the ministry to carry whatever it pleased through Parliament, Jackson had added that "*the Opinion of the Bulk of Mankind without Doors*" [that is, outside the government] is the only Restraint that any Man ought reasonably to rely on for securing what a Ministry, or those that can influence a Ministry, wish to deprive him of." In stressing the power of opinion to restrain government, Jackson may have been talking, like Hume, about the enduring beliefs that make government feasible. But he was also hinting that government might be constrained by what we now call public opinion, the changing, not to say fickle, views of the bulk of mankind about current issues. Franklin knew more than most people about that kind of opinion and how to make use of it. He had been manipulating it in favor of his projects in Philadelphia for thirty years. He was ready to take a hand in lining up opinion in England against the proprietors and in favor of the Assembly.

Franklin's friend Strahan printed the leading London newspaper, the *Chronicle,* and was a partner in several other papers. During Franklin's illness, when he was forbidden by Dr. Fothergill to do any writing, Billy undertook to refute the charges spread by the proprietors that the Assembly had failed to levy taxes to support the war effort against the French. In a piece published in the *Chronicle* and in other newspapers and magazines, Billy drew on the Assembly's records not only to show its eagerness in voting supplies but also to turn the charges against the proprietors. It was they who had stood in the way of the Assembly's efforts, and it was a matter of principle "that neither the proprietaries nor any other power on earth, ought to interfere between them and their sovereign, either to modify or refuse their free gifts, and grants for his majesty's service."

Meanwhile, Franklin had secured Jackson's collaboration in

producing *An Historical Review of the Constitution and Government of Pennsylvania*, to be published at the opening of the January 1759 session of Parliament. There, he assured his friend Joseph Galloway, a leader of the Assembly, "the Proprietors will be gibbeted up as they deserve, to rot and stink in the Nostrils of Posterity." It would thus "prepare the Minds of the Publick" for depriving them of power without depriving the Assembly of anything.

The *Historical Review* (in 444 pages!) was finally published in May 1759, but Franklin was slow to learn that public opinion could not be mobilized in England as easily as in Pennsylvania. Nor did it matter as much. While Jackson's diagnosis of the influence that the bulk of the populace could exert on public policy was perceptive, it was more valid as a prediction than as a description of current practice. By the middle of the eighteenth century, the English public was certainly being courted for support of different public policies in newspapers, pamphlets, cartoons, and books whose very numbers suggested that public influence must be large. And by the end of the century it was. But in 1759, when Franklin set out to bring the ministry and Parliament to his way of thinking, the men who made decisions were not listening much to what was said "without doors." They listened, instead, to people on the inside, like the proprietors, who had an official authority by virtue of their royal charter.

The agents like Franklin, whom American colonies employed to carry messages to England, were on the outside, because they had never been officially recognized as spokesmen for their governments. If they had been, if men like Lord Granville had recognized that people were more easily governed when they had a hand in government, Franklin's dream of an Anglo-American empire might eventually have been realized. But in 1759, as in 1776, the people who made decisions for the colonies, as for England itself, were a small group, engaged in political contests and maneuvers among themselves. Outsiders, with or without public support, were not invited to take part. Though they might be called on for information or advice, decisions depended more on the outcome of party divisions within the group than on what outsiders told them or on what they read in newspapers and pamphlets.

It was this set of people that Franklin was up against. The Board of Trade, the Privy Council, the Parliament. Direct negotiations with the proprietors having failed, he had somehow to affect the deliberations of their superiors, through propaganda in print, through face-to-face appearances before them, through any contacts he could make with people who could pull strings. He was handicapped not only by his unofficial status as agent of a colonial assembly but also by his misreading of the climate of opinion among the insiders. Why he should have thought they were looking for an excuse to cancel all the powers of the proprietors is a mystery. The Assembly's postponement of their petition relieved him of any immediate need to test his belief by that method. Instead they required him to carry on with his original purpose—they did not accept his offer to resign—of getting the authorities to overrule the proprietors in the matter of taxing their lands and of giving binding instructions to their governors.

That contest came to a head in 1760, when the Assembly passed another act to raise £100,000 by a tax on land that included the proprietors' estates (without the limitations they had agreed to in November 1758). The governor in Pennsylvania had succumbed to the Assembly's pressure and signed the act.

Franklin won a small victory when the Privy Council allowed the act to stand. But he seems to have misread an accompanying report of the Board of Trade, deploring the excessive powers of the Assembly in Pennsylvania and the weakness of its governors. Such weakness, the Board averred, was bound to occur "while the Prerogatives of Royalty are placed in the feeble hands of Individuals, and the Authority of the Crown is to be exercised, without the Powers of the Crown to support it."

The board's remarks could be read as an invitation to the crown to resume the powers granted to the proprietors. That was the way Isaac Norris interpreted the passage when Franklin sent him the Board of Trade's report. But neither Norris nor Franklin seems to have noticed that the board's intention, if it undertook such a resumption, would be, as Richard Jackson had feared, to new model the whole constitution of Pennsylvania so as to reduce the role of the Assembly and to magnify the executive authority exercised from England. Norris eventually came to see the danger and backed off from any move for royal government. Franklin did not, but he did not pursue the issue at this time, perhaps because a larger question was occupying him. While he found time to advise his many new friends about smoking chimneys, invent a new musical instrument (the glass "armonica"), instruct Polly Stevenson about tides in rivers, and tour the Low Countries with Billy and Richard Jackson, he was also thinking about his Anglo-American empire and the way the outcome of the war might affect the prospects for it.

From at least as early as his speculations about population growth in 1751, Franklin had seen encounters of English settlers with the Indians and the French as only the first episodes in a larger conflict that would require resolution sooner or later, before it cost more lives in the relentless English expansion. What Braddock had failed to do in 1755 was accomplished when the French and Indians destroyed and abandoned Fort Duquesne as General John Forbes advanced cautiously toward it late in 1758. Forbes renamed the site Pittsburgh, after the minister who was now conducting the war from London. When Franklin received the news in London, his first thought was of the importance of keeping the fort in English hands. With the surprising success of the British expedition in capturing Quebec in 1759, it appeared likely that England would win the war. North America had been the principal battleground, but the war extended around the globe to the West Indies, India, and Africa. Franklin knew that peace negotiations would involve some swapping of territories. In 1745, as we have seen, he had been eager to show Pennsylvanians their stake in helping the New Englanders capture Louisbourg, from which French privateers had harassed Philadelphia shipping. But in the peace of Aix-la-Chapelle in 1748, the British had returned that threatening fortress to France. After the British captured Quebec, with the likelihood of eventual French surrender of all Canada, Franklin's worries extended from Pittsburgh to Canada itself. Three months before the fall of Quebec a British expedition had taken the French island of Guadeloupe, highly prized for its exports of sugar. By December 1759 people were already talking about the relative value of Guadeloupe and Canada, for the sugar trade was far more valuable than the fur trade.

Franklin's thoughts on population growth now acquired a more immediate relevance than even he could have foreseen when he wrote them down. He sent a copy to his Scottish friend Lord Kames with a letter applying them to the opportunity that the conquest of Canada would offer for the Anglo-American empire he envisaged. "No one can rejoice more sincerely than I do on the Reduction of Canada," he wrote in January 1760, nine months before the total surrender. He rejoiced, he assured Kames, "not merely as I am a Colonist, but as I am a Briton. I have long been of Opinion, that the Foundations of the future Grandeur and Stability of the British Empire, lie in America." There lay the possibility of "the greatest Political Structure Human Wisdom ever yet erected." The crucial step toward that greatness now was to keep Canada in British hands after the war. "If the French remain in Canada, they will continually harass our Colonies by the Indians, impede if not prevent their Growth; your Progress to Greatness will at best be slow, and give room for many Accidents that may for ever prevent it."

For the next year or two it was popularly believed that the peace negotiations with France would turn on a choice between Canada and Guadeloupe. In fact there was never much doubt among the negotiators themselves about keeping Canada, but pamphlets and newspapers weighed the question at length. Franklin entered the debate first with a satirical piece for Strahan's *Chronicle* and then with a carefully argued pamphlet ("the Canada Pamphlet") to show that the future of the British Empire lay in the fecundity of its American colonists. They would spread across the continent and furnish a limitless market for British manufactures, far exceeding the value of all the sugar production in the world. If cooped up on the Atlantic seaboard, they would turn to manufacturing for themselves and hasten the day when they might seek a political independence to match the economic independence that manufacturing for themselves would give. To bolster his arguments, Franklin appended his essay on population growth.

Franklin was certainly not the only one who thought that public opinion might swing the peace negotiations one way or the other. His was one of sixty-five pamphlets on the subject that appeared by the time the Treaty of Paris was signed in 1763. But did he have in mind the possibility of bringing his public arguments before the men who mattered by a private channel? As soon as the pamphlet was published he sent a copy to Lord Kames, with a letter suggesting that he had written it "to comply with your Request, in writing something on the present Situation of our Affairs in America, in order to give more correct Notions of the British Interest with regard to the Colonies, than those I found many sensible Men possess'd." Franklin knew that Kames was on intimate terms with the other great Scottish intellectuals of the time, with David Hume, Adam Smith, and William Robertson. Did he also know that the circle extended to the Scottish members of Parliament, that James Oswald, until 1759 a member of the Board of Trade and now on the Treasury Board, had long been a protégé of Kames's and sought his advice on public matters? Did the circle perhaps extend to Lord Bute, who would become the principal negotiator of the peace treaty after George III succeeded to the throne in October 1760? Did Franklin write and send his pamphlet to Kames with a view to reaching other insiders?

Possibly, but Kames was not his only avenue of access to people who mattered. By 1758 Franklin had become a close friend of Dr. John Pringle, a member of the Royal College of Physicians, whom he joined every Sunday evening along with yet another collection of friends. Who were they? The only surviving letter from Pringle about the group tells us that after Franklin departed for Philadelphia the members continued to assemble in expecta-

Benjamin Franklin, 1763

tion of his return and spoke of him "with the greatest affection and esteem." That was the way most people who knew Franklin spoke of him, but the friends he shared with Pringle were likely to have been people high in both political and intellectual circles. Pringle, who like Franklin had become active in the meetings of the Royal Society, was interested in Franklin's electrical work and consulted him about its possible use in medicine. And who else had a special interest in electricity? Lord Bute, who was said to have a fine collection of electrical apparatus. Pringle's letter about the Sunday evening group also indicates that he had passed on to Bute some proposals from Franklin about preserving gunpowder and about securing the health of British troops in Africa. Pringle in return passed on to Franklin directions from Lady Bute about collecting American seashells for her, which Franklin had apparently promised to do.

There is nothing to suggest that Bute was actually a member of Pringle's Sunday group, but Pringle's association with Bute and with the royal family was close. In 1761 he became personal physician both to the queen and to Bute. There is no evidence that Franklin used his acquaintance with Bute to influence the peace negotiations, but he did use it in a way that demonstrated his ability to reach the people who were then deciding American affairs. In 1762, through Bute's influence, he got Billy appointed royal governor of New Jersey, to the consternation of the proprietors of neighboring Pennsylvania. Billy too had promised to collect seashells for Lady Bute.

By 1762, when Franklin was preparing to return home, with the sense that there was nothing more he could do for Pennsylvania in London, he must have felt that he had learned to navigate the treacherous waters of British politics. Strahan was urg-

William Franklin, ca. 1790

ing him to run for a seat in Parliament. He had made friends with insiders and taken a hand in molding public opinion. He was tempted to stay and admitted it to Strahan. And, in fact, he probably did not intend to let the inside knowledge he had gained lie fallow. He hinted to Strahan that he would be returning before long. He had not for a moment lost sight of his Anglo-American goal, nor had he lost his impatience with the proprietors, whom he saw as the immediate obstacles to be overcome. But he had been absent from Pennsylvania for five years, and the next steps had to be taken there. With Billy's appointment for New Jersey in hand, and his own weight with English authorities thus confirmed, he set sail for Philadelphia to consolidate the backing there for a royal seizure of proprietary powers.

Making Enemies

At this stage in Franklin's career, when we have come to know him as well as the surviving paper and ink will let us, we are perhaps entitled to ask how well he knew himself. His five years in London had been a heady experience. He had faced the contempt of Thomas Penn but enjoyed the admiration and friendship, not to say the veneration, of better men than Penn. They included some of England and Scotland's leading intellectuals and a few of its more powerful political figures. With no official position, his charm, his genuine interest in other people, and his way of dealing with them had made him a figure to reckon with. Although he still took pains to keep himself inconspicuous, that had always been his recipe for power. And it must have seemed to him that it was working in England as it had in Pennsylvania. His vanity was of too refined an order to permit exposure. As he himself observed later, by letting others indulge their vanity in claiming credit for something you had done, you eventually would be discovered as the true author and thus win a higher merit. He was not without ambition, he was simply too shrewd to show it. How far did it now extend?

Franklin knew what he had done in England. It fell short of what he had hoped for, but it had prepared him to do much more. What he most wanted was the Anglo-American empire he had first hinted at in his thoughts on the growth of American population. After five years in London, mingling in circles that expanded ever higher, he was preparing, probably without quite admitting it to himself, to become the architect of that empire. But his success in winning the esteem and affection of everyone around him must have given him signals of how important a figure he had become, important not just as a Philadelphian, not just as a Pennsylvanian, and not just, seemingly, as an American, but as a Briton, as a builder of empire, someone who carried weight on both sides of the ocean. It should not surprise us if he erred a little in his assessment of just how much weight this amounted to on either side.

There can be no doubt that he erred. During the next two years he now spent in America, from November 1, 1762, to November 7, 1764 (his longest spell at home until 1785), he made mistakes, mistakes that make us wonder if *we* have made mistakes in our attempts to understand him. Perhaps the most remarkable thing about the man as we have come to know him has been his ability to make friends with all kinds of people and to win their support and admiration. He is capable of writing angry diatribes against measures and policies imposed from above by distant authorities, but the only clue we have of a failure in dealing with people face to face is his confrontation with Thomas Penn. And in that case it is easy to excuse his impatience with a supercilious overlord. His anger even adds a little spice to a personality that would be almost too lovable without it. But in the two years after his arrival back in Philadelphia, we find him embroiled in disputes where his customary confidence in utility and reason combine strangely with his anger at Penn to afflict him with a prolonged fit of political blindness.

The years began auspiciously. In the weeks after his arrival his house was filled with friends welcoming him home, "a Succession of them from Morning to Night ever since my Arrival," as he wrote to Strahan in December. Despite his absence, the people of Philadelphia had continued to elect him their representative to the Assembly every year; and when it met in January, Franklin immediately took his seat there. In March his fellow members in a show of confidence awarded him £500 a year for his services in England, in addition to the expenses he had incurred. He devoted most of the next six months to visits, first to Virginia and then to all the northern colonies from New Jersey to New Hampshire, in his capacity as joint deputy postmaster for America. He thus had the opportunity to assess the range of American opinion on public affairs, and to make and renew friendships with people sharing his scientific interests, with people in high office like Governor Francis Bernard of Massachusetts, and with young admirers like Katy Greene in Rhode Island, who had long been Polly Stevenson's American counterpart for him. He had met her on a visit in 1754, when she was Catherine Ray, and he had kept up a regular correspondence with her, a correspondence that was audaciously flirtatious until she married William Greene, son of Rhode Island's colonial governor and himself a future governor of that state. While Franklin was in New England, John Penn, son of Richard and nephew of Thomas, arrived in Pennsylvania as governor and was greeted warmly and optimistically in Philadelphia. As soon as Franklin returned from his postal inspection journey in November, he called to pay his respects. Writing to Collinson, Franklin expressed his determination not to let his dislike of the uncle prejudice him against the nephew: "He is civil, and I endeavour to fail in no Point of Respect; so I think we shall have no personal Difference, at least I will give no Occasion."

As his first year at home ended, Franklin had an opportunity to do the new governor a service. The final cession of Canada to Britain in 1763 was followed by an Indian uprising in the Ohio country ("Pontiac's Rebellion") that threatened settlers in western Pennsylvania. In December a number of them from the Paxton region in Lancaster Country—"the Paxton Boys"—vented their wrath in the massacre of two small groups of friendly Indians who had settled at Conestoga and Lancaster. By the end of January 1764, the Paxton Boys were preparing to pursue a band of 140 more Christian Indians who had fled to Philadelphia for protection. Franklin had always favored fair treatment of Indians as a way of preventing war. When war came, though, he was no pacifist. He even suggested the use of bloodhounds to hunt down warriors who struck at isolated farms. He was an admirer and adviser of Colonel Henry Bouquet, who commanded the forces suppressing Pontiac's Rebellion. But the cowardly slaughter of friendly Indians aroused Franklin's indignation, as it did that of most Pennsylvanians in the East. At the end of January he published an account of the massacres, denouncing the perpetrators as "Christian White Savages," more barbarous than the people they persecuted.

The Paxton Boys, undeterred, gathered supporters for a march on Philadelphia, not only to destroy the Indians under protection there but also, it was feared, to bring down the government that protected them. Franklin resisted any temptation he may have felt to exploit their attack in support of his own objections to proprietary government and instead took the lead in organizing resistance to mob rule. As he told it in a letter to John Fothergill, he "promoted an Association to support the Authority of the Government and defend the Governor by taking Arms, sign'd it first myself, and was followed by several Hundreds, who took Arms accordingly; the Governor offer'd me the Command of them, but I chose to carry a Musket, and strengthen his Authority by setting an Example of Obedience to his Orders. And, would you think it, this Proprietary Governor did me the Honour, on an Alarm, to run to my House at Midnight, with his Counsellors at his Heels, for Advice, and made it his Head Quarters for some time." Franklin wrote this on March 14, 1764, five weeks after the event; and, as the tone of his words suggests, by this time the governor was no longer seeking shelter or advice from him, and Franklin was no longer prepared to give it. By the following November he was on his way back to England with a petition from the Pennsylvania Assembly for royal government. We know that Franklin had wanted to oust the proprietors in favor of the king long before this. And more than any other single individual he was responsible for the chain of events in 1764 that produced the petition. He got what he wanted from the Pennsylvania Assembly, but at a cost that he failed to reckon.

To understand how large a mistake he made, and how he could have let himself make it, we have to consider the people who tried to stop him and why they tried, as well as some of the people who encouraged him and why they did.

From the beginning of his public career Franklin had accepted the dominance of the Quakers in the colony they had founded. In organizing its defense in the militia Association of

1747, in negotiating with the local Indians, in the fruitless effort to create a colonial union at Albany, he had always managed to work with Quaker leaders like James Logan and Isaac Norris. He could not accept their religious beliefs, but their principled informality and toleration of other sects suited him better than the rigidities of the church he had been brought up in. In becoming the leader of the Assembly, he necessarily became the political leader of the Quakers, recognized as such by Collinson and Fothergill in London as much as by Norris in Philadelphia. Quakers needed someone like Franklin to speak for them in politics, where their overload of principles often involved them in contests with authority but inhibited their conduct of them. They had quarreled with the proprietors of Pennsylvania, even with William Penn himself, from the beginning. And when Penn's successors abandoned Quakerism, the adversarial relationship was intensified.

When Franklin stepped into leadership of the Quakers in the Assembly, he took on as adversaries not only the proprietors but also those Pennsylvanians who supported them and were supported by them. That meant members of the Governor's Council, the principal judges of the colony's courts, and many of the non-Quaker immigrants who flocked to the colony in the 1730s and 1740s. The Germans, who were escaping from religious persecution at home and who mainly settled in the eastern counties, were generally sympathetic to the Quakers, but the Scots-Irish Presbyterians (like the Paxton Boys) who moved into the new western counties were less so. And there were many immigrants from England in the eastern counties who felt that the Church of England should occupy a more prominent place in the government of an English colony. By the late 1750s there had developed a Proprietary Party drawn mainly from Presbyterians and Anglicans to contest the Quakers in the annual elections to the Assembly. It was not much of a contest, because the twenty-six seats of the three eastern counties automatically constituted a majority, and the Quakers, with the assistance of the Germans, could usually count on winning them. But the Proprietary Party contained some important men. Among them were three whom Franklin should have taken more seriously than he did.

The first, William Smith, was a plausible scoundrel. He had come to America from Scotland in 1751 as tutor in a New York household, and two years later he wrote a tract on education that pleased Franklin and induced him to offer Smith an appointment in his academy. In 1756, when the academy became the College of Philadelphia, Franklin arranged for Smith to head it. By this time Smith had visited England to take holy orders in the Anglican church and had made the acquaintance of Thomas Penn. Smith, who always had his eye on the main chance, evidently saw Penn as a man with deeper pockets than Franklin. From then on he served the proprietor by attacking Franklin and the Assembly in tracts that accused the Quakers of neglecting, if not preventing, the defense of the province against the Indians. He even proposed that both Quakers and Germans be disqualified from public office. In 1758, while Franklin was in England, the Assembly responded by jailing Smith for libel, but Smith, with his gift for ingratiating himself in the right places, appealed to the king and eventually got an order from the Privy Council rebuking the Assembly.

In May 1764 Smith was back in Pennsylvania, still a pensioner of Thomas Penn's, with an honorary doctor's degree from Oxford and an inside track to people in authority in England that was at least as effective as Franklin's. Unbeknownst to Franklin, he was in close communication with Lord Kames's protégé on the Board of Trade, James Oswald, and furnished him with recommendations on American affairs, including a suggestion that Parliament "interfere, and ascertain the particular Powers both of Governors and Assemblies, that now at last we may enjoy some Respite from those eternal Questions that distract us, and have thrown us almost into the Hands of the Enemy." The intervention Smith favored would have been the opposite of what Franklin wanted: to strengthen the powers of the proprietary governor and his Council against the Assembly. In 1764 Smith was still at the head of the College of Philadelphia, for which he had just collected more than £7,000 on a trip to England. He was a force among Pennsylvania's Anglicans, whom he was currently seeking to join with New Jersey's in a convention over which he would preside. He would soon be agitating for a bishopric over them. Franklin had no illusions about Smith's character or ambitions, but his contempt may have led him to underestimate the man's talent for making mischief.

No one in Pennsylvania, neither Franklin nor any of his Quaker allies, could have underestimated another supporter of the proprietors, William Allen, the wealthiest man in the colony. He had worked with Franklin in many public enterprises and helped secure him the deputy postmastership for America. He was a member of the Governor's Council and chief justice of the colony. In 1764 he too had just returned from England (on August 13), where he had held lengthy conversations not only with Richard Jackson but with the secretary of state, Lord Halifax, and of course with Thomas Penn. Despite his indebtedness to Penn for his appointment as chief justice, Allen was his own man, as he was to prove later in supporting American resistance to British taxation but then refusing to join in the movement for independence. He was a person whose opinions were worth listening to, but when he greeted Franklin on his return from England with a stern warning against the political and economic consequences of a shift to royal government, Franklin complained to Jackson of his disrespect. "You know," Franklin wrote, "I always spoke respectfully of him. Has he done the same by me? I respect even the Ashes of a departed Friendship. But he is at this time [September 1, 1764] abusing me to the Quakers, as many as come in his Way, by a very unfair Account of some private Conversation that pass'd between us many Years ago, when we were great Friends."

The third man who supported the proprietors against Franklin at a critical juncture entered Pennsylvania politics as a partisan of the Quaker party. John Dickinson, a wealthy lawyer, had moved to Philadelphia from Delaware, and was sitting in the Assembly when Franklin returned from England late in 1762. Like Franklin he was not himself a Quaker but sympathized with Quakers in their contests with the proprietors. He was married to the daughter of Isaac Norris, the Speaker of the Assembly, who had been encouraging Franklin's thinking about the readiness of British authorities to revoke proprietary powers. Dickinson was a thoughtful man, slow to make up his mind on political issues but extremely effective in argument once he did. He was to play a significant role both in colonial opposition to British taxation and in delaying the Declaration of Independence until every avenue of reconciliation had been pursued. He was, like Allen, a man most people found worth listening to.

Of the three people whom Franklin found in his way in 1764,

Dickinson alone was present in the first half of the year, when Franklin began his campaign to engage popular support for a change in government. He took his first step in March with a set of twenty-six resolutions for the Assembly reciting the familiar sins of the proprietors and closing with a move to adjourn, so that the members could consult their constituents about petitioning for a royal government. Franklin had such a petition ready to hand, which he printed in many copies and circulated for signatures to demonstrate the results of the consultation. To guide people to the right results, he published in April *Cool Thoughts on the Present Situation of Our Public Affairs,* delineating the benefits other colonies (the Carolinas and New Jersey) had gained earlier by the substitition of royal for proprietary government. When the members of the Assembly returned in May, Franklin had a formal petition ready for them, and only three voted against it.

It looked like an easy triumph for Franklin, but the circumstances should have given him pause. Isaac Norris, at the last minute, had resigned from the speakership, ostensibly for reasons of health but also because he had finally decided that a move to royal government would be bad for Pennsylvania. He did not want the petition to go in his name. It went instead, and appropriately, under Franklin's name, for he was at once elected to replace Norris. What was more ominous than Norris's defection was the fact that Dickinson was one of the three men voting against the petition. Dickinson agreed with all the objections to the proprietors' conduct of government, but he thought that this was the wrong time to seek a change because of the possible loss of the religious and political privileges unique to Pennsylvania under the government established by William Penn's Charter of

Liberties: the guaranteee of religious liberty and the absence of any legislative powers in the Governor's Council.

Dickinson's concerns were not imaginary. His objection to the timing of the petition rested on reports from England of a new determination to bring the American colonies under stricter control by the mother country. When the negotiators of the peace with France decided, as Franklin had hoped they would, that Canada was more important than Guadeloupe, that decision was not quite an admission that the future of the British Empire lay in North America, as Franklin had argued and fervently believed. But it was a step in that direction. And in taking that step, the authorities in London turned their attention to the existing American colonies with a view to more careful supervision of them and to the costs involved in protecting them from any renewed French threat.

Strict enforcement of the regulations governing colonial trade began with an act of Parliament in April 1763 requiring the British navy to act as an arm of the customs service in America. By March 1764, while preparing his resolutions against proprietary goverment, Franklin had observed "much Commotion among our Merchants" over the interference with their ships. Jackson had warned him the previous November of worse to come, that Parliament was contemplating not only an overhaul and expansion of the trade regulations to secure more revenue but also the imposition of "inland duties," that is, direct taxation. On April 5, 1764, Parliament enacted the Sugar Act, raising duties and establishing regulations on a variety of colonial imports and exports. At the same time the ministry made known its intention to devise a set of stamp taxes on documents used in American commercial and legal transactions. By the time Franklin drove his petition for royal government through the Assembly in late May, news of these developments had traveled through all the colonies. Franklin himself reported, in the same letter to Richard Jackson that enclosed the petition, that "The Men of War station'd in our several Ports are very active in their new Employment of Custom house Officers; a Portmanteau cannot go between here and New York without being search'd: Every Boat stopt and examin'd, and much Incumbrance by that means brought upon all Business." It was a bad time to be asking for a revamping of Pennsylvania's government by royal officials who were already engaged in establishing greater control over the daily transactions of the inhabitants. That was what Dickinson meant when he argued against the timing of a move that might otherwise or eventually be desirable.

Dickinson was not the only one who thought so. In the absence of William Smith and William Allen, the Proprietary Party had done little to oppose the petition, but Smith returned in June and began organizing popular opposition and circulating counterpetitions against royal government. Allen returned in August with word that English officials were ready to show Pennsylvania what royal authority would be like: "the King's little Finger we should find heavier than the Proprietor's whole Loins." A new election to the Assembly was coming up in October, and Smith and Allen saw to it that the press was filled with attacks on Franklin of a kind he had never before encountered, dwelling on his lechery (begetting an illegitimate son) and the insult he had offered the province's Germans (the essay on population growth, where his reference to "Palatine boors" was now translated for the public as meaning Palatine hogs). Franklin had procured some 3,500 signatures to his popular petitions for royal government. Smith rounded up 15,000 against it. When the elections were held on October 1, Franklin stood as a candidate in both the city and the county of Philadelphia. He lost in both, though by a narrow margin. The proprietary party, hitherto scarcely represented at all in the Assembly, gained a dozen of the forty-six seats. It was not a majority of the Assembly, but it may have represented a majority of the population. Franklin's defeat at the polls should have prompted second thoughts about royal government in the entire Assembly, and above all in Franklin. But the Assembly not only turned back a motion to recall the petition, it also voted to send Franklin back to London to assist Richard Jackson in securing its objective. On November 7 he set sail.

Franklin was now fifty-eight years old. Before him lay eleven years of unremitting efforts in England against the exercise of Parliamentary authority in America. After those efforts failed, he helped write the Declaration of Independence, then secured the American alliance with France, negotiated the treaty of peace with England, and sat in the convention that drafted the United States Constitution to replace the Articles of Confederation. If he was to do all those things after 1764, what possessed him in that year to try to bring Pennsylvania under stricter control of a government he spent most of the rest of his life trying to limit and ultimately to defy?

We have to admit at the outset that his mission to England included instructions to himself and Jackson to work with other colonial agents against the "unequal, oppressive and unjust" measures for more direct control and taxation of all the colonies. Before he left Philadelphia the assemblies of Massachusetts and Rhode Island had sent messages to the Pennsylvania Assembly urging cooperation against attempts "to deprive the Colonists of some of their most essential Rights as British Subjects, and as Men." Franklin, in informing Jackson of his appointment, reported that the Assembly had instructed him not only to assist with the petition but also expected him to "be of some Use in our general American Affairs."

This aspect of his mission may already have loomed larger in his mind than his obsessive urge to be rid of the proprietors. But his view of the impending taxation of the colonies was obviously more optimistic than that of the people who sent him to deal with the problem. Moreover, he did not have quite the same ideas they did about the rights they wanted him to protect. As early as March 1763, shortly after the signing of the definitive treaty granting all Canada to England, Jackson had told him of the ministry's intention to keep ten thousand troops in America and to require the Americans to pay for them. Franklin's response was characteristic: "I shall only say, it is not worth your while. All we can spare from mere Living, goes to you for Superfluities. The more you oblige us to pay here, the less you can receive there." Six months later, when Jackson, himself a member of the House of Commons, informed him that "£200000 a year will infallibly be raised by Parliament on the Plantations," Franklin's reaction was the same: "I am not much alarm'd about your Schemes of raising Money on us. You will take care for your own sakes not to lay greater Burthens on us than we can bear; for you cannot hurt us without hurting your selves." In the ensuing months, as the ministry pursued its plans, Franklin remained unperturbed. To Collinson he admitted that "We are in your Hands as Clay in the Hands of the Potter," but "as the Potter cannot waste or spoil his Clay without injuring himself; so I think there is scarce anything you can do that may be hurtful to us, but what will be as much or more so to you. This must be our chief Security." He went on, in a letter to Jackson, to point out an additional folly in the Parliamentary plans: "Two distinct Jurisdictions or Powers of Taxing cannot well subsist together in the same Country. They will confound and obstruct each other. When any Tax for America is propos'd in your Parliament, how are you to know that we are not already tax'd as much as we can bear? If a Tax is propos'd with us, how dare we venture to lay it, as the next Ship perhaps may bring us an Account of some heavy Tax impos'd by you. If you choose to tax us, give us Members in your Legislature, and let us be one People."

Franklin's reliance on Parliament's coming to its senses was only indirectly related to any expectations that it would recognize taxation as a violation of colonial rights. Questions of right and wrong, and hence of "rights," entered Franklin's calculations the way they always had, as adjuncts of what was useful or beneficial to the people involved. He had earlier abandoned his youthful freethinking dismissal of morality because it proved to be "not very useful." In its place he had made right and wrong depend on usefulness, on practical results. Parliamentary taxation of the colonies was wrong because it would harm both England and the colonies. That it would violate colonial "rights" was a warning sign of its harmfulness, for those rights had grown from the fact that they were beneficial, and they were right because they were beneficial. Government worked better, more easily, if rights were respected. Rights were obstacles wisely devised against harmful, mistaken government actions.

This was the view Franklin had pressed on William Shirley ten years earlier: the English believed they had rights to a share in their government. They were therefore more easily governed if the government could sustain that belief. In a letter to Jackson on March 14, 1764, Franklin made much the same point in a different form. "I wish," he said, "some good Angel would forever whisper in the Ears of your great Men, that Dominion is founded in Opinion, and that if you would preserve your Authority among us, you must preserve the Opinion we us'd to have of your Justice." But in thinking of colonial rights as opinions or beliefs, Franklin deprived them of any absolute character and made them merely instrumental and thus, by implication, negotiable. His task in England would be to prevent Parliament from making the mistake of taxing the colonies. If Parliament persisted in that mistake, his task would be to reduce the damage.

That was not quite the way Franklin's constituents viewed the matter. For them rights were sacred. They would not have liked to hear that they were clay in the hands of England's potter and that their security depended on the potter's care of his clay. They did not want to hear calculations of how great a burden they could bear without breaking. Just how strongly they felt about this would become apparent when Parliament did persist in the mistake of taxing them without their consent. When Franklin was confronted with their intransigence, he realized—indeed, before many of them did—that Parliament's persistence would make government not merely difficult but impossible. But in 1764 he misjudged the character of their beliefs. Why? He had spent two years in America, and he was usually sensitive to the views of people around him. Perhaps part of the trouble came from the kind of people he had been mingling with, the elevated social circles in which he had been moving, in both countries.

In 1764 there were a number of Americans who would have

liked to see something like a colonial nobility (themselves included) ensconced in the governments of the colonies. In that year Governor Francis Bernard of Massachusetts drafted a proposal for reorganizing all the colonial governments, with royal governors and a nobility appointed by the king for life, to serve in the upper houses of colonial legislatures. There is no evidence that Bernard confided this plan to Franklin, but Franklin was on intimate terms with him (he received eight letters from Bernard about the education of Bernard's son in 1763 and 1764). In his tour of the northern colonies Franklin consorted with many people in Rhode Island and Connecticut who would have been happy to see the kind of change Bernard envisaged. They encouraged Franklin in his petition for a royal government in Pennsylvania for the same reason that fifteen thousand Pennsylvanians opposed it. In Rhode Island some of them asked his support for a secret petition already on its way to England for a royal replacement of the popular government there. In Connecticut, Samuel Johnson (whom Franklin had earlier tried to recruit to head his academy) was equally impatient with the popular character of government there: "Would to God," he wrote to Franklin about the time of his departure, "you were charged with pleading the same Cause in behalf of all the Governments, that they might all alike be taken into the Kings more immediate Protection."

There is no reason to suppose that Franklin wanted the government of Pennsylvania or any other colony to be less popular. But he was keeping company with people who did, and he seems to have been out of touch, at least temporarily, with the larger public he was dedicated to serve. He was due for a deserved unpleasant surprise.

5 The Importance of Opinion

By early December 1764, Franklin was back in London, settled in his old quarters with Mrs. Stevenson at Number 7, Craven Street. As on his return to Philadelphia two years earlier, he was quickly surrounded by friends eager to renew old ties: Strahan and Jackson, Collinson and Fothergill, Polly Stevenson and her young circle. Everyone sought his company, and everyone needed his advice. Lord Kames was having trouble with a smoking chimney and wanted the "universal Smoke Doctor" to tell him what to do about it. The Earl of Morton asked him to join friends for dinner and at the same time instruct the earl's workmen about placing lightning rods on his Bond Street house. Joseph Priestley was writing a history of electricity and hoped to revive Franklin's interest in doing more experiments, for everyone agreed that his participation was the way to advance the subject. ("My great ambition would be to act under your auspices.") Young Matthew Boulton, who was trying to build a steam engine with James Watt, sent him a model of the one they were developing, begging him for any thought that "occours to your fertile Genius which you think may be usefull or preserve me from Error in the Execution of this Engine." Franklin obliged with some suggestions about the firebox, and ultimately Boulton and Watt did produce a working steam engine that would revolutionize the industrial world.

It was flattering to be sought out as the universal genius that in many senses he was—Franklin was not immune to flattery. But it was the company he valued, the company of people who could talk on the same wavelength with him. There had always been a few in Philadelphia, men like James Logan, the learned fur trader, and John Bartram, the self-taught botanist. And there were the men of large minds he encountered incidentally in his visits to other colonies as deputy postmaster: John Mitchell, the cartographer in Virginia; Jared Eliot, the experimental farmer in Connecticut; the men who came to the Albany Congress and agreed on colonial union. Not accidentally, they were mostly people "of the better sort." They held large acreages, high office, and high opinions of their own importance. They may have taken care not to exhibit those opinions to a man of Franklin's stature, whom they knew—that was itself a sign of their familiarity with a larger world—to rank a cut above themselves in the esteem of people who mattered. Franklin was less impressed than most people by social standing, but as we have guessed (who can do more than guess about this man?) Franklin's mingling in their company during his two years' stay in America may have made made him less aware than he should have been of popular opinion. And in England, where people of the better sort were more plentiful, more powerful, and on the whole—he would not have denied it—more interesting, Franklin found himself continually rubbing elbows with them. The old weekly dinners with convivial, highly placed friends resumed. Sir John Pringle, the queen's physician, became his closest companion, with whom he shared the lengthy travels he liked to take in the summer. The two went to Paris in 1767, where Louis XV and his queen entertained them at Versailles. Franklin wrote a long, joking letter about it to Polly Stevenson. The French were dressing him up like one of them, he said, transforming him into a Frenchman, and to conform to the mode he would soon have to make love to his friends' wives!

Right and Rights

It was great fun, an exercise of the extraordinary social and intellectual talents that had been submerged and too easily neglected in the familiar, narrow politics of provincial Pennsylvania. Franklin thrived in the company of exciting people, and the excitement went on for more than ten years, as one thing after another kept him in England. But as provincial politics had engulfed him in Pennsylvania, imperial politics took hold of him in London and gradually came to exclude almost everything else. He had come on a political mission, a mission he had brought on himself. And in his dedication to public service he knew that his public stretched beyond Philadelphia and Pennsylvania to America. America, Franklin had long ago decided, was the future center of the British Empire, and the future would have to grow out of the present. The task he must set himself, had already set himself, was to guide the growth, to make life useful and beneficial to the people of what must become the greatest empire in the world.

As Franklin saw it the task was not an impossible one, and need not be a difficult one. It required only that people do what was useful and right for themselves, and they could easily do that without interfering with what was useful and right for others. The British Empire in 1764 was a working system. Its government mostly did what was right and useful for everybody in it. But it had flaws that needed correcting. Some of its laws favored some of its subjects at the expense of others, especially the acts regulating trade and manufacturing that restricted subjects in America for the benefit of subjects in England. If the future strength of the empire lay in its American colonies, it was high time to correct that inequity, the more so as the successful war with France had opened the way for American growth to proceed as never before.

Franklin had outlined to Shirley in 1754 a way to make corrections, and he was on hand in London to direct them in 1764. But the principal obstacle that made difficult what should have been easy was embodied in his own status. He had come as the agent of Pennsylvania's Assembly, and in the years ahead the assemblies of other colonies would make him their agent as well. The trouble lay in the fact that colonial agents were little more than propagandists. They were not officers of government. They could make humble requests to the ministers assigned to deal with the colonies, they could offer petitions to the king or to Parliament, but no one had to listen to them. They had no power, no platform from which to gain an official hearing for measures that would be useful and right for everybody. Instead of acting to get things done, they could only react in ineffectual response to the succession of mistakes that misinformed people in power continued to make.

As an agent, Franklin had the advantage of his international prestige and his closeness to many of the people who mattered. But he was never close enough to direct what the government did. He could only make suggestions, in print or in person, to whoever would read or listen, about why the latest government action was wrong and what would be a better one. For the next ten years he tried. It was an educational experience that required him continually to examine, apply, and adjust the ideas that had guided him for nearly sixty years.

The experience began as soon as he was settled in London. Franklin, as we know, was more interested in right than in rights. He liked to devise schemes that would benefit everybody. He knew what Edmund Burke wisely remarked, that when people start talking about rights, it is a sure sign of a poorly conducted government. That sign had made its appearance before Franklin arrived in London. George Grenville, speaking for the ministry in Parliament, had started the talk about rights at the very moment when he proposed to raise money in the colonies by a direct stamp tax on the papers used to transact business there. Grenville sensed that this was a new thing, and he took pains to deny that it could violate colonial rights before anyone ever said that it did. The colonial agent of Virginia had been present in the gallery of the House of Commons and heard Grenville challenge any member to dispute the power of Parliament to levy taxes anywhere in the empire. Even as he did so, however, he betrayed an unspoken doubt by proposing to give the colonies a year to suggest some other tax than the one he had in mind.

After arriving in London, Franklin met with the other agents and learned of Grenville's insistence that it was one of Parliament's rights to tax the colonies. He knew already of the response contained in the messages to the Pennsylvania Assembly from Connecticut and Massachusetts, that the exercise of such a supposed right of Parliament would deprive the colonists of "some of their most essential Rights." Franklin wanted both sides to stop talking about rights, and he had thought of a way to do it: a measure that would raise money for Parliament by a tax that would not seem like a tax to the colonists. Parliament had previously hampered the conduct of business in America by forbidding the colonial assemblies to make paper money legal tender for payment of debts. Since gold and silver coins were scarce in America, being constantly sent abroad to pay for imports, the colonists needed paper money simply as a medium of exchange. So when Grenville invited the colonial agents, as he had promised, to suggest an alternative to the stamp tax, Franklin offered one that would supply the colonies with paper money and at the same time collect what was really a tax for the service. Parliament should establish a colonial loan office, which would issue bills of credit. The bills would be legal tender, but they would be redeemable only on payment of a yearly interest of 6 percent.

It was an ingenious scheme and might have worked in 1765. Two years later Grenville himself was ready to propose it, but by then the talk of rights had gone on too long for it to work. At the meeting with the agents, Franklin recalled, "Mr. Grenville paid little Attention to it, being besotted with his Stamp Scheme." Grenville, he believed, had the whole Stamp Act "cut and dry'd, and every Resolve fram'd at the Treasury ready for the House [of Commons], before I arriv'd in England."

As Franklin later heard, Grenville's insistence on a clear-cut tax arose from an ignorance of American attitudes that was common in England, the same ignorance that had prevented Parliament from considering a union of the colonies against the French in the preceding war. The English suspected that Americans wanted to become independent, and any union among them might be used as a step in that direction. Grenville wanted a tax as a way to suppress an opinion that did not, as yet, exist. He wanted a demonstration of Parliament's sovereignty, its *right* to tax the colonists, its right, as Franklin saw it, to do what was wrong.

Franklin was certain that Americans harbored no yearning for independence. He had tried a few years earlier in the Canada pamphlet to disabuse the English of the illusion that they did. But he also knew that the power of the empire itself, like all forms of rule, rested on opinion. He himself still misjudged the strength of American opinion about rights, but he could foresee a needless disagreement between Parliament and the colonies arising from an ignorance that the very rights in question had been originally designed to avoid. Parliament, and particularly the House of Commons, had come into existence in the distant past as a way of informing the king about his dominions and in particular as a way of informing him about what taxes and what kinds of taxes his subjects were able and willing to pay. From this way of getting things right had grown the right to consent to taxes through elected representatives, and Franklin found the proof in Parliament's later extension of representation to Wales and to the counties of Chester and Durham. The preamble to the statute enfranchising Durham less than a century earlier, in 1672, specified the reason: the people of Durham were subject to the same taxes as other counties and were "therefore concerned *equally* with others the Inhabitants of this Kingdom to have Knights and Burgesses [that is, representatives] in Parliament of THEIR OWN ELECTION to represent *the condition of their Country.*" From the words of the statute Franklin made the obvious application to the colonies:

> This contains the strongest Parliamentary Acknowledgments and Authority of this Truth.
>
> That a People liable to Rates and Subsidies granted by Parliament, are THEREFORE intitled to have Representatives in Parliament
> "Of their own Election."
> "To represent the Condition of their Country."
> Which could not otherwise be so well understood or taken care of.

Here was an obvious example of how doing what was right begot rights. And to recognize the colonists' rights would be just as right now as recognizing Durham's was in 1672. Franklin's friend Jackson, who had become a member of Parliament, made the point for him when Grenville's stamp tax came up for debate. But to no purpose. The act was passed in February, to go into effect the first of November, 1765. There were no members from America to "represent the Condition of their Country" or to inform the members of Parliament how their actions would affect Americans' opinion of them and their supposed power.

Franklin knew that the Stamp Act would offend Americans and erode their loyalty to their mother country, but he still did not realize just how offended they would be or how closely the act would come to creating the urge for independence it was designed to suppress. Once the act was passed, he bent his efforts toward getting it repealed, but meanwhile he clearly expected it to take effect on November 1. As long as it was there, his instinct was to make the best of it. He continued to tell people that it would cause England to "Lose more in Trade then they can get in Taxes." And he urged his friends in America to respond with industry and frugality, for "Idleness and Pride Tax with a heavier Hand than Kings and Parliaments; if we can get rid of the former we may easily bear the Latter." George Grenville, equally mistaken about the American reception of his tax, thought to make it go down easier by appointing Americans to collect it. He asked the colonial agents to nominate collectors, who would receive a commission on the proceeds. Franklin displayed his own miscalculation of the American reaction by nominating his friend John Hughes for the post in Pennsylvania.

When he heard from Hughes in early August of the resolves passed in May by the Virginia House of Burgesses, Franklin was shocked. The Virginians had declared Parliamentary taxation "illegal, unconstitutional and unjust." And they had gone on, as reported in the newspapers, to say that "the Inhabitants of this Colony, are not bound to yield Obedience to any law or Ordinance whatever, designed to impose any Taxation whatsoever upon them, other than the Laws or Ordinances of the General Assembly [of Virginia]." The Virginia Resolves were the signal for riots against stamp tax collectors throughout the colonies and for similar resolves by other colonial assemblies. By the end of October, all the designated collectors, including Hughes, were coerced into promising not to collect the tax. With the act already, in effect, nullified, a congress in New York with representatives from nine colonies declared it to be the essential right of the colonists as Englishmen "that no Taxes be imposed on them, but with their own Consent, given personally, or by their Representatives."

Franklin finally grasped what had happened to American opinion and what it meant for his empire. He was correct in thinking that Americans did not want independence from Britain, but he now saw that they did want some kind of independence from Parliament. Nor would they be satisfied by representation in that body. They had their own representative assemblies and wanted no others. The congress in New York had stated flatly that "the People of these Colonies are not, and from their local Circumstances cannot be, Represented in the House of Commons in Great-Britain." Franklin had been thinking of colonial representation in Parliament as a possible solution to the problem, and in August 1765 had written his friend in Massachusetts, Lieutenant Governor Thomas Hutchinson, asking what he thought about an application from the colonies for the purpose. That Franklin should have sought advice about popular rights from Hutchinson, perhaps the most unpopular man in Massachusetts (however undeservedly), is symptomatic of how far he had drifted from the people to whose service he was devoting himself.

By the time Hutchinson answered him in January 1766, Hutchinson's house was in ruins, destroyed by the Boston mob, and Franklin had long since come to recognize what Hutchinson told him, that the rift between Parliament and the colonies had opened too wide to be bridged by admitting colonial representatives. "The Time has been," Franklin wrote, before he could have received Hutchinson's letter, "when the Colonies, would have esteem'd it a great Advantage as well as Honour to them to be permitted to send Members to Parliament; and would have ask'd for that Privilege if they could have had the least hopes of obtaining it. The Time is now come when they are indifferent about it, and will probably not ask it; though they might accept it if offered them; and the Time will come when they will certainly refuse it."

They were never given the opportunity to refuse, and Franklin had already dismissed that option as a real possibility. By the time the Stamp Act was supposed to go into effect, he had come to a full realization of the determination of his countrymen to resist it in force and of the danger that Parliament would use the army in an impossible attempt to make them knuckle under. As usual he was thinking of ways to defuse the situation, which as usual meant getting people to stop talking and stop thinking about rights that both sides claimed and that neither side was likely to give up. A lucky change in the ministry, which had nothing to do with American affairs, had brought in men more sympathetic to the colonists. Some of Franklin's friends took advantage of the change to arrange for him to meet with Lord Dartmouth, newly placed at the head of the Board of Trade. Franklin was pleased with the chance to offer him a typically Franklinian proposal, namely, "to suspend the Execution of the Act for a Term of Years, till the Colonies should be more clear of Debt [contracted in the French and Indian War], and better able to bear it, and then drop it on some other decent Pretence, without ever bringing the Question of Right to a Decision." He went on to warn Dartmouth of the probable consequences of sending fleets and armies to back up the tax collectors: "the Inhabitants would probably take every Method to encourage the Soldiers to desert, to which the high Price of Labour would contribute, and the Chance of being never apprehended in so extensive a Country, where the Want of Hands, as well as the Desire of wasting the Strength of an Army come to oppress, would encline every one to conceal Deserters, so that the Officers would probably soon be left alone." The end result would be the creation of a "a deep-rooted Aversion between the two Countries, and laying the Foundation of a future total Separation."

The new ministry did not accept Franklin's proposal, but it decided on one that might work just as well: to repeal rather than suspend the Stamp Act and at the same time to make a declaration to the effect that Parliament nevertheless had total authority over the colonies. Franklin thought that the declaration would cause no great problem because it would probably never be put to use. Such a "declaratory act" already existed in relation to Ireland and had never been put to use there. And the declaration contemplated for the colonies avoided any specific mention of taxation. Once the Stamp Act was gone, Parliament, he felt sure, would not soon walk into the hornets' nest of colonial taxation again. The problem would be to get the repeal through the House of Commons, for despite the accompanying Declaratory Act, repeal looked like backing down in the face of colonial intransigence. And here the new ministry, headed by Lord Rockingham, needed Franklin's assistance. He was the arch-American, the famous scientist, the spokesman of reason. He should appear before the House of Commons to soothe the bad temper of the opposition and explain away the bad temper of the Americans.

From Caution to Confrontation

In the examination that took place on February 13, 1766, Franklin was at his best. His friends among the members of the

House of Commons fed him leading questions to give him the opportunity to show what a misguided measure the Stamp Act was. Members opposed to repeal unwittingly obliged with questions that he was able to turn against the questioners. Asked by friends about "the temper of America" before 1763, he could honestly emphasize the colonists' loyalty: "They were governed by this country at the expence only of a little pen, ink and paper. They were led by a thread. They had not only a respect, but an affection, for Great Britain." That respect and affection, he assured the Commons, had been "very much altered" by the levying of an "internal tax." The colonists had never objected to the customs duties (that is, external taxes) and other regulations of their trade, and, by implication at least, they would not object now to the regulation of their trade by external taxes. It was only internal taxes that bothered them. And when an unfriendly member asked whether the objection to internal taxes could not be equally applied to external taxes, Franklin had an answer ready: "Many arguments have been lately used here to shew them that there is no difference, and that if you have no right to tax them internally, you have none to tax them externally, or to make any other law to bind them. At present they do not reason so, but in time they may possibly be convinced by these arguments."

What Franklin did not say was that he himself had long been been convinced by such arguments, made to himself by himself. His own view of the rights of the colonies was actually more radical than that of his constituents in America. But preserving the empire so that it could be reformed was more important than insisting in advance on all the rights that ought to be recognized in any reform. He was not mistaken in saying that Americans had not objected (except perhaps by smuggling) to the regulation of their trade or to the duties used for regulation. And he believed that they would have accepted the concealed tax in his proposal for a Parliamentary loan office. He did not personally think that acceptance of indirect taxes conferred a right in Parliament to levy them. But he kept that view to himself. He believed the colonists would swallow external taxes without raising the question of rights. And if the question of rights could be taken out of the picture, it might be possible to reorganize the empire on a more equitable basis, or at least to prevent any new measures that would resuscitate an irreconcilable quarrel. First it was necessary to get rid of an act that the colonists had made plain they would not accept. On that point he did not attempt to belittle their intransigence.

> Q. Don't you think they would submit to the stamp-act if it was modified, the obnoxious parts taken out, and the duty reduced to some particulars, of small moment?
> A. No; they will never submit to it. . . .
> Q. If the stamp-act should be repealed, would it induce the assemblies of America to acknowledge the rights of parliament to tax them, and would they erase their resolutions?
> A. No, never.

Franklin's strategy worked, or at least seemed to. Parliament repealed the Stamp Act and made a declaration of its own rights (the Declaratory Act) directly contrary to the declarations by the colonial assemblies. In doing so it contrived to overlook the actual nullification by the colonists of one of its laws. Franklin was delighted because the empire had shown itself to be a working system in spite of the flaws that came near to destroying it, as an attempt to enforce the Stamp Act might have done. The existing ministry had backed the repeal against the opposition's efforts to reduce the tax to a token "merely to keep up the Claim of Right." He advised his American friends to follow suit by a show of gratitude. "We now see," he wrote, perhaps more optimistically than he felt, "that tho' the Parliament may sometimes possibly thro' Misinformation be mislead to do a wrong Thing towards America, yet as soon as they are rightly inform'd, they will immediately rectify it, which ought to confirm our Veneration for that most August Body, and Confidence in its Justice and Equity." If there were to be a reform of the empire, it would have to come through that august body, and Franklin had high hopes that the ministry would now begin to undertake the needed measures. To the Speaker of the Pennsylvania Assembly he wrote, "The House [of Commons] will next proceed to reconsider all the Acts of Trade, designing to give us every reasonable Relief." He told his old partner David Hall the same thing and added his hope "that Harmony between the two Countries will be restor'd, and all Mobs and Riots on our Side the Water totally cease."

Franklin's optimism may have been genuine, but it was short-lived, as the Rockingham ministry quickly gave way to a succession of others, all of them more committed to Parliamentary rights than to right, more eager to teach the colonists a lesson in sovereignty than to give them reasonable relief. In the surviving papers that came from his hand in the next nine or ten years, the greater part of them having to do with the empire, Franklin can be seen year after year trying to patch up the empire, trying to undo the mistakes of a heedless ministry, trying to guide colonial protests in constructive ways, trying to interpret them constructively to an uncomprehending English public. Seldom in his public statements do we get a glimpse of his larger hopes for the empire, because to achieve them would have required changes that he knew to be out of reach.

The closest glimpse we get is in the private comments he wrote in the margins of books and pamphlets in which uninformed Englishmen offered their views about how to treat the colonies. After the repeal of the Stamp Act, seventy-one members of the House of Lords published a protest against this coddling of rebellious colonists. In his copy Franklin recorded his own view of the structure of the empire, namely that it consisted of several separate societies, each with its own representative assembly, united by their allegiance to a single king. Parliament was the assembly for Great Britain, but no assembly had powers extending beyond the borders of the particular society it represented. In the absence of a larger general assembly, with representatives from each of the empire's societies, the American assemblies had submitted as a matter of convenience to regulations passed by the British Parliament. But where the Lords spoke of Parliament as "the supreme legislature" for the whole empire, Franklin wrote in the margin, "There is yet no such Thing. It is indeed wanted and to be wish'd for." Where the Lords complained that the colonists had shown "contempt of the *Sovereignty* of the *British Legislature*," Franklin wrote, "The Sovereignty of the Crown I understand. The Sov[ereignt]y of the British Legislature out of Britain, I do not understand." The Lords objected that the majority in Parliament had given in to "the *Clamour of Multitudes*." To this Franklin offered another version of his recognition of the fact that government rested on opinion: "the Clamour of Multitudes. It is good to attend to it. It is wise to foresee and avoid it. It is wise, when neither foreseen nor avoided, to correct the Measures that give Occasion to it. Glad the majority [in repealing the Stamp Act] have that Wisdom."

There is nothing in these comments that cannot be found, at least implicitly, in Franklin's earlier writings, in his letters to Governor Shirley, or even in his objection to proprietary rule in Pennsylvania because it placed a private subject in England in command of other subjects in Pennsylvania. Franklin did not forget his petition to the king asking him to assert his sovereignty over Pennsylvania. He had presented the petition on his arrival in England, but the king's Privy Council had delayed considering it (a delay that turned out to be permanent), and he heard from his colleagues in Pennsylvania that they were thus left "to groan . . . under the Tyranny of a private Subject." But the claims of Parliament to sovereignty over the colonies dwarfed the proprietor's claim. It made every subject of the king in England a tyrant over the king's subjects in America.

In a long letter to Lord Kames, to whom he sometimes unburdened himself more freely than to most other correspondents, Franklin expressed his dismay at the possessive attitude toward the colonists that he found not only in Parliament but in the people who elected it. "Every Man in England," he said, "seems to consider himself as a Piece of a Sovereign over America; seems to jostle himself into the Throne with the King, and talks of OUR *subjects in the Colonies.*"

Franklin was writing just a year after the repeal of the Stamp Act, his optimism gone. Instead of measures for relieving the colonies, the British press was full of complaints against them. The New York Assembly had refused to comply in every detail with an act of Parliament requring them to supply quarters and provisions for the troops stationed there. The act could be seen as a tax, and in order to avoid acknowledgement of a right to tax them, New York had treated the act as a request and in complying had taken care to omit a few provisions the act specified. It could thus be seen as the Assembly's own voluntary act. The royal governor and the ministry in England chose to see this token denial of Parliament's authority as an act of rebellion. "And now," Franklin reported, "all the Talk here is to send a Force to compel them." It was another quarrel over asserting rights for the sake of asserting them; and Franklin as usual did what he could in the English newspapers to reduce the conflict to absurdity. "It used to be thought," he wrote, "that Rebellion consisted in *doing* something; but this is a Rebellion that consists in *not doing* something, or in doing nothing. If every man who neglects or refuses to comply with an act of Parliament is a rebel, I am afraid we have many more rebels among us than we were aware," including "the acting rebels that wear French silks and cambricks" smuggled into the country.

It was clear that Americans, aroused by the Stamp Act, would never submit to a direct tax by a body in which they had no representatives, and they were becoming alert to indirect taxes. Franklin had abandoned any expectation that they would be offered representation in Parliament or that they would accept it if offered. He was also sure that the Americans, growing in numbers and strength as they were, would one day be more powerful than the British. In the long run the only way the empire could be preserved was through a union of all its parts, in a general assembly comparable to the one he had suggested for the colonies at Albany but embracing the British Isles and the colonies as equals. Franklin longed for such a union, but as he confessed to

Kames, he saw no likelihood of its coming to pass. In closing his letter he explained why, in a passage that predicted and lamented what would happen during the remainder of his life:

Upon the whole, I have lived so great a Part of my Life in Britain, and have formed so many Friendships in it, that I love it and wish its Prosperity, and therefore wish to see that Union on which alone I think it can be secur'd and establish'd. As to America, the Advantages of such an Union to her are not so apparent. She may suffer at present under the arbitrary Power of this Country; she may suffer for a while in a Separation from it; but these are temporary Evils that she will outgrow. Scotland and Ireland are differently circumstanc'd. Confined by the Sea, they can scarcely increase in Numbers, Wealth and Strength so as to overbalance England. But America, an immense Territory, favour'd by Nature with all Advantages of Climate, Soil, great navigable Rivers and Lakes, &c. must become a great Country, populous and mighty; and will in a less time than is generally conceiv'd be able to shake off any Shackles that may be impos'd on her, and perhaps place them on the Imposers. In the mean time, every Act of Oppression will sour their Tempers, lessen greatly if not annihilate the Profits of your Commerce with them, and hasten their final Revolt: For the Seeds of Liberty are universally sown there, and nothing can eradicate them. And yet there remains among that People so much Respect, Veneration and Affection for Britain, that, if cultivated prudently, with kind Usage and Tenderness for their Privileges, they might be easily govern'd still for Ages, without Force or any considerable Expence. But I do not see here a sufficient quantity of the Wisdom that is necessary to produce such a Conduct, and I lament the Want of it.

Franklin was not content to lament the folly that he saw destroying his empire. He would save it if he could by persuading British politicians that their authority in America rested on

American opinion and by persuading Americans to be patient with British mistakes until they were corrected, as they had been in repeal of the Stamp Act. Unfortunately, the assertion of rights by both sides had not subsided with repeal. It had become a major element in American determination to set limits to British rule, matched by British determination to demonstrate that there were no limits. Franklin was sure that the limits must eventually be set at the shores of the British Isles. Most other Americans did not reach that opinion until the 1770s. They were currently setting the limits, Franklin (mistakenly) supposed, at the levying of internal taxes. His immediate objective therefore was to prevent anything that could be seen as an internal tax (including his own earlier scheme of a parliamentary loan office) and at the same time to discourage unnecessary American assertions of rights and shows of resistance that might provoke corresponding exercises of Parliament's supposed authority.

At the time when he wrote so pessimistically to Kames (February 25, 1767), Franklin was most disturbed by the anti-American sentiment he found not only in Parliament but in the popular press, and he set himself to clearing up the many damaging misconceptions he encountered about his countrymen, in particular about their views of Parliament's power. Because of their opposition to the Stamp Act, many people in England seemed to believe "That the colonies contend the parliament of Britain has no authority over them." That was, in fact, Franklin's own view, but the last thing he wanted to do was exacerbate British irritation by expressing it. In his examination before the House of Commons he had insisted that Americans objected only to internal taxes. When an unfriendly member pointed out that the resolutions passed by the colonial assemblies had objected to any taxes, Franklin had soothed him by saying that what they meant was internal taxes. And he seems to have believed that to be the case. In a newspaper article he stated flatly, "The truth is, that all acts of the British legislature, expressly extending to the colonies, have ever been received there as laws, and executed in their courts, the right of parliament to make them being never yet contested, acts to raise money upon the colonies by internal taxes only and alone excepted."

Franklin was wrong. Colonial views of Parliament's authority were not quite as far behind his own as he supposed. The colonial resolutions against the Stamp Act had not objected to Parliament's legislation (for the regulation of trade), but they had indeed denied its right to levy taxes of any kind, without distinction. Franklin, rather than eliminating misunderstanding, contributed to it by stating, "The colonies submit to pay all external taxes laid on them by way of duty on merchandizes imported into their country, and never disputed the authority of parliament to lay such duties."

To English politicians intent on establishing Parliament's rights, the distinction between internal and external taxes was nonsense (as it actually was to most Americans); and in 1767 the Chancellor of the Exchequer, Charles Townshend, decided to establish Parliament's right to tax by a series of external taxes levied on various English manufactures (paper, glass, paint) and also on East India tea imported into the colonies. He also provided for a new Board of Customs Commissioners to reside in America and oversee their collection. As Franklin had earlier underestimated Americans' reaction to the Stamp Act, he now seems to have believed that they would have no objection to these external taxes. The Townshend Acts were passed at the end of June 1767, and Franklin's earliest surviving letter to his Pennsylvania correspondents after that date (August 8) reports an opinion among the "profess'd Adversaries of America" that "it is high time to put the Right and Power of this Country to tax the Colonies, out of dispute, by an Act of Taxation effectually carried into Execution." He apparently did not consider the Townshend Acts to fit that description. He mused that if a bill to tax the colonies should be brought before Parliament, "it is hard to say what would be the Event of it, or what would be the Effects." He thought it possible that something like his Parliamentary loan office scheme might be tried and warned that "It is our Interest to prevent this," for "The Plan of our Adversaries is to render Assemblies in America useless; and to have a Revenue independent of their Grants, for all the Purposes of their Defence, and Supporting Government among them."

Franklin makes no mention of the fact that the proceeds from the Townshend duties were directed to those very purposes, though he later explained American objections on that ground. He evidently considered the duties themselves to be export duties and, as such, within the authority of Parliament by any definition. As he explained to his son William, "not only the Parliament of Britain, but every state in Europe claims and exercises a right of laying duties on the exportation of its own commodities to foreign countries." In the summer of 1767 Franklin worried that Parliament *would* tax the colonies, not that it had just done so. To prevent a tax, he advised his friends in Philadelphia "that we should all do our Endeavours on both sides the Water, to lessen the present Unpopularity of the American Cause; conciliate the Affections of the People here towards us; increase by all possible Means the Number of our Friends, and be careful not to weaken their Hands and strengthen those of our Enemies, by rash Proceedings on our side, the Mischiefs of which are inconceivable."

The first rash proceedings came from Massachusetts. On October 28, 1767, the Boston town meeting called on the people of the colony to subscribe to an agreement not to buy any of a list of thirty-eight articles imported from abroad. Existing regulations already required the colonists to purchase any imported manufactures from England and forbade the direct importation of articles not produced in England, for example, wines. The meeting voted to encourage, presumably by bounties, the local manufacture of glass and paper, the two principal products on which the Townshend duties were to be collected. In subsequent meetings the town called on the colony's Assembly to seek a repeal of the Townshend Acts as "an infringement of their natural and Constitutional Rights." They were taxes imposed without the colony's consent or consultation, and it was "immaterial to us by what mode the Taxes are to be levied, or by what Name they are called." When news of the Boston nonimportation resolutions reached England in December, on top of reports from Governor Bernard "that he daily expected a rebellion," Franklin wrote to his Philadelphia friends that "The Boston People pretending to interfere with the Manufactures of this Country, makes a great clamour here against Americans in general." He hoped that if Pennsylvanians followed the Boston example, "they will among other things give this reason, that 'tis to enable them more speedily and effectually to discharge their debts to Great Britain; this will soften a little and at the same time appear honourable and like ourselves." It would be better, too, "if we meddled only with such manufactures as England does not attend to." The London press was treating the Boston agreement as a malicious attempt to undermine British prosperity, a blatant move toward total independence. As the nonimportation movement spread through the other colonies, unaccompanied by any "softening" rationale, the English papers filled with talk of sending troops to put the Americans in their proper place.

Franklin's first public response was a piece for the newspapers on January 7, 1768. In it he tried to turn the tables by focusing attention on the change in British policy, beginning with the Stamp Act, that ignored the universal opinions of Americans about their rights. "It has," he wrote, "been thought wisdom in a Government exercising sovereignty over different kinds of people, to have some regard to prevailing and established opinions among the people to be governed . . . how absurd so ever such popular opinions may be in their natures." Without discussing the constitutionality of the Townshend duties as taxes, he explained the prevailing opinion that the royal governors and judges, to be supported by the duties, were "sometimes men of vicious characters and broken fortunes, sent by a Minister merely to get them out of the way." If the assemblies were deprived of any control in voting their salaries, governors would be able to dispense with assemblies altogether, "having nothing to hope from their meeting, and perhaps something to fear from their enquiries." Americans had submitted to regulation of their trade, despite the fact that the regulations favored some of the king's subjects (in England) over others (in America). Americans were loyal subjects of the king. "But a new kind of loyalty seems to be required of us, a loyalty to P[arliamen]t; a loyalty that is to extend, it is said, to a surrender of all our properties, whenever a H[ouse] of C[ommons], in which there is not a single member of our chusing, shall think fit to grant them away without our consent." Americans were united to Britain, he said, by "respect and love. . . . But this unhappy new system of politics tends to dissolve those bands of union, and to sever us for ever."

Franklin regarded this piece as a plea for moderation. He seems to have been more concerned with quieting popular British resentment of American nonimportation agreements than he was with the Townshend Acts themselves. But as the year wore on and the papers printed more and more proposals for sending the mighty British army to whip the Americans into shape, Franklin responded with his characteristic satirical pragmatism. Writing as an Englishman, he calculated that it had taken five years to subdue one American colony, namely Canada, even with the assistance of all the others. Now there would be fifteen (including Florida) to conquer all at once. At the rate of five years per colony, it would take seventy-five years to subdue them.

Franklin was only half joking. It is difficult in hindsight to recover his or anyone else's perspective on the relations between England and America in the 1760s and early 1770s. We know that the fighting in the American War for Independence would begin less than seven years after he made this humorous calculation. We know that both he and the people he argued with were aware of the danger that such a war might be in the offing. What we cannot recapture is the expectation on both sides that it could be, probably would be, avoided. The British extremists thought war would be avoided by a simple show of force, in the face of which colonial discontent, the product of a few agitators, would quickly subside. Franklin, under no such illusion, still hoped in 1768 that it could be avoided if the men in power in England could be made to understand how much they had to lose by alienating the Americans and if Americans could be persuaded to wait for such an understanding to operate.

Franklin continued throughout 1768 in his efforts to placate the British and quiet the Americans. In meetings with members of Parliament he emphasized "that tho' the Right has been deny'd, the Payment of the Duties has nevertheless been every where submitted to . . . That the Honour of Parliament and of the Nation, is best maintain'd by rectifying what it has done improperly as soon as it can be convinc'd of it, and not by being obstinate in the Wrong. . . . That Government is not establish'd merely by *Power;* there must be maintain'd a general Opinion of its *Wisdom* and *Justice,* to make it firm and durable." He continued to preach this sermon, but he made few converts, and sometime in 1769 he must have decided that British abuse of power had to be met with something more than patience. Not with mobs of the kind that stopped the Stamp Tax collectors. Franklin hated mobs and the power of mobs, whether in England or America; and it bothered him when Americans cheered, albeit from a distance, the London mobs that supported the demagogic John Wilkes in his contest for a seat in Parliament. Wilkes was an ally Franklin could do without. But the nonimportation agreements that so offended the English were another matter. Although his first reaction had been to write excuses for them, they gave the English a taste of the growing strength that would inevitably surpass England's in the not too distant future. At the same time they contributed to the growth of that strength by fostering an economic self-sufficiency and by encouraging Franklin's favorite virtues of industry and thrift. By the end of January 1769 he was writing home that "if News can come of all the Colonies having join'd in the Determination to buy no more British goods, the Acts must be repeal'd." He had been convinced that talk was not enough and that closing the American market for British manufactures was perhaps "the only way in which we can yet contend with this powerful People with any Prospect of Success." Franklin still wanted to save the empire, but his vision of it as a collection of different societies united in affection and allegiance to a common king was fading behind a contest between two peoples, two countries. "Losing our Commerce must certainly weaken this Country," he wrote to his friend Galloway. "Possibly they may think of some equal means of hurting us; but something must be try'd and some Risque run, rather than sit down quietly under a Claim of Parliament to the Right of disposing of our Properties without our Consent."

This is a different Franklin from the one who had been so disturbed by the offense which the Boston agreement gave to the English. His next letter to Galloway urged that not only the Pennsylvania Assembly but "all the Inhabitants" of the colony engage in the agreement not to buy British goods. Opening a correspondence with the Reverend Samuel Cooper of Boston, he told him that "The Tide is yet strong against us. . . . But it must turn; if your frugal and industrious Resolutions continue." By the end of 1769 the tide had turned to the extent that Parliament was considering the repeal of all the Townshend duties except the one on tea. William Strahan asked Franklin if that would satisfy the colonists. It would not, Franklin told him, because among other reasons "their Agreements not to import till the Repeal takes place, include the whole, which shows that they object to the whole; and those Agreements will continue binding on them if the whole is not repealed."

In March 1770 Parliament did repeal the other duties but left the one on tea, intent once again on making at least a token exercise of its supposed right to tax. The members, Franklin believed, had been "persuaded by Governor Bernard and some lying Letters said to be from Boston" that the agreements were breaking up, that the Americans could not go on much longer without their customary imports from Britain, "and must of course submit to any Terms Parliament should think fit to impose upon us." These misconceptions, along with "the idle Notion of the Dignity and Sovereignty of Parliament, which they are so fond of, and imagine will be endanger'd by any farther Concessions, prevailed I know with many to vote with the Ministry" in retaining the tea tax.

While Franklin had once hoped to avoid a contest over rights, it had come down to that, and Franklin was convinced that the empire could be saved only by Parliament's withdrawing from the contest. Even his son William, who as royal governor of New Jersey was disposed to favor Parliament, told him that "nothing can make them [the colonists] acknowledge the Right of Parliament to tax them." Franklin therefore encouraged his American correspondents to stand firm in their rejection of all British goods until their rights were acknowledged. If any of the merchants gave way, he hoped "the Country People will have the Good Sense and spirit not to buy." To Charles Thomson, a former teacher in his academy who was becoming a power in Pennsylvania politics, he offered his opinion that "if we do not now persist in this Measure till it has had its full Effect, it can never again be used on any future Occasion with the least prospect of Success, and that if we do persist another year, we shall never afterward have occasion to use it." He sent the same message to Galloway, adding, "what is more to be considered and valued than everything else, our Rights will finally be established, and no future Attempts will be hazarded here to deprive us of them."

Franklin's letters, widely publicized, helped to maintain the agreements in Pennsylvania and Massachusetts, but in July, despite strong popular opposition, New York merchants broke the united front and began importing everything but tea. In September, Philadelphia merchants gave way, and in October so did Boston's. Perhaps Franklin was right, that if the agreements had held, Parliament would have repealed the tea duty and allowed the situation to revert to what it had been before 1763. The question of rights might then have been allowed to fall away. But Parliament held fast to the duty on tea as a matter of rights; the colonists resisted it as a matter of rights; and for the remainder of his stay in England Franklin's quest to save the empire became more and more a matter of establishing American rights and dissolving British pretensions to rights.

Franklin still loved England and the English. The mission on which he had come, to secure royal government for Pennsylvania, had been definitively settled against him by 1768, and from time to time thereafter he planned to return to Philadelphia, but he always found reason to stay a little longer in London. In 1767, when his daughter Sally, once destined by Franklin to be the bride of Billy Strahan, married Richard Bache, a debt-ridden young Philadelphia merchant, he did not think of returning for the wedding. He did not approve of Sally's choice and became fully reconciled to the match only after Bache met with him four years later on a trip to England. Franklin continued his exile there contentedly, enjoying old friends and making new ones.

He spent a lot of time at Twyford, the country home of Jonathan Shipley, Bishop of St. Asaph, who was something of a kindred spirit and an unwavering supporter of the American cause. It was at Twyford in the summer of 1771 that Franklin began his never-finished autobiography, and the Shipleys would have welcomed him there to complete it.

The five Shipley daughters joined the ranks of the young women like Polly Stevenson and Katy Greene who claimed a special place in his affections. As surrogate father, he gave Polly Stevenson in marriage to a distinguished young physician, William Hewson, in 1770. The young couple came to live and to lighten his life at Craven Street. (Polly remained devoted to him, and after the Revolution, when she was a widow, she moved to Philadelphia to be near him.) He did not have time for electrical experiments, but other scientists could not do without his advice, and he wrote several pieces for an expanded edition of his *Experiments and Observations*. A new friend in France, Jacques Barbeu-Dubourg, flooded him with lively letters on a variety of scientific and political subjects and translated his writings for publication in Paris. He joined the governing council of the Royal Society and secured the election of his friend Sir John Pringle as president. He designed lightning rods to protect the Royal Arsenal at Purfleet. As he told his son William in 1772:

> As to my situation here nothing can be more agreeable, especially as I hope for less embarrassment from the new minister. A general respect paid me by the learned, a number of friends and acquaintance among them with whom I have a pleasing intercourse; a character of so much weight that it has protected me when some in power would have done me injury, and continued me in an office they would have deprived me of; my company so much desired that

I seldom dine at home in winter, and could spend the whole summer in the country houses of inviting friends if I chose it. Learned and ingenious foreigners that come to England, almost all make a point of visiting me, for my reputation is still higher abroad than here; several of the foreign ambassadors have assiduously cultivated my acquaintance, treating me as one of their *corps*, partly I believe from the desire they have from time to time of hearing something of American affairs, an object become of importance in foreign courts, who begin to hope Britain's alarming power will be diminished by the defection of her Colonies; and partly that they may have an opportunity of introducing me to the gentlemen of their country who desire it. The K[ing]. too has lately been heard to speak of me with great regard.

But neither the king's regard nor the esteem and affection of so many friends could turn him from what he now saw as his duty: to secure the recognition of American rights in their full extent. No longer did he refrain from stating his own views of that extent. In 1768 he had feared the damage from less sweeping assertions in the reports of the Boston town meeting. At the time, the town was still distinguishing between Parliament's authority to legislate and its nonexistent authority to tax and had included in its protests against the Townshend Acts a statement of "our acknowledged and Constitutional subordination to the supreme Legislative power of the Nation." By June 1770 Franklin wanted an end to any such acknowledgements. Writing to Cooper, who in the past year had become a regular correspondent, he expounded his own view that no subordination to Parliament existed.

That the Colonies originally were constituted distinct States, and intended to be continued such, is clear to me from a thorough Consideration of their original Charters, and the whole Conduct of the Crown and Nation towards them until the Restoration. Since that Period, the Parliament here has usurp'd an Authority of making Laws for them, which before it had not. We have for some time submitted to that Usurpation, partly thro' Ignorance and Inattention, and partly from our Weakness and Inability to contend. I hope when our Rights are better understood here, we shall, by a prudent and proper Conduct be able to obtain from the Equity of this Nation a Restoration of them. And in the mean time I could wish that such Expressions as, *The supreme Authority of Parliament; The Subordinacy of our Assemblies to the Parliament* and the like (which in Reality mean nothing if our Assemblies with the King have a true Legislative Authority) I say, I could wish that such Expressions were no more seen in our publick Pieces. They are too strong for Compliment, and tend to confirm a Claim [of] Subjects in one Part of the King's Dominions to be Sovereigns over their Fellow-Subjects in another Part of his Dominions; when [in] truth they have no such Right, and their Claim is founded only on Usurpation, the several States having equal Rights and Liberties, and being only connected, as England and Scotland were before the Union, by having one common Sovereign, the King.

Franklin must have known that Cooper would not keep these pronouncements to himself, for Cooper had told him of sharing Franklin's earlier letters with prominent people in Massachusetts. He showed this one to "some of the leading Members" of the colony's Assembly, with the result that the Assembly elected Franklin as their agent on October 24, 1770. The Georgia Assembly in 1768 and the New Jersey Assembly in 1769 had already made him their agent, and Pennsylvania had continued to retain him in that capacity, even though the whole issue of royal government there had subsided into the larger issue of Parliamentary taxation. Franklin was thus the appointed spokesman for four colonies and able to spread widely on both sides of the ocean his views of American rights. Thomas Cushing, Speaker of the Massachusetts Assembly, became, along with Cooper, as much a purveyor of Franklin's principles as Franklin was of the Assembly's. And Massachusetts became, even more than it already was, the collision point between Parliamentary and colonial assertions of rights.

Hillsborough and Hutchinson

Boston, Franklin's hometown, had been at the forefront of American resistance to British taxation from the time of the Stamp Act in 1765. Franklin had visited the town often, the last time in 1763, and had kept in touch with people there, among them Governor Francis Bernard and Lieutenant Governor Thomas Hutchinson. He had no sympathy with the riots or the rioters who destroyed Hutchinson's house in 1765, and we have seen his initial disapproval of the Boston town meeting's inauguration of the nonimportation agreements late in 1767. His conversion to wholehearted support of the agreements may have been prompted by his encounters in London with ministers who turned a deaf ear to American opinion and a blind eye to American strength. But his personal experience of ministerial arrogance coincided with the political experience of the people of Massachusetts.

The Massachusetts Assembly on February 11, 1768, had adopted a "Circular Letter" addressed to the assemblies of the other colonies, inviting them to join in denouncing the Townshend Acts, including the appointment of the customs commissioners, headquartered in Boston, who were using their powers in an arbitrary manner. The Circular Letter arrived in England

Thomas Hutchinson, 1741

shortly after the creation of a new secretary of state to deal exclusively with the colonies. Franklin had welcomed the step in the hope that it would mean a more informed treatment of the colonies by an officer whose sole business it would be to communicate with them. But the first man to hold the office became a principal instrument first in escalating colonial opposition and second—and perhaps equally significant—in suppressing Benjamin Franklin's disposition for moderation. The earl of Hillsborough, to whom Franklin later dedicated his *Rules by Which a Great Empire May Be Reduced to a Small One,* was a prime example of the heedless aristocrat whom British politics could drop into positions of power. Franklin's description of him, if scarcely impartial, will suggest at least the sort of effect he had on a man who was initially disposed to like him. Hillsborough, Franklin confided to Cushing, was "proud, supercilious, extremely conceited (moderate as they are) of his political Knowledge and Abilities, fond of every one that can stoop to flatter him, and inimical to all that dare tell him disagreeable Truths."

Hillsborough responded to the Massachusetts Circular Letter with an order to Governor Bernard to make the Assembly rescind it and to the governors of the other colonies to prevent their assemblies from receiving it. He followed up these orders, which in their nature could not be carried out, with one that could. On the basis of frivolous calls for help from the customs commissioners, he ordered two regiments of British troops stationed in Halifax, Nova Scotia, to proceed to Boston. There, after a year and a half of abrasive encounters with the inhabitants, they were goaded into the "Boston Massacre," in which five civilians were killed. Meanwhile, in February 1769, Hillsborough had persuaded Parliament to pass a series of resolutions denouncing as illegal, unconstitutional, unwarrantable, dangerous, and subversive various proceedings against the Townshend Acts by Massachusetts in general and Boston in particular. An address to the king attached to the resolutions called for the apprehension of "the chief authors and instigators" of the disorders, to be tried for treason without a jury under an archaic statute of Henry VIII's.

It seems likely that Hillsborough's hostility was the product not merely of his own headstrong nature but of the reports he received from Franklin's old friend Governor Bernard. William Bollan, formerly an agent of Massachusetts, somehow obtained copies of Bernard's letters to Hillsborough and sent six of them, dated in the preceding November and December (1768), to Boston. The letters described the breakdown of government, the approach of insurrection, and the need to deprive the Assembly of some of its powers. They made their public appearance with a scathing commentary by the governor's refractory Council in a pamphlet printed in Boston in April 1769. The Massachusetts Council and Assembly immediately demanded Bernard's recall, but Bernard did not wait (although the Privy Council later pronounced the charges against him "groundless, vexatious, and scandalous"). On the first of August he boarded ship for England, bearing with him a letter for Franklin from Hutchinson, who was left in charge of the province, first as Bernard's deputy and then, from 1770 on, as royal governor in his own right.

Hutchinson relied on Bernard to fill Franklin in on "all our late occurrences." "Only give me leave," he added, "to remark upon them that the air of indecency and contempt which our publick proceedings carry with them can have no other tendency than further to provoke a power it cannot Reach. And yet I hope some allowances will be made for them. They are artful performances of one or two designing men whose political existence depends upon keeping up a Clamour." Hutchinson had reason to think that Franklin would welcome a briefing from Bernard about the performance of designing men in Massachusetts, for Hutchinson and Franklin had much in common. They had both been born in Boston, five years apart, and had both been brought up in the Congregational church without forming any attachment to its dogmas. "The longer I live," Hutchinson once wrote, in words that could have been Franklin's, "the less stress I lay upon modes and forms in religion, and do not love a good man the less because he and I are not just of the same way of thinking." Franklin had joined with Hutchinson at the Albany Congress in planning a union and reconstruction of colonial governments that both men continued to dream of. Hutchinson was no apologist for parliamentary taxation. Before the Stamp Act was passed, while Franklin was devoting himself to his project of unseating the Penn family, Hutchinson had written an essay demonstrating why a parliamentary tax would violate what the colonists considered their rights. He did not publish the essay but sent it to his and Franklin's friend Richard Jackson, who passed it on to Henry Seymour Conway. Conway, as secretary of state, may well have drawn on it in arguments for repeal. There is no evidence that Jackson or Conway showed the piece to Franklin, but Hutchinson's arguments foreshadowed most of those that Franklin used in his many newspaper articles, even including his predictions of America's growing strength.

Hutchinson and Franklin shared also a pragmatic attitude toward politics, a concentration on doing what was possible, what would work. In the early stages of the colonies' quarrel with England they both counseled moderation, for they both cherished the empire and saw the conflict as needless. As they saw eye to eye on a union of the colonies at Albany, they could have worked together on a more equitable union of Britain and the colonies. Even in 1769 in Hutchinson's letter to Franklin about the disorders in Boston he hopes that "some allowances" can be made for the behavior he deplores. That the two men wound up on opposite sides when the chips were down can be explained at least in part by their being on opposite sides of the water. Since 1764 Franklin had been dealing in England with people who insisted on rights that they could not exercise without alienating the colonists and destroying the empire. Hutchinson had been dealing in America with people who insisted on rights that they could not exercise without alienating the British and destroying the empire. Both men blamed the people they had been contending with, represented in both cases, as they thought, by a few designing men. And in both cases their opponents' insistence on asserting rights forced them into doing the same, on opposite sides.

It was, of course, not quite that simple. Franklin's vision of a reconstructed empire had always been a union of equals. Hutchinson, while he wanted Americans to have a larger share in their own government, envisioned their continued subordination to the mother country. The British Parliament, he believed, with or without American representatitves must remain supreme. If it made mistakes, it alone could correct them. The most effective opponents of the Stamp Act had taken that position in 1765. It was implied at least in Franklin's own advice to Americans after the successful campaign for repeal in 1766, when he wrote, "tho' the Parliament may sometimes possibly thro' misinformation be mislead to do a wrong Thing towards America, yet as soon as they are rightly inform'd, they will immediately rectify it."

Three years later Franklin could not be so confident that Parliament would correct itself, when men like Hillsborough were in the ministry, controlling access to the information or misinformation Parliament received from royal officials in America. After the Massachusetts Assembly made Franklin their agent, Hillsborough characteristically stuck his head in the sand by refusing to recognize the appointment. The only colonial agent Hillsborough would deign to listen to would be one approved by the royal governor, which would mean, in effect, that the agent would carry to London only what the royal governor was already sending in his reports. In a stormy interview, when Franklin presented his credentials Hillsborough refused to read them and forbade the Board of Trade even to record them. Franklin

Benjamin Franklin, 1767

closed the exchange with apologies for taking his Lordship's time and the icy riposte: "It is I believe of no great Importance whether the Appointment is acknowledged or not, for I have not the least conception that an Agent can *at present* be of any Use, to any of the Colonies."

Franklin nevertheless continued to be of use by reporting to Massachusetts on the proceedings of Parliament, with advice about the best means of defeating its pretensions to authority. In a long letter to Cushing on June 10, 1771, he noted a disposition among the members to give up any further attempt to tax the colonies. He wondered hopefully again whether it might be possible "gradually to wear off the assum'd Authority of Parliament," without openly challenging it, but he declined to urge any such evasion of the issue "because I see, in this seemingly prudent Course, some Danger of a diminishing Attention to our Rights." It was important, he insisted, never to "adopt or acknowledge an Act of Parliament but by a formal Law of our own." He counted on the rapid growth of American strength and thought it critical to maintain "our military Spirit" through an active militia. Sooner or later England would need American help in another war. Then would be the time to wring from Parliament a formal relinquishment of its authority in the colonies, in return for American military support.

Franklin could scarcely have escaped the implication that American military strength might well be used against an England that abused its colonies. But he was still thinking of America's role inside the empire, not outside it. He had for some time been engaged with a number of English and Pennsylvania investors in a company formed to plant a new colony in the Ohio country. That project required the approval of the secretary of state for the colonies, and in this instance Hillsborough found himself arrayed against people who carried more weight than an unrecognized (if world-renowned) colonial agent. Thomas Walpole, the banker for whom the company was named, had spread shares of stock widely among influential members of Parliament. When Hillsborough denied them the needed grant of land, they forced his resignation. He was succeeded in August 1772 by the Earl of Dartmouth, who lost no time in recognizing Franklin as agent of the several colonies he represented.

Dartmouth was already known as a man of piety and peace. He had been a member of the Rockingham ministry that repealed the Stamp Act. He was in many ways the opposite of Hillsborough, always ready to listen to reason, always eager to please with words of sympathy and promise. Franklin was to learn that kind words were Dartmouth's specialty and that the expectations they raised were seldom fulfilled. But in the early months of Dartmouth's ministry it was easy to hope that men of goodwill on both sides of the ocean could find a way to let the assumed authority of Parliament fall into atrophy and to revive the old affection and allegiance of the colonies.

That possibility suddenly looked real to Franklin in December 1772, when he came into possession (how he never revealed) of a series of letters from America to Thomas Whately, a recently deceased undersecretary of the Treasury. Whately had been a principal author and defender of the Stamp Act and remained a major influence in British colonial policy. He was no longer in office at the time of his death, but his many American correspondents had continued to bombard him with accounts of Americans' subversion of British authority. It is not impossible that the letters that came into Franklin's hands had passed under

Hillsborough's eyes. They had been written from 1767 to 1769, most of them by people whose views had been colored by their suffering in the Stamp Act riots. They painted a picture of a people still on the verge of rebellion who deserved the treatment that Hillsborough had certainly been prepared to give them. Without British intervention, they warned, "the country and particularly N. England, will soon and forever be in perpetual anarchy and disobedience": "A bridle at present, may accompish more than a rod hereafter." Specifically, there must be an alteration in the Massachusetts government of the kind that Governor Bernard had recommended. The most alarming statements came in letters from Franklin's old friend Hutchinson and from Hutchinson's brother-in-law Andrew Oliver, alarming because the two men were now respectively governor and lieutenant governor of Massachusetts. "There must be," Hutchinson had written in January 1769, just as Hillsborough was taking office, "an abridgment of what are called English liberties." If no serious measures were taken to secure colonial dependence, if Parliament came up with "nothing more than some declaratory acts or resolves, *it is all over with us.*" In a later letter he insisted that Parliament should require the dissolution of the nonimportation agreements and subject "all who do not renounce them to penalties adequate to the offence."

Hutchinson was recommending what he thought was needed to save the country he loved from the disaster he was sure would follow its separation from the empire. "I wish the good of the colony," he wrote, "when I wish to see some further restraint of liberty rather than the connexion with the parent state should be broken; for I am sure such a breach must prove the ruin of the colony." To Franklin, reading those words, it was a "further restraint of liberty" that would spell ruin both to the colony and to the empire. Hutchinson had told him that the troubles in Massachusetts were all the work of "one or two designing men." Franklin now agreed, but he identified the designing men as Hutchinson and his friends, who had depicted the colonists' assertions of their rights as sedition. They had translated a widespread popular defense of liberty as the work of a few "incendiaries," and helped to perpetuate a clash over matters of principle that should have ended with the repeal of the Stamp Act.

It was still necessary, Franklin was sure, for Americans to remain on guard against restraints on their liberty. But with the new ministry already more sympathetic, Americans might return the sympathy if they learned that the measures against them had been prompted by a few designing men among them. If Franklin had been closer to Hutchinson, perhaps he would not have done what he did. But he evidently decided that Hutchinson and the others deserved the contempt that disclosure of their recommendations would bring, that the hostility of Americans to Parliament could thus be transferred to the people who had misled it. In December 1772 he sent the letters to Cushing. "For my own part," he told Cushing, "I cannot but acknowledge, that my Resentment against this Country, for its arbitrary Measures in governing us, conducted by the late Minister, has, since my Conviction by these Papers, that those Measures were projected, advised and called for by Men of Character among ourselves, and whose Advice must therefore be attended with all the Weight that was proper to mislead, and which could therefore scarce fail of Misleading; my own Resentment, I say, has by this means been considerably abated."

It was only two and a half years from December 2, 1772, when

Franklin shipped the Hutchinson-Oliver letters to Cushing, until he arrived back in Philadelphia on May 6, with the Revolutionary War already begun. During those two and a half years the confrontation between American rights and Parliamentary sovereignty proceeded in a chain of action and reaction, assertion and denial, challenge and defiance, interrupted only by the time it took for news to travel three thousand miles of ocean (anywhere from six weeks to three months in each direction). The angry exchanges, viewed from this century, seem to take place in slow motion. People on one side of the water could respond to events on the other side only after succeeding events might already have rendered the response inadequate. The time lag meant that any incipient disposition to accommodate the other side would give way to renewed anger when news arrived of a provoking response to something done several months before. But there was never much room for accommodation. Face-to-face communication, if it had been possible, might have resulted in some negotiation of differences; but as long as each side insisted on absolute rights that the other refused to recognize, more rapid communications could only have hastened the transition from words to blows.

Looking back on these years, John Adams reflected that "the Revolution was effected before the war commenced. The Revolution was in the minds and hearts of the people." Adams may have been thinking of a longer period of time than the two and a half years before Lexington and Concord. But the events of those thirty months were crucial in changing the minds and hearts of many. And they changed Franklin more personally, we might say more intimately, than others because he was a principal actor in so many of them.

6 Endgame

The particular series of exchanges that led to Lexington and Concord can be said to have begun at a Boston town meeting in November 1772. Franklin, though three thousand miles from Boston, was involved from the start. He was not simply the intermediary who conveyed petitions, remonstrances, rebukes, and news back and forth. He did all that, and like other messengers was often blamed for the message. But in his case there was some substance to support the impression among British statesmen that he was the éminence grise behind the defiant pronouncements he delivered. As we have seen, Franklin was a latecomer to the Americans' intransigent assertion of rights. Negotiation was more to his taste. But he had believed from the outset that the Americans were right and Parliament wrong. By 1772 he was convinced that an absolute insistence on American rights was the only way to sustain America's relationship with the country he loved almost as much as his own.

Delivering Messages

In November of that year, 1772, while Franklin was in the process of obtaining the letters which he hoped would help explain British mistakes, the Boston town meeting was denouncing those mistakes. It was a little unusual for a town meeting to enter into imperial politics. This one acted in default of a special session of the Massachusetts Assembly, which the town had unsuccessfully asked the governor to call. The problem was still the Townshend Acts. The continuing duty on tea had been dedicated to pay the governor's salary, thereby depriving the Assembly of a possible control over him. Franklin already had in his hands a petition from the Assembly to the king against this threat to its powers. Late in September it was learned in Boston that the judges of the Superior Court would also be freed from local control in the same way. When the governor refused to convene the Assembly to consider the new threat, the Boston town meeting undertook to lead the whole colony in resistance. In a declaration of their rights as men, as Christians, and as subjects, the members listed as violations of those rights virtually everything Parliament had done to the colonies. In effect they denied, as Franklin had been denying more and more openly, that Parliament had any authority to do anything in America. They published their denial in a pamphlet, which they sent to the other towns in Massachusetts—and of course to Franklin—inviting them to make similar declarations.

To the Governor of Massachusetts, Franklin's former friend Hutchinson, the Boston declaration bordered on treason, and he saw it as the work of his former friend Franklin: "although at its first appearance it was considered as their own work, yet they had little more to do than to make the necessary alterations in the arrangement of materials prepared for them by their great director in England, whose counsels they obeyed, and in whose wisdom and dexterity they had an implicit faith." Hutchinson was writing several years later and greatly exaggerated Franklin's influence, as he had at the time in reports to England. The Boston declaration's wholesale indictment did include a number of charges that Franklin had emphasized, such as the longstanding prohibitions on colonial manufactures, which infringed "that Right with which God and Nature have invested us, to make Use of our Skill and Industry in procuring the Necessaries and Conveniences of life." It also pointed out what Franklin repeatedly reminded his constituents, that "The Inhabitants of this Country, in all Probability, in a few Years, will be more numerous, than those of Great Britain and Ireland together." But the bulk of the declaration was not a mere rearrangement of Franklin's words. Samuel Adams, one of the probable authors, needed no tutoring from Franklin in his defiance of Parliament, and Adams had been guiding both Boston and Massachusetts in that direction for some years. Nevertheless, the declaration did reflect the views that Franklin had been sharing with Cushing. In England the solicitor general saw in it "the lessons taught in Dr. Franklin's school of politics." As soon as Franklin received a copy from Cushing (February 1773), he gave it his imprimatur by having Strahan print it, with a preface stressing for English readers the losses the country sustained from Americans' rejection of taxed East India tea.

For some reason Franklin delayed the English publication until June. Perhaps he waited because anti-American sentiment in Parliament seemed to be subsiding, and he hoped, as he told

Cushing in March, "that great Care will be taken to keep our People quiet." He too would be quiet in order not to stir up adversaries in Parliament who, for the moment at least, were distracted by other concerns. But by June "our people" in Massachusetts were far from quiet. The Hutchinson letters had arrived with their evidence of the governor's earlier disparagement of colonial rights, and Hutchinson himself had reacted to the Boston declaration in a speech to the Assembly that carried the quarrel to a new level.

Hutchinson had seen the Boston declaration as an assertion of independence not merely from Parliament but from the empire. It was the work of only one town, but its denunciation, indeed its renunciation, of Parliament was being repeated, at Boston's urging, by the colony's other towns. Hutchinson felt duty bound to set the whole population straight about its subjection to Parliament in an address to the regular session of the Assembly that opened on January 6, 1773. What the people must recognize, he told them, was that there could be no constitutional separation of king and Parliament, no allegiance to the king without subordination to Parliament. "I know of no line that can be drawn," he told the Assembly, "between the supreme authority of Parliament and the total independence of the colonies." There could not, he said, be "two independent Legislatures in one and the same state." For the Massachusetts Assembly to be coequal with Parliament under the same king would be to make Massachusetts a separate kingdom, "as distinct as the kingdoms of England and Scotland before the union." Hutchinson apparently regarded this as an absurdity. The Assembly, like Franklin, regarded it as fact. "Very true," they said in answer, "and if they interfere not with each other, what hinders, but that being united in one head and common Sovereign, they may live happily in that connection and mutually support and protect each other?" Hutchinson had depicted the perils the colony would face if it became totally independent by rejecting Parliament. The Assembly replied ominously that "there is more reason to dread the consequences of absolute uncontroled power, whether of a nation or a monarch, than those of a total independence."

Hutchinson answered the Assembly's answer in a lengthy history lecture, and the Assembly answered the answer in another one. With these speeches the fat was in the fire. Franklin's collection of Hutchinson's letters from the 1760s arrived in a colony already disgusted with its governor. Meanwhile, in England both of Hutchinson's speeches and the Assembly's rejoinder to the first one had been printed in the London newspapers. When Franklin met with Dartmouth on May 6, he found him dismayed at Hutchinson's incitement of the Assembly to public articulation of principles that would be a red flag to Parliament. Dartmouth, Franklin reported to Cushing, had intended "to let all Contention subside, and by Degrees suffer Matters to return to the old Channel . . . but what Difficulties, says he, that Gentleman has brought us all into by his Imprudence." It would be difficult, either for Dartmouth or for Parliament, to ignore the Assembly's denial of Parliament's authority. Could the Assembly not be persuaded to rescind it? "There is," said Franklin, "not the least Possibility they will ever do that," for in spite of what Hutchinson or other royal governors might claim to the contrary, "the country is all of one Mind upon the Subject." And if Parliament responded with some act to penalize them, Americans would invent some way of retaliating, "and so we shall go on injuring and provoking each other."

Injuries and provocations were what lay ahead, leapfrogging and overlapping each other, as each side reacted to an earlier affront while news of another was crossing the Atlantic. Cushing had anticipated that the Assembly's response to Hutchinson might not go down well in England. While Franklin talked with Dartmouth, a letter was on its way advising Franklin that "any high Measures" taken against Massachusetts would be resented by all the colonies. In March 1773 the Virginia Assembly had appointed a committee of correspondence to communicate with similar committees in other colonies about British actions infringing colonial rights. The Massachusetts Assembly's altercation with Hutchinson had "arrested the attention of the whole Continent." Letters approving the Assembly's position were pouring in from everywhere, and possibly, Cushing suggested, "if the Colonies are not soon relieved, a Congress will grow out of this Measure."

A congress did grow out of British measures but not immediately from this one. Dartmouth was able to keep the Massachusetts Assembly's answers to Hutchinson from formal consideration by Parliament for several months, during which he officially reprimanded Hutchinson for bringing on a dispute with the Assembly "upon Points that cannot be kept too much out of sight." At the same time, ignoring Franklin's dictum, Dartmouth wrote secretly to Cushing begging him to get the Assembly to rescind its answer to Hutchinson and assuring him of his private view that Parliament's right to tax "should be suspended and lie dormant." Cushing responded with a private letter agreeing that it was a good idea to avoid the "entangling question" of Parliament's right but suggesting that the way to keep it out of sight was for Parliament to do the rescinding and to redress the grievances that brought it up in the first place. The Massachusetts Assembly, he said, echoing Franklin, " never will be brought to rescind or revoke what they have advanced."

Even as Dartmouth's letters were crossing to America, he and Franklin delivered messages that brought the question of Parliament's right to center stage. Shortly after his meeting with Dartmouth on May 6, Franklin received from Cushing another petition to the king (pointedly not a petition to Parliament) against the payment of the governor's and judges' salaries. Cushing complained about the delay that Dartmouth had persuaded Franklin to accept in not presenting the first petition on the subject six months earlier. At that time, Franklin had reported Dartmouth's fears that the king would find the petition offensive and might lay it before Parliament. Cushing thought it strange that a petition, itself a sign of loyalty to the king, could offend him: "if the Colonies are reduced to this deplorable Situation, that every new Petititon they prefer is to be Considered as a fresh offence to his Majesty, what have they left to do?" Cushing wanted both petitions presented at once.

Dartmouth obliged on June 2 and received the king's immediate response. It was as bad as Dartmouth had feared. The king affirmed Parliament's absolute authority as inseparable from his own "and therefore His Majesty could not but be greatly displeased with the Petitions and Remonstrance." The king thought that "the unwarrantable Doctrines" in them must be the work "of a few who seek to create groundless Jealousy and Distrust" among his faithful subjects. Franklin dispatched this response to Cushing on the same day, and two days later, on June 4, sent him news of Parliament's latest challenge to the colonies, adopted almost casually and incidentally as part of a deal to help the East India Company out of financial troubles. The company needed to sell more tea. Americans were great tea drinkers, and to avoid the Townshend duty on it, they were smuggling large quantities from the Dutch. The company agitated for repeal of the Townshend duty, but Parliament devised a better deal for the company. It retained the Townshend duty but eliminated larger duties collected in England en route to America. East India tea, even with the Townshend duty paid, would thereby become cheaper than smuggled Dutch tea. It looked like, and may have been intended as, a subterfuge to bribe Americans to pay the Townshend tax and thus acknowledge Parliament's right to levy it. Franklin saw it that way. "They have no idea," he told Cushing, "that any People can act from any Principle but that of Interest; and they believe that 3d. in a Pound of Tea, of which one does not drink perhaps 10 lb. in a Year, is sufficient to overcome all the Patriotism of an American!"

Franklin seldom did anything without knowing what he was doing; but the time lag in communications with America meant that he and everyone else in the developing dispute had frequently to act in the dark. It was impossible to predict with any certainty what the consequences of any action would be, and it was easy to guess wrong. Franklin had guessed wrong in 1765 when he thought he was doing John Hughes a favor by getting him appointed to collect the Stamp Tax in Pennsylvania. It is hard to believe that he knew quite what he was doing in 1772 when he sent Hutchinson's letters to Cushing. He betrayed his uncertainty in the accompanying letter, asking Cushing not to copy or publish them (the unnamed person from whom he obtained them forbade it). But Cushing could show them around, not only to some other correspondents of Franklin but to "a few such other Gentlemen as you may think it fit to show them to." Having given such an indeterminate permission, Franklin could scarcely have expected that the letters would not become common knowledge. The whole point of sending them was to transform public opinion. They did not transform it, but arriving as they did after Hutchinson's exchange with the Assembly, they confirmed it.

On June 2, after virtually everyone who cared to do so had seen them, Cushing officially read the letters aloud to the Assembly. By June 17 they were in print and quickly reprinted and published in newspapers and pamphlets throughout the colonies. On June 23, by a vote of 80 to 11, the Assembly petitioned the king for the removal of both Hutchinson and Oliver from office. Franklin, whom Cushing had not disclosed as the person who revealed the letters, received the petition and presented it to Dartmouth on August 21. With it he sent a conciliatory letter from the Assembly to Dartmouth and a brief note of his own, stating, seemingly in all innocence, that the people of Massachusetts, "having lately discovered, as they think, the authors of their grievances to be some of their own people, their resentment against Britain is thence much abated."

But an abatement of colonial resentment did not mean a relaxation of American insistence on rights. Franklin seems to have believed that the publication of the letters could be used in England to discredit not only Hutchinson but the ministries responsible for the Townshend Acts and for other measures that were alienating the Americans. At the same time he hoped to use the growing strength of the colonies as a bargaining chip with Dartmouth in the likely event of Britain's involvement in another European war. He had already written to Cushing on July 7, suggesting the need for calling a continental congress, now, in peacetime, to ensure unity when the opportunity came to trade recognition of American rights for American help in war. It was a complex and risky strategy. The Hutchinson-Oliver letters were published in London in late August, as soon as Franklin received the recall petition. Franklin followed them with a succession of newspaper squibs and pamphlets to pave the way for the reversal of British policy that he hoped to effect. On August 31, he suggested in *The Public Advertiser* that the example of the Hutchinson letters showed the need to require publication of "all the confidential Letters received from America on public Affairs, and from public Men" so that "the incendiary Writers should be exposed and punished." Then on September 11 came his *Rules by Which a Great Empire May Be Reduced to a Small One*, designed to discredit Hillsborough and the things that incendiary writers had prompted him to do. Three days later he published, as by *"A Sincere Well-Wisher To Great Britain and her Colonies,"* a piece commending his own pamphlet and rejoicing that Hillsborough had been replaced by a true Englishman (Dartmouth): "Be it *his* Glory to *reverse* those baneful and pernicious Measures which have too long harassed the Colonies." On September 22 he published one of his most famous hoaxes, "An Edict by the King of Prussia," purporting to restrict and tax trade and manufacturing in England. The people of England had originally come from Germany, and the King of Prussia was simply exercising his rights over them as subjects. It was a clever parallel that reduced Parliament's claims over the colonies to an absurdity. The people who at first took it seriously and denounced it were left to realize that they were denouncing Parliament's pretensions.

In the remainder of the year, perhaps only coincidentally, Franklin engaged himself in designing lightning protection for the Royal Arsenal, a symbolic piece of advance military aid from a colonist. But his overall strategy ran afoul of provocations and reprisals on both sides that he had not anticipated. The publication of the Hutchinson letters in England had resulted in a flood of speculation and gossip about how they had been procured. Cushing had kept Franklin's name secret, and he was not even suspected. The original recipient, Thomas Whately, had died six months before Franklin got the letters. Gossip seized on a friend of Whately's, John Temple, as a likely suspect. The gossip provoked a duel on December 11, 1773, between Temple and William Whately, Thomas's surviving brother, in which Whately was wounded. When a second duel was threatened, Franklin could no longer keep silent. On December 25 he placed in the *London Chronicle* a notice stating that "I alone am the person who obtained and transmitted to Boston the letters in question." He did not say then or ever from whom he obtained them but it was not, he said, from William Whately, "because they were never in his possession; and, for the same reason, they could not be taken from him by Mr. T."

Significantly, Franklin did not say that Temple could not have taken them from someone else. In an attempt to get the name of the person who first stole, borrowed, or was given the letters, William Whately brought suit in chancery against Franklin to retrieve the originals. But long before the case could be brought to trial, Franklin, Massachusetts, and England were in deeper trouble than any lawsuit could settle. On January 20, 1774, news reached London in record time of an event in Massachusetts the preceding December: the Boston Tea Party.

Blaming the Messenger

Seventeen seventy-four was probably the most difficult year of Franklin's life. It was not just the vicious denunciation of him, officially delivered by the solicitor general to degrade his public image. He could endure insults. He was never so unsure of himself that he could let them affect him. He could endure the coolness of a few of his English friends—most of them remained loyal. He could endure the death of his wife in Philadelphia, whom he dearly loved despite distance and differences. They had both reached an age when life slopes toward the end anyhow. What made the year so painful was not what happened to him personally but the headlong plunge toward destruction of the imperial community he valued like life itself.

It was so unnecessary, so heedless, so foolish. He knew how to stop it. He was right there where it was happening, and he was not an inconsiderable figure among the people who made it happen. They knew who he was. They listened to what he said. But he could not make them understand.

By 1774 Franklin knew that the only way to preserve his beloved empire was for the British Parliament to give up any authority over the colonies. Americans' good opinion of the mother country was the cement of empire, the only tie that could hold the burgeoning people of a continent to those of an island three thousand miles across the ocean, really the only tie that had ever held them. And the exercise of Parliamentary authority had already stretched that tie to the breaking point. It did not require genius to see it. It should have been as obvious to British statesmen as it was to Franklin. He could scarcely believe, refused to believe, that the people who mattered in England would continue to leave their government in the hands of men who could not see something so obvious.

The irony of their blindness to the obvious was that it may have been Franklin himself who blinkered their eyes. In his unrelenting insistence that they recognize American rights, he came to personify the American cause. In the eyes of the ministry in power he became the source of the disaffection he sought to explain and remove. The Boston Tea Party, in which leading citizens, thinly disguised as Indians, destroyed East India tea, would not have been Franklin's idea of the way to assert American rights. But it was a signal of how far American opinion of British rule had deteriorated. As soon as he heard of it, Franklin wrote to the Massachusetts Assembly of his concern "that there should seem to any a Necessity for carrying Matters to such Extremity, as, in a Dispute about Publick Rights, to destroy private Property." To the English he explained it as the action of a mob, to the Massachusetts Assembly he recommended that they "repair the Damage and make Compensation to the Company."

Franklin was still trying to hold the empire together, and the Tea Party was one more obstacle to deal with. It was actually a symptom of the damage already done, but the British chose to treat the symptom, which they mistook for the disease, and the treatment was to punish the perpetrators, not least the man ready at hand whom they could conveniently blame for it all. No one accused Franklin directly of instigating the Tea Party, but the news of it arrived just as the Privy Council was meeting (in the leisurely way it handled American affairs) to consider the petition to the king that Franklin had presented to Dartmouth five months earlier for the recall of Hutchinson and Oliver because of their letters. Franklin never uttered a word of regret for sending the letters to Cushing. If he ever had second thoughts, if he ever considered what he had done as underhanded or a betrayal of trust, he seemingly did not admit it, even to himself. Whatever the cost to Hutchinson and others, it was an opportunity to restore American affection for England, to make Hutchinson and a few other unworthy Americans the scapegoats to carry off American distrust of the British. By recalling Hutchinson and Oliver in answer to the petition, the British would demonstate respect for American opinion. That was what the petition asked. It did not accuse Hutchinson or Oliver of malfeasance in office. It recited their misrepresentation of American loyalty and asked for their removal simply because they had "rendered themselves justly obnoxious to your loving subjects, and entirely lost their confidence."

On January 29, before anyone in the government had time to respond directly to the news of the Boston Tea Party, the Privy Council met to hear the Massachusetts petition. Far from seizing the opportunity to show their respect for American opinion, the councillors made the meeting the occasion for denouncing the man they saw lurking behind all England's troubles in America. Franklin, not Hutchinson, would be their scapegoat to send to the wilderness. Meeting in the "cockpit," a kind of indoor amphitheatre, open to the public, they sat and cheered to hear their solicitor general, Alexander Wedderburn, heap abuse on Franklin in language too coarse for newspapers to print. Franklin, wearing a full dress suit of Manchester velvet, stood before them erect and unblinking for nearly an hour of relentless invective. Wedderburn scarcely mentioned the petition except as an example of Franklin's machinations. Franklin was "the true incendiary" whose minions "have been inflaming the whole province against his Majesty's government." He was not so much the agent of the Massachusetts Assembly as the "first mover and prime conductor of it . . . the inventor and first planner" of its petition against Hutchinson. Hutchinson's only offense, in private letters to friends, had been to relate the doings of people under Franklin's thumb, people "so very bad that it cannot but offend his Majesty to hear of them," the same people who have now "with their usual moderation destroyed the cargo of three British ships."

Franklin answered not a word and kept his face totally blank. He was too proud to dignify the solicitor general's billingsgate with any kind of defense before a jeering audience. The councillors rejected the petition itself as "groundless, Vexatious and Scandalous and calculated only for the Seditious Purpose of keeping up a Spirit of Clamour and Discontent." The wicked man who had dared present it, they knew, was also deputy postmaster general for America. Within two days they had him dismissed from that position.

Franklin recognized that his usefulness as agent of the Massachusetts Assembly had been destroyed, and he resigned at once, leaving the agency to Arthur Lee, an irascible Virginian whom Massachusetts had earlier deputized to help him. But when Lee departed for a tour of the Continent, Franklin stayed on to give "what Assistance I could as a private Man." Whatever offices he held or did not hold, he could never really be a merely private man. He was still the embodiment in London of the bad Americans whom the British would have to deal with across the ocean. Wedderburn might humble him in the cockpit, but England would have to dole out stronger medicine to the wicked people he had misled into seditious mischief (especially after those people demonstrated their impenitent devotion to him by burning Wedderburn in effigy).

The remarkable thing is that Franklin did not at once abandon all his hopes for the empire. His ordeal at the cockpit confirmed what almost all his transactions with the government had been demonstrating, that it lacked, as far as the colonies were concerned, any sense of the need for consent of the governed. After reporting the incident to Cushing, he added:

> When I see that all petitions and complaints of grievances are so odious to government, that even the mere pipe which conveys them becomes obnoxious, I am at a loss to know how peace and union is to be maintained or restored between the different parts of the empire. Grievances cannot be redressed unless they are known; and they cannot be known but through complaints and petitions: If these are deemed affronts, and the messengers punished as offenders, who will henceforth send petitions? and who will deliver them? It has been thought a dangerous thing in any state to stop up the vent of griefs. Wise governments have therefore generally received petitions with some indulgence, even when but slightly founded. Those who think themselves injured by their rulers, are sometimes, by a mild and prudent answer, convinced of their errour. But where complaining is a crime, hope becomes despair.

And yet he did not despair. Three weeks after Wedderburn's tirade he wrote to Joseph Galloway of the anger in England over the general colonial resistance to the East India Company's tea. He almost found reason for hope in the fact that some part of the blame had fallen on himself, "perhaps from a Suspicion that I instigated the Opposition to its importation." He told Galloway for the first time about his role in sending the Hutchinson letters to Boston and his expectation that "If the Ministry here had been disposed to a Reconciliation, as they sometimes pretend to be, this was giving a fair Opening, which they might have thanked me for; but they chuse rather to abuse me." In answer to a suggestion by Galloway in a preceding letter, Franklin wrote a requiem to his earlier hopes for a general reconstruction of the empire on more equitable principles: "I wish most sincerely with you that a Constitution was formed and settled for America, that we might know what we are and what we have, what our Rights and what our Duties, in the Judgment of this Country as well as in our own. Till such a Constitution is settled, different Sentiments, will ever occasion Misunderstandings. But if 'tis to be settled, it must settle itself, no body here caring for the Trouble of thinking on't."

A Heedless Ministry

What people in the government were thinking on, after having dealt with Franklin in the cockpit, was the best way to punish Boston for the Tea Party and Massachusetts for the Assembly's daring to oppose its royal governor. What they came up with first was an act of Parliament on March 31, 1774, closing the port of Boston to all commerce. At the same time they decided to send General Thomas Gage to relieve Hutchinson temporarily as governor, accompanied by four British regiments, whose muskets would serve to gain the acquiescence, if not the consent, of the governed to whatever else might be needed. The whatever else was three more Parliamentary acts, known ever since, along with the Boston Port Act, as the Coercive or Intolerable Acts. These reorganized the Massachusetts government, reduced the powers of the Assembly, shut down town meetings, limited trial by jury, and provided that troops, which would obviously be needed, could be quartered anywhere in Boston at the pleasure of their commander.

Franklin joined with other Americans in London to protest against the passage of these measures. He continued to write pieces for the newspapers, including his proposal that the British castrate American males to stop population growth. He knew that the Coercive Acts spelled war. Even before they were passed, the English newspapers were full of the need for the British army to teach the colonists a lesson. In response Franklin warned against the assumption "that this War with the Colonies (for a War it will be) is a *national* Cause when in fact it is merely a *ministerial* one." It remained his hope, which he clung to throughout the year, that a change in the ministry would reverse the suicidal plunge. In informing Cushing of the imminent passage of the Boston Port Act and of a plan to seize the ringleaders of the Tea Party (which might include himself), he still wanted the Assembly to make restitution for the tea, "for such a Step will remove much of the Prejudice now entertain'd against us, and put us on a fair Footing in contending for our old Privileges as Occasion may require." But while he thus counseled moderation and worked behind the scenes to develop a Parliamentary opposition, he counted on American strength as the only way to save both the empire and the rights of Americans within it.

The time lag in transatlantic communications now left him in the dark for months as events developed rapidly toward revolution. When he heard in July of the impending Continental Congress, he saw it, as did many Americans, as a possible step toward reconciliation. Such a congress had been talked of ever since the one at Albany in 1754, and in 1765 it had materialized in the

Stamp Act Congress, where the colonies had demonstrated that they could join to state their common rights despite the much-publicized disagreements among them about their boundaries, their different religious views, and their economic rivalries. In 1768 the merchants in the various colonies had joined for a time in nonimportation agreements against the Townshend Acts without benefit of any general intercolonial meetings. The collapse of the agreement suggested the need for more coordination. But when General Gage arrived in Boston in May with the Port Act in hand, the town meeting swung into action with an appeal to other colonies to join Massachusetts in shutting down all consumption of British goods without waiting for any collective deliberation.

The Bostonians were right in thinking that the other colonists would share their outrage. The Coercive Acts were designed to make an example of Massachusetts, but the lesson they taught Americans was not to avoid the bad example but to follow it. What was happening to Massachusetts could happen to them. Better to make common cause with the offender now than to wait. Nevertheless, the objective for most Americans, as for Franklin, was still to secure recognition of their rights within the empire. The response to Boston's appeal was not an immediate willingness to shun all intercourse with Britain but a call, from several colonies, for a congress to consider what to do. A congress was the preference of those who did not want to rush into an uncoordinated confrontation with an acknowledged superior. But even the most cautious welcomed the opportunity it might offer for defining and establishing American rights within the empire; perhaps a permanent continental congress could become part of the imperial structure. For those who felt that membership in the empire was no longer a viable option, it could still be the opportunity to convince other leading colonists to join in a united resistance.

Whether the congress would be a vehicle of conciliation or an instrument of revolution was not at all clear when the Massachusetts Assembly officially voted on June 17 to send delegates and set the place as Philadelphia and the time as the first of September. General and Governor Gage immediately dissolved the Assembly, and it never sat again under British rule. Other royal governors acted in time to prevent their assembles from choosing delegates, but officially or unofficially every colony but Georgia had a delegation ready to go before September.

Franklin had suggested a congress to the Massachusetts Assembly the year before as a means of putting on record a united colonial declaration of rights. At that time he thought of demanding Parliamentary recognition of the rights thus defined as the price of colonial assistance in a future British war. Now, with the congress actually in the offing, he saw it as a means not only of working out a firm statement of rights but also of gaining recognition for them through a unanimous nonimportation, nonexportation, and nonconsumption agreement, to last until Parliament gave up all pretense to authority in America. He was confident that the loss of American business would bring down the existing ministry and result in one that would accept an American bill of rights as defined by the congress.

There is no surviving letter in which any of the delegates asked his advice before the congress met. But in England, John Pownall, brother of a former Massachusetts governor and himself an undersecretary of state for the colonies, reported Franklin's opinion on what the congress would do before it was even scheduled to meet. Pownall thought that "they will probably do what he bids them to do, and he says that they will draw up a State of their Claims in the form of a petition or rather a *Bill of Rights* and annex to it a Resolution of Non Importation to continue until those Claims be yielded to." Pownall may have been expressing only the prevailing English view that Americans did everything at Franklin's bidding, but what Pownall attributed to Franklin was pretty close to what the congress did do and to what Franklin hoped that it would.

What neither Franklin nor Pownall could know was how rapidly events and opinion in America were moving. A friend in Philadelphia wrote Franklin in May, predicting that "there is a set of people in New England, that before they Would lose their priviledges Would oppose force by force and Numbers" and that Britain did not have enough men or ships to "bring the Americans under." Franklin answered calmly in June that the letter gave him great satisfaction and assured his friend that American firmness would oblige the present ministry to "quit their Places to Men of more Moderation and Wisdom." Franklin continued to urge his American friends to stand firm, but he only gradually learned of the effective dissolution of royal government in Massachusetts and its replacement by popular committees and conventions that were ready indeed to oppose force by force. In the first week of September, as the Continental Congress convened in Philadelphia, a rumor spread that Gage had sent a detachment of soldiers to seize the arsenal that colonists were amassing at Cambridge. In a matter of hours armed men were marching to the site from all over the colonies. Three thousand had arrived, and they had started coming from as far as Virginia, before it was discovered to be a false alarm. Franklin heard of the incident from Cooper along with the news that a revolutionary legislature in Massachusetts was already planned, to replace the old Assembly.

Meanwhile, Massachusetts towns were defying the prohibition on town meetings and sending men to county conventions. One met in Suffolk County early in September and adopted a set of resolves calling for disobedience to the Coercive Acts, dissolution of the law courts, seizure of public monies, and preparation for war. Paul Revere carried the resolves posthaste to Philadelphia, and on September 18 the Congress voted to approve them all. In the weeks that followed, the Congress prepared a bill of rights that condemned virtually everything Parliament had ever done concerning America. And in an act misnamed an "Association" the Congress provided for the formation of local committees throughout the colonies to prevent anyone from buying, selling, or consuming any products of Great Britain.

Joseph Galloway, a delegate for Pennsylvania, offered a plan of union, calling for a colonial parliament like that in Franklin's Albany Plan, which would have joint authority with Parliament over the colonies: every act affecting America would require the assent of both bodies. This was what many members had been hoping for as a mode of reconciliation. But Patrick Henry of Virginia showed how far American opinion of British authority had come by stating that the plan would only free the Americans from a corrupt House of Commons to subject them to an intercolonial legislature that would be corrupted in the same way by "that nation which avows in the Face of the World, that Bribery is a part of her System of Government." The Congress voted down the plan and expunged all record of its discussion from the minutes. When Franklin later heard of it he agreed with Henry. Even while working in London for a change of ministry and assuring his American friends that their steadiness would achieve it, he was expecting, not very realistically, a ministry that would lead Parliament to renounce its powers in America. At the very time that Galloway was presenting his plan to the Congress, Franklin was writing to him from London that the British Parliament was "a very expensive Machine, that requires a vast deal of oiling and greasing at the People's Charge for they finally pay all the enormous Salaries of Places, the Pensions and the Bribes, now by Custom become necessary to induce the Members to vote according to their Consciences." A few months later he confessed to Galloway "that when I consider the extream Corruption prevalent among all Orders of Men in this old rotten State, and the glorious publick Virtue so predominant in our rising Country, I cannot but apprehend more Mischief than Benefit from a closer Union. . . . To unite us intimately, will only be to corrupt and poison us also."

By the time he wrote these words, on February 25, 1775, Franklin knew that war was almost certain, but to prevent it he was willing to "try any thing, and bear any thing that can be borne with Safety to our just Liberties." Despite all evidence to the contrary, he believed, as he prepared to depart for Philadelphia in March, that American strength, displayed in united rejection of British manufactures, would so discredit the existing ministry that it would "be overthrown, and routed, and the Friends of America come into Administration."

To understand how he could be so mistaken, we have to remember that hardly anyone else at the time, even those on both sides preparing for war, expected war to result in American independence. Some kind of settlement short of that seemed more likely. And Franklin in the preceding six months had been working among the British friends of America to make clear what kind of settlement would be required to keep Americans in the empire. Though Franklin held no authority, formal or informal, official or unofficial, to speak for America or to negotiate in its name, people in England were convinced that he did. Wedderburn had heaped scorn on him for acting like an ambassador from Massachusetts. Now well-wishers insisted on seeing him, in spite of his demurrals, as ambassador for America, who might be able to work out a settlement before war began. Without authorization of any kind, Franklin was nevertheless willing to "try any thing," that is, to specify the conditions that he thought his countrymen might agree to.

From early December through the middle of March, therefore, a series of intermediaries carried messages back and forth between him and unnamed members of the ministry, who took pains never to admit who they were or what they were doing. It began when two of Franklin's old friends, John Fothergill and David Barclay, persuaded him to set down in writing what he thought Britain must do to halt the rush toward war. While Barclay and Fothergill discussed this document with people in the ministry or close to it, amending, proposing, and pleading, another unauthorized diplomat, Admiral Lord Richard Howe, undertook the same task. Howe concealed his role in comic-opera fashion under the guise of arranging and appearing at a chess match between Franklin and Lady Caroline Howe, his sister. Franklin was impatient with the deviousness that everyone seemed to think necessary in these dealings with a ministry that made mistreatment of Americans a badge of honor. He stated flatly what he took to be the sine qua non of American demands. Along with a few specifics, like repeal of the Tea Act and the Coercive Acts, he insisted on a renunciation by Parliament of any legislative authority over the internal affairs of any American colony. He made one large concession in allowing that the acts restricting American manufactures should be "reconsidered" rather than "repealed." He agreed, pledging his own credit, to reimburse the East India Company's loss in the Tea Party, provided the town of Boston was compensated for the much larger loss resulting from the closing of the port. He was willing to continue the charade as long as the others were, and it went on until the middle of March. But the nameless ministers to whom his demands were presented balked at all the crucial points, and he knew better than to mislead them into thinking that Americans would or should settle for anything less.

Meanwhile, the results of the Continental Congress had reached London in mid-September, with assertions of American rights more sweeping even than Franklin's and with the establishment of the Association enforcing nonimportation, nonexportation, and nonconsumption. A petition to the king was included, which Franklin dutifully presented to Dartmouth with the usual results. As he reported to Charles Thomson, who was now leading Pennsylvanians toward rebellion, "from the constant Refusal, Neglect or Discouragement, of American Petitions, these many Years past, our Country will at last be convinc'd that Petitions are odious here and that petitioning is far from being a probable Means of obtaining Redress. A firm, steady, and faithfull, Adherence to the Non-Consumption Agreement is the only Thing to be depended on."

Franklin retained a dim hope that the Continental Congress

might become part of a reorganized empire, presided over by a royally appointed commissioner (Lord Howe was a possibility). The government's disdain of the Congress as an unauthorized assembly made that contingency remote until American firmness, as Franklin desired, should produce the longed-for change in the ministry. His hope for such a change may have been bolstered by the support of Britain's most celebrated empire builder. When Franklin first arrived in England in 1757 he had tried in vain to obtain an audience with William Pitt, who was engaged at the time in wresting North America from the French. Now the empire Pitt had won was threatened with dissolution, and he invited Franklin to visit him to discuss ways of saving it. The first visit came in August, and Franklin was overjoyed not only at getting the great man's attention but at finding him in agreement about the ministry's disastrous policies. As soon as Franklin received the proceedings of the Congress in mid-December, he sent copies to Pitt, now Lord Chatham, and met with him again on the twenty-sixth.

Chatham's view of the Congress, coming from one who had once been the most powerful man in England, was more than encouraging: "They had acted, he said with so much Temper, Moderation and Wisdom, that he thought it the most honourable Assembly of Statesmen since those of the ancient Greeks and Romans in the most virtuous times." He had only one or two reservations about their stand on minor matters that Franklin would have considered negotiable. Chatham himself proposed sending a commission to work out an agreement. Three days later, on December 29, Franklin spent the afternoon and evening with another great figure from the golden age of imperial relations, Lord Camden, who had been Pitt's attorney general in 1757 and Lord Chancellor from 1766 to 1770. Along with Pitt he had opposed all the Parliamentary measures that alienated America, and Franklin now "had the great Pleasure of hearing his full Approbation of the Proceedings of the Congress." With two such giants waiting to succeed the men who were driving the Americans to rebellion, Franklin may be excused for thinking that reconciliation required only a sustained demonstration of American will.

Chatham, who had seldom appeared in Parliament in recent years, was evidently prompted by Franklin's visit in December to take a hand in defusing the existing tension. In their conversation Franklin had stressed the danger posed by the presence of British troops in the colonies: some "unpremeditated unforeseen Quarrel" between soldiers and civilians could trigger an explosion. On January 19 Chatham sent him a message asking him to be present at the House of Lords the next day, when Chatham proposed to introduce a motion. While Fothergill, Barclay, and Howe continued their surreptitious goings and comings to the ministers they dared not name, Chatham felt no need to conceal his admiration for Franklin or his contempt for the men who were losing his empire. He met Franklin in the lobby of the House, where his unaccustomed presence caused a considerable stir, especially after he pointedly took Franklin by the arm and led him past the doorkeepers posted at the entrance to keep out the public. Chatham's motion was to withdraw General Gage's troops from Boston, in order to "soften Animosities" and prevent any "sudden and fatal Catastrophe." Franklin was flattered by the attention to his suggestion. Camden and other lords familiar with the American scene supported the motion, "but all avail'd no more than the whistling of the Winds" against the ministerial control of the House.

It had to be an extraordinary satisfaction to Franklin to have the open support of the great imperial statesman, not only for himself but for his country. The automatic rejection of Chatham's gesture confirmed his view that only a new ministry, with men like Chatham at the helm, could reverse the anti-American policy of the government. And he soon had another, culminating, experience of the ministry's madness and of the futility of his own efforts to set them straight.

Chatham's motion to remove the troops from Boston was only the first step in a plan he was devising for a general settlement. Again he wanted the advice of the man who spoke for Americans. And again he disdained to keep it a secret. On a Sunday afternoon, January 29, a year to the day from Wedderburn's seeming destruction of the incendiary, Chatham arrived in his well-known coach at Franklin's door in Craven Street. For two hours they talked, as people coming from church saw the coach and set all London gossiping about the alliance. Chatham had already drafted a plan, which he left with Franklin, and the two met again to discuss it the following Tuesday at Chatham's estate. They conferred for four hours, Chatham doing most of the talking, so that Franklin actually had little opportunity to make the changes that he thought would improve the plan. But when Chatham introduced it as a bill in the House of Lords the next day, with Franklin again conspicuously present, its provisions were sufficiently generous to have made it a likely basis for a settlement. It would have limited Parliament's authority in America mainly to the regulation of trade, forbade taxation of any colony without consent of its legislature, recognized the Continental Congress, and suspended or repealed the statutes from 1764 to 1774 that the Congress had objected to.

It was not everything that Franklin would have wished, but it was close enough to what he had long been advocating for the Lords to attribute it to him. When Dartmouth proposed, and Chatham consented, that it lie on the table for consideration, Lord Sandwich rose to demand its immediate rejection "with the Contempt it deserv'd." So disgraceful a proposal, he said, could surely not have originated with a British peer of the realm. Turning toward Franklin, who was leaning on the railing that separated the members from the select audience, Sandwich said that "he fancied he had in his Eye the Person who drew it up, one of the bitterest and most Mischievous enemies this Country had ever known." Dartmouth with his usual flabbiness immediately joined the chorus and declared himself persuaded to reject it. Chatham with his usual grace declared that the bill was entirely his own: "But he made no Scruple to declare, that if he were the first Minister of this Country, and had the Care of Settling this momentous Business, he should not be asham'd of publickly calling to his Assistance a Person so perfectly acquainted with the whole of American Affairs, as the Gentleman alluded to and injuriously reflected on, one, he was pleas'd to say, whom all Europe held in high Estimation for his Knowledge and Wisdom, and rank'd with our Boyles and Newtons; who was an Honour not to the English Nation only but to Human Nature."

Franklin found the praise more embarrassing than the denunciation but managed to maintain through both a woodenly immovable countenance. What he witnessed at the House of Lords that day epitomized his experience of England over the preceding ten years. He had encountered men of goodwill, men of vision like Chatham, men of learning like Richard Jackson, men of science like Sir John Pringle and Joseph Priestley, and they had all recognized him as their equal, sought his company, cherished his opinion. At the same time he had encountered the men of small mind and mean spirit who guided goverment in ignorance and indifference toward the total alienation of his countrymen. They stood before him now, a Sandwich, a Hillsborough, the silly Dartmouth, and proceeded to vote down without hesitation the only proposal put before them that might have undone their unthinking mischief. Franklin's reaction can be read as an epitaph for an empire that did not deserve the greatness its American colonies could bring to it:

> To hear so many of these *Hereditary* Legislators declaiming so vehemently against, not the Adopting merely, but even the *Consideration* of a Proposal so important in its Nature, offered by a Person of so weighty a Character, one of the first Statesman of the Age, who had taken up this Country when in the lowest Despondency, and conducted it to Victory and Glory thro' a War with two of the mightiest Kingdoms in Europe; to hear them censuring his Plan not only for their own Misunderstandings of what was in it, but for their Imaginations of what was not in it, which they would not give themselves an Opportunity of rectifying by a second Reading; to perceive the total ignorance of the Subject in some, the Prejudice and Passion of others, and the wilful Perversion of Plain Truth in several of the Ministers; and upon the whole to see it so ignominiously rejected by so great a Majority, and so hastily too, in Breach of all Decency and prudent Regard to the Character and Dignity of their Body as a third Part of the National Legislature, gave me an exceeding mean Opinion of their Abilities, and made their Claim of Sovereignty over three Millions of virtuous sensible People in America, seem the greatest of Absurdities since they appear'd to

have scarce Discretion enough to govern a Herd of Swine. Hereditary Legislators! thought I. There would be more Propriety, because less Hazard of Mischief, in having (as in some University of Germany,) Hereditary Professors of Mathematicks! But this was a hasty Reflection: For the *elected* House of Commons is no better, nor ever will be while the Electors receive Money for their Votes, and pay Money where with Ministers may bribe their Representatives when chosen.

Franklin remained in London for another seven weeks of the fruitless fussing of Fothergill, Barclay, and Howe. He still hoped that a change of ministry would enable him to remain an English American. But if that should not occur, he was prepared to lead his countrymen independently to the strength that awaited them.

7 Becoming American

Franklin was sixty-nine when his ship docked at Philadelphia on May 5, 1775, old enough to retire comfortably to a life of leisure and contemplation and the pursuits of his not-so-idle curiosity. But during the next year and a half, as his countrymen edged into independence, they needed his help and did not hesitate to ask it. The day after he landed, the Pennsylvania Assembly hastened to make him a delegate to the Second Continental Congress, which assembled four days later to weigh the consequences of what had happened at Lexington and Concord on April 19. With Pennsylvania moving toward revolution, a Committee of Safety took charge and made Franklin its president. As he wrote to his friend Priestley in London, "My time was never more fully employed. In the morning at 6, I am at the committee of safety, appointed by the assembly to put the province in a state of defence; which committee holds till near 9, when I am at the congress, and that sits till after 4 in the afternoon."

Breaking Ties

In the intervals of public business Franklin maintained a bitter-sweet correspondence with his English friends. They kept him abreast of what the government was doing there; he kept them abreast of what its troops and ships were doing in America. What they were doing was carry out a misguided colonial policy with fire and sword. Before he left England, Franklin had concluded that reasoned argument was lost on the existing ministry. Now his impatience with the government's pretensions to superiority turned into anger against its indiscriminate use of the military to subjugate the people whose rights he had spent the preceding ten years defending. To Franklin the engagements at Lexington and Concord, along with the burning of Falmouth, Maine, amounted to sheer murder. He vented his feelings in letters that strangely combined contempt for the whole English nation with undiminished affection for the men and women (Mary Stevenson and Polly Stevenson Hewson) who had been his close companions for so many years. To Anthony Todd, his amiable supervisor at the English post office, he recited British atrocities and asked, "Do you think it prudent by your Barbarities to fix us in a rooted Hatred of your Nation, and make all our innumerable Posterity detest you?" Then he closed by hoping that "your dear little Girl is well, and that you continue happy."

In these letters Franklin can use the words *you* and *your* in the singular to express endearments, but he does not hesitate to use the same words in the plural to designate the entire nation of which his friends were unmistakeably a part. Remaining as they did in England, they had to be "other." He reserves the words *we* and *our*, which he once applied to the whole empire, exclusively now for America and Americans. He could send and receive greetings from people like Lord Shelburne, Chatham's right-hand man, and members of the Club of Honest Whigs, who had sympathized with America and who, Priestley assured him, "think themselves much honoured by your having been one of them." But he was no longer one of them: no longer a British American but decisively an American.

He could not refrain from reminding his friends of what Britain was losing. He still saw America, with its growing strength and population, as the future seat of the greatest political structure human beings would ever erect. While exchanging news with Priestley and others he offered them a not-quite-playful application of the statistics he had first suggested in 1751. On his way to a conference with General Washington, in October 1775 (helping to reorganize the Continental Army), Franklin dashed off a note to Priestley, assuring him that he was still "well and hearty" and suggesting that Priestley pose a question to their common friend Richard Price, who was fond of statistical calculations: "Britain, at the expence of three millions, has killed 150 Yankies this campaign, which is £20,000 a head; and at Bunker's Hill she gained a mile of ground. . . . During the same time 60,000 children have been born in America. From these *data* his mathematical head will easily calculate the time and expence necessary to kill us all, and conquer our whole territory."

On the same day, as this thought percolated in his mind, he wrote more seriously to another friend that "A separation will of course be inevitable. 'Tis a million of pities so fair a plan as we have hitherto been engaged in for increasing strength and empire with *public felicity*, should be destroyed by the mangling hands of a few blundering ministers. It will not be destroyed.

God will protect and prosper it: You will only exclude yourselves from any share in it."

The otherness of the English was something that Franklin's transfer from London to Philadelphia brought home to him more abruptly than it came to others on either side of the ocean. To them the war that began at Lexington and Concord was either a rebellion or a civil war. To Franklin it was already an international war, a war between an old (and corrupt) nation and an emerging (and virtuous) one. His English friends bombarded him with letters begging him to broker a reconciliation on the terms he had once thought feasible, a return to the way things were in 1763 with perhaps some guarantees to keep them that way. Proposals of that kind died quickly in Parliament anyhow; but Franklin knew, before most of his countrymen, that it was too late for a reconciliation that acknowledged any kind of subordination of Americans to England. All the proposals he received from England envisaged the colonies remaining as colonies. And even in America, despite the organization of a Continental Army to fight a sustained war, Franklin had to wait for his countrymen to catch up to his recognition of their separateness from the country they had habitually called "home."

Many never did catch up, including his son Billy, royal governor of New Jersey, with whom he had continued to correspond from London in the warmest terms, as he had with his old political ally, Galloway. A few weeks after Franklin arrived, he met with the two of them at Galloway's house for a discussion that lasted far into the night. When it was over, so was their friendship. Billy clung to his office longer than other royal governors, but in 1776 he was interned under guard in Connecticut. When Elizabeth, his wife, begged Franklin to intercede for him, per-

haps in exchange for American prisoners, Franklin was un-
moved. William Franklin and Joseph Galloway ended their lives
in England, estranged from independent America and from
Franklin.

A Cautious Congress

In their place Franklin found a few men in Congress who had arrived at his position without benefit of his ten years in London.
The New Englanders had experienced directly the consequences
of the policies that had finally sent him back to Philadelphia in
disgust. In Congress, joined by a few southerners, they were taking the lead, which was entirely to his liking. As in all public
meetings, Franklin was careful not to talk too much, not to rush
things, to let others take charge until they were ready to go his
way and ask his advice. He was now a figure of national and international renown, as he had earlier become a figure of local
renown in Pennsylvania, with the result that his advice would
sooner or later be asked. It would count for more if it came without any trace of self-promotion.

We get a glimpse of his quiet effectiveness in the impression
he made on two delegates who wrote home about him. Silas
Deane, a prominent Connecticut lawyer, reported in a letter to
his wife, Elizabeth, on July 1, "Doctor Franklin is with us but he
is not a Speaker tho' we have I think his hearty Approbation of
and assent to every Measure." John Adams wrote in much
more detail to his wife, the formidable Abigail, on July 23: "Dr.
Franklin has been very constant in his Attendance on Congress
from the Beginning. His Conduct has been composed and grave
and in the Opinion of many Gentlemen very reserved. He has

not assumed any Thing, nor affected to take the lead; but has seemed to choose that the Congress should pursue their own Principles and sentiments and adopt their own Plans: Yet he has not been backward. . . . He does not hesitate at our boldest Measures, but rather seems to think us, too irresolute, and backward." Adams went on, in characteristic Adams fashion (we shall encounter his character again), to let Abigail know, if a little obliquely, that a Congress with an Adams in it needed no other leadership. "The People of England," he acknowledged, "have thought that the Opposition in America, was wholly owing to Dr. Franklin: and I suppose their scribblers will attribute the Temper, and Proceedings of this Congress to him: but there cannot be a greater Mistake. He has had but little share farther than to cooperate and assist. He is however a great and good Man."

The great and good man was actually exerting more influence in Congress than Adams wanted to recognize. His care not to get too far ahead required Franklin to straddle the gap between the cautious majority and the firebrands who shared his own radical views. He was willing to join the majority in a last petition to the king, though he had long since concluded that petitions were a waste of time. Informing an English friend of this "Olive Branch Petition," adopted two months after he came home, he surmised that it would be treated with the same contempt as earlier ones, "for tho' this may afford Britain one chance more of recovering our Affections and retaining the Connection, I think she has neither Temper nor Wisdom enough to seize the Golden Opportunity." He was right, of course. Congress waited for an answer that never came. Members may have learned by October or November from the London newspapers that it was "thought beneath the dignity of government" to answer a petition from such an irregular body as the Congress. The only answers were a proclamation from the king, issued August 23, declaring the colonists to be rebels and out of his royal protection and, in December, an act of Parliament—the Prohibitory Act—extending the blockade of Boston to all American ports and declaring American ships and their cargoes forfeit.

While Congress waited hopefully for the British to relent and repent, Franklin did his best to prepare the members for independence, wheedling them into incremental steps toward that end. In July they established a post office with Franklin as postmaster general, a minor act of defiance. In the same month Franklin sent up a trial balloon in a set of articles of confederation, amounting to a constitution for a permanent United Colonies. Congress allowed him to read the articles aloud and to place them on the table, but only on condition that no record of their presentation be made in official journals. The majority of the Congress were still yearning for something that was not going to happen; and in October and November, to hurry them up, Franklin showed them some of his letters from England, which made clear, as one member noted, "that the Ministry is determined at all events to conquer America." The members asked him whether he thought the letters were "a sufficient Foundation for America to proceed upon." He told them of his belief that they were, but in deference to their timidity, "He observed that it was not certain; for that upon the Arrival of the Petition the Ministry might think best to relax a little but it was by no means to be trusted to. We ought to be prepared for the worst."

Preparing for the worst meant preparing to defeat not only Britain's armies but a British navy that commanded the world's oceans. Franklin had no illusions about the costs of defying so much power. At one point in his fruitless, last-minute negotiations in London, David Barclay had "hinted how necessary an Agreement was for America, since it was so easy for Britain to burn all our Sea Port Towns." At this, Franklin "grew warm, said that the chief Part of my little Property consisted of Houses in those Towns, that they might make Bonfires of them whenever they pleased." In the long run, Franklin believed, Britain could burn every town and still never subdue a country of farmers, spread out into an interior that held all the natural resources for self-sufficiency. Until those resources could be discovered and developed, however, Americans would have to fight with what they had and what they could borrow. Despite previous wars with the French and Indians, guns had always been scarce in the colonies, and there were too few gunsmiths to supply an army. But pikes and bows and arrows could be made in quantity at once and could still be effective in the hands of determined men against better-armed troops. He recommended prompt preparation and use of both. As president of the Pennsylvania Committee of Safety he also arranged for the quick construction of twenty galleys to defend Philadelphia against Britain's almighty men-of-war, which could not maneuver easily in the confines of the Delaware River.

But there was no point in relying for long on such makeshifts, no point in a long-drawn-out guerrilla war to tire the British into giving up. He waited with growing impatience for Congress to bite the bullet and go all out for an independent America. Until it did the country would never exert its real strength. As he put it privately to Silas Deane, who shared his eagerness for action, "I lament with you the Want of a naval Force. I hope the next Winter will be employ'd in forming one. When we are no longer fascinated with the Idea of a speedy Reconciliation, we shall exert ourselves to some purpose. 'Till then Things will be done by Halves."

Without a truly formidable navy of its own, which at best would take much longer than a single winter to build, America would need the assistance of a country that had one. France, still smarting from defeat in the Seven Years' War, was the most likely candidate. And until America could establish its own munitions factories and foundries on a large enough scale for a war that went beyond bows and arrows, France was also the most likely source of arms and ammunition. In September, Congress heeded George Washington's appeal for arms and put Franklin on a secret committee to procure them abroad. By the end of November, Congress was ready to look for direct foreign support and put Franklin on a secret Committee of Correspondence to find it. At some point, perhaps at the formation of this committee, Franklin expressed his reluctance to have Americans seek aid through alliance with other nations. There is no record of what he said at the time, but in 1777, while in Paris deeply engaged in seeking an alliance with France, he confessed, "I have never yet changed the Opinion I gave in Congress, that a Virgin State should preserve the Virgin Character, and not go about suitering for Alliances, but wait with decent Dignity for the applications of others. I was over-ruld; perhaps for the best." Having been overruled, Franklin was not one to sulk. If the colonists needed allies, he knew better how and where to look for them than anyone else in Congress. He quickly dispatched a letter to a European friend who had assured him earlier that "Le cri général est que votre cause est celle de la nature, celle du genre humain" (the general view [in Europe] is that your cause is that of nature, that of the human race). Charles-Guillaume-Frédéric Dumas, a European savant with whom Franklin had been exchanging thoughts and books, was living at The Hague, a center for European diplomacy and intrigue. Franklin now (December 9, 1775) asked Dumas to take soundings about the possibility of gaining more than good wishes. Would Dumas find out "whether if, as it seems likely to happen, we should be obliged to break off all connection with Britain, and declare ourselves an independent people, there is any state or power in Europe, who would be willing to enter into an alliance with us for the benefit of our commerce, which amounted, before the war, to near seven milllions sterling per annum, and must continually increase, as our people increase most rapidly."

As it happened, before Dumas could have received this inquiry, Franklin and his Committee of Correspondence learned that a French agent had been taking soundings in America. The French secretary of state, the Comte de Vergennes, had sent the Chevalier de Bonvouloir to observe the extent of American resistance to England. The aptly named Bonvouloir (Goodwill) was in Philadelphia as Franklin's committee began its secret deliberations, and he appropriately met with them secretly to convey Vergennes's message.

The secret committees offered a golden opportunity to move the colonies another step closer to independence and at the same time to obtain the arms and the allies needed to make independence work. Secrecy hid American moves not only from the British but also from a Congress still hesitant to step out of its colonial identity. Congress had agreed to appoint the committees, but Franklin and his companions did not feel obliged to report back on the diplomatic maneuvers they took to place the United Colonies in the rank of nations, capable of dealing independently with the rest of the world. Early in March, encouraged by Bonvouloir, the Committee of Correspondence sent Silas Deane as its agent to Paris, instructed to meet directly with Vergennes and ascertain "whether if the Colonies should be forced to form themselves into an independent state [note the singular *state*], France would probably acknowledge them as such, receive their ambassadors, enter into any treaty or alliance with them, for commerce or defence, or both."

By this time Franklin and his fellow workers for independence had gained sudden support from a pamphlet published in January and quickly republished throughout the colonies. The author was Thomas Paine, a journalist and jack-of-all-trades whom Franklin had encountered in London and furnished with letters of introduction to notable Philadelphians. The pamphlet Paine now published was a wake-up call for Americans, asking them why they should shed their blood merely to return to a condition in which they had already been betrayed. *Common Sense*, the title of the pamphlet, dictated a repudiation not merely of George III but of monarchy itself. With Paine's eloquence converting Americans by the thousands and Deane off to France, Congress found another task for Franklin. From the time when the fighting began, Washington had hoped to bring Canada into the cause, but the troops he sent there, after capturing Montreal, had bogged down before Quebec and found the inhabitants cool to all entreaties to join the revolution. Perhaps Franklin could persuade them. With two colleagues he set off at the end of March 1776 and encountered only disaster. The American forces, logistically unsupported, had lived off the land, alienating the inhabitants and suffering humiliating defeat at the hands of the British occupying forces. The American troops, Franklin reported on May 12, "must starve, plunder, or surrender."

Both the commissioners and the troops were soon in full retreat. By the end of May, Franklin was back in Philadelphia, crippled by edema and gout in his legs, but heartened by what had happened in Congress during his absence. Under the prodding of the Adamses, both John and Samuel, a resolution had squeaked through recommending that every colony suppress whatever British authority remained within its bounds and henceforth rest all government on popular consent. The reluctant conservatives in Congress had gradually accepted the fact that they were now embarked on independence, and on June 11 Franklin found himself on a committee to draft a formal declaration of that fact. Franklin and the other members left it to Thomas Jefferson to find the words and made only minor revisions to the document that Congress, after a few more revisions, adopted on July 4.

Independence and Union

We have little from Franklin's hand in these days when colonists became Americans. The declaration was perhaps anticlimactic to him; his own independence from Britain had come after his negotiations with Lord Howe had made it clear that Parliament would never acknowledge American rights. At that time neither he nor Howe had been authorized to speak for the people they undertook to represent. In the two years since then, they had both acquired a kind of authorization. Franklin was a principal member of the secret congressional committee to conduct foreign correspondence, and England was now a foreign country. Admiral Lord Howe had a double authorization. His Majesty had placed him in command of 78 warships and had given his brother William command of 23,800 troops to put an end to the American rebellion. The Howes were separately authorized to accept American submission without the punishment thus prepared for them, on roughly the same terms that Lord Howe had unofficially proposed and Franklin unofficially rejected two years earlier. The Howes had both departed for America well before the Declaration of Independence. General Howe landed his troops on Staten Island on June 25, but Admiral Howe's fleet, having endured many delays, did not anchor there until July 12. General Howe was not eager to test his troops against Washington's, encamped on Long Island, and Admiral Howe wanted to make another try at reconciliation. He had prepared circular letters to governments no longer in existence, offering pardons to rebels who submitted to the authority of Parliament. From his flagship, *Eagle*, he sent these notices to Franklin to forward to the appropriate recipients, along with a personal note expressing his hope that they would be the means of "promoting the reestablishment of lasting Peace and Union with the Colonies."

In reply Franklin was able to write his own special declaration of independence. It was a time of eloquence, when men at war could express their convictions without restraint: Paine's literary demolition of monarchy, Jefferson's ringing affirmation of human rights. Franklin's reply to Howe was perhaps the most eloquent letter he ever wrote, a declaration not so much of human rights as of human feelings. He must have been astonished, and was certainly angry, to receive from Howe a proposal demonstrating that neither Howe nor other British officers of government had taken seriously anything that Franklin had told them in the preceding ten years. He began the letter by saying that "it must give your Lordship Pain to be sent so far on so hopeless a Business." Then he went on to spell out just how hopeless a business it was, rendered much more so by what the British had done in the time since the two men had gone over the same ground to the accompaniment of chess games with Howe's sister. In what became a famous passage Franklin expressed the profound love he had once felt for the empire he had longed to preserve.

> Long did I endeavour with unfeigned and unwearied Zeal, to preserve from breaking, that fine and noble China Vase the British Empire: for I knew that being once broken, the separate Parts could not retain even their Share of the Strength or Value that existed in the Whole, and that a perfect Re-Union of those Parts could scarce even be hoped for. Your Lordship may possibly remember the Tears of Joy that wet my Cheek, when, at your good Sister's in London, you once gave me Expectations that a Reconciliation might soon take place. I had the Misfortune to find those Expectations disappointed, and to be treated as the Cause of the Mischief I was labouring to prevent.

It was not his own treatment that concerned him now but the treatment the British had given his countrymen in the past two years and the contempt that Howe's terms showed for them.

> Directing Pardons to be offered the Colonies, who are the very Parties injured, expresses indeed that Opinion of our Ignorance, Baseness, and Insensibility which your uninform'd and proud Nation has long been pleased to entertain of us; but it can have no other Effect than that of increasing our Resentment. It is impossible we should think of Submission to a Government, that has with the most wanton Barbarity and Cruelty, burnt our defenceless

Towns in the midst of Winter, excited the Savages to massacre our Farmers, and our Slaves to murder their masters, and is even now bringing foreign Mercenaries to deluge our Settlements with Blood.

Franklin, it is true, shared his countrymen's prejudices against "savages" and slaves. But he now read Howe a lesson in human relations that few have ever learned.

These atrocious Injuries have extinguished every remaining Spark of Affection for that Parent Country we once held so dear: But were it possible for *us* to forget and forgive them, it is not possible for *you* (I mean the British Nation) to forgive the People you have so heavily injured; you can never confide again in those as Fellow Subjects, and permit them to enjoy equal Freedom, to whom you know you have given such just Cause of lasting Enmity. And this must impel you, were we again under your Government, to endeavour the breaking our Sp[i]rit by the severest Tyranny, and obstructing by every means in your Power our growing Strength and Prosperity.

In other words, the victim can sometimes learn to forgive but can seldom be forgiven. The only friendly relation now possible between Britain and America was one between "distinct States." It took several years of warfare before the English government was ready or willing to think of the colonies as distinct states. Lord Howe, with a commission to make some kind of peace with the rebels, and an army and navy to do the pacifying, seems to have thought that his brother's success against Washington in the Battle of Long Island on August 27 would induce the Americans to treat with him as British subjects. He sent messages to the Congress, endeavoring at the same time to imply that the body he was addressing did not exist. Congress humored him to the extent of sending a delegation of three to meet with him on Staten Island. Franklin, of course, was one; John Adams and Edward Rutledge of South Carolina the others. Howe declared that he could not talk with them as delegates of the body that sent them; they told him to consider them in whatever light he wished, but there was no way in which they would consider themselves as anything but the representatives of independent states. Howe tried to tell them of the good things that he could get done for them as colonists of Great Britain, to which they could only answer that Americans were no longer in that position and that neither they nor Congress could or would place them in it again. The former colonies were now independent both of Great Britain and of the Congress in which they had joined to protect themselves from Great Britain.

The meeting was a waste of time, but the Americans' insistence that they represented independent states concealed an ambiguity they all felt. Not about independence from Britain: none of them entertained any doubts about that, then or ever after. But it was Congress, not Pennsylvania or Massachusetts or South Carolina, that had sent them to Staten Island. And in talking with Howe, they undertook to speak for all the colonies, as though they were a single people. Franklin told Howe that "*America* could not return again to the Domination of Great Britain." (emphasis added) The same ambivalence had been apparent in the declaration that announced independence. It begins by justifying the separation of "one people" from another, but at the end it declares "That these United Colonies are, and of Right ought to be Free and Independent States." In specifying the rights of free and independent states, it says that "they have full Power to levy War, conclude Peace, contract Alliances, establish Commerce, and to do all other Acts and Things which Independent States may of right do." But it was Congress that was levying war, Congress that was preparing to contract alliances, Congress that would make peace. And in Congress more than one member had already shown his sense that Americans were one people. At its first meeting Patrick Henry, a dyed-in-the-wool Virginian, announced with enthusiasm, "I am not a Virginian, but an American." And John Adams, who at the meeting with Howe told him "that it was not in their power to treat otherwise than as independent States," would argue in Congress for a union of the states that would "make us one individual only, . . . one common mass. We shall no longer retain our separate individuality."

Neither Henry nor Adams meant quite what he said. Henry would later lead the opposition in Virginia to joining the other states under the Constitution of 1787. John Adams, before becoming President of the United States, would be the principal author of a separate state constitution for Massachusetts. Franklin shared this dual allegiance. During his absence in Canada the conservatism of the old Pennsylvania Assembly had reduced it to impotence. The Assembly was replaced in July by an elected revolutionary convention that assumed the government of the independent state. Franklin was chosen a member from Philadelphia and immediately became the Convention's president as well as its delegate to the Second Continental Congress. In these capacities he had to think about the best way to replace both the old authorities, proprietary and royal, which he had spent his previous political career opposing. He had long been a little more American than Pennsylvanian, and he has left us more of his views about the kind of government he wanted for a union of the states than of what he wanted for Pennsylvania.

Franklin had first started thinking about union when the colonies were part of the empire, when he already foresaw America as the future center of the greatest political structure in human history. At Albany in 1754 he had devised a preliminary plan of union as a first step toward his empire of equals. Now Britain would be excluded, but he still thought in imperial terms. A year before the colonies were ready for independence, when he laid his plan before them, he envisaged a confederation that would embrace not only the colonies represented at Philadelphia but, if they should choose to join: "the West India Islands, Quebec, St. Johns, Nova Scotia, Bermudas, and the East and West Floridas."

He did not think of dissolving all into one common mass. Each state in his plan was to retain "as much as it may think fit" of its existing laws and customs and could "amend its own constitution as shall seem best to its own Assembly or Convention." But as far as the rest of the world was concerned, Americans would be one people, in effect one state. From the time he took the lead in trying to get Pennsylvania to join the other colonies in defending themselves against the French, Franklin had been been telling Americans that their strength lay in union. He had made the point in a famous depiction (sometimes called the first American political cartoon) of a snake divided into segments, each marked with the name of a colony, over the motto, "Join or Die." In his efforts as colonial agent to bring Britain to terms, he had counseled his constituents again and again that their only hope of overcoming a ruinous British policy lay in sticking together. Now that they had declared independence, their only hope of overcoming a British army and navy lay in staying together. They had joined as separate colonies, now turned independent, but from the first they had recognized themselves as one people in forming a Continental Congress and a Continental Army. Their union, as Franklin saw it, must be not simply a union of states but of people. It should be a union of equals, and in order to succeed it would have to recognize in its structure the human equality affirmed in its Declaration of Independence. Although each state would have its own government to serve its people in their local affairs, Congress would serve the same people in dealing with the outside world, and it must serve them as equals.

When the First Continental Congress met in 1774, everyone recognized that some colonies were much larger than others and ought to exercise power and bear burdens proportionately, but there was no time to take a count of the population in each of them. As a matter of temporary convenience, it was decided to vote by colonies, one vote for each colony, with the stipulation that this was not a precedent for the future. The future had now arrived, and Franklin proposed a confederation in which the people of each state would be represented in Congress in proportion to their numbers, to be determined annually by a count of all males between sixteen and sixty. These were the able-bodied, income-producing men; and for every five thousand of them a state would be entitled to one delegate and one vote and would be assessed a corresponding share of the expenses that the American people as a whole might incur in war and peace.

Franklin's proposal had been shelved for future consideration in 1775, but in June of 1776, with independence in the offing, Congress appointed a committee, without Franklin, to draft a plan of confederation. He was assigned instead, on the same day, to the committee that drafted the Declaration of Independence. His old adversary in the petition for royal government in Pennsylvania, John Dickinson, led the congressional committee to draft articles of confederation, and the result he presented in the last days of July violated the principle that Franklin regarded as crucial; the equality of people in the distribution of power and payment. In Dickinson's Articles of Confederation, though otherwise much amended before their final adoption in 1781, each state retained a single vote in Congress. In the initial debate Franklin broke his customary silence to object. According to John Adams, who was taking notes, Franklin said, "Let the smaller Colonies give equal Money and Men, and then have an equal Vote. But if they have an equal Vote, without bearing equal Burthens, a Confederation upon such iniquitous Principles, will never last long."

Franklin did not prevail. In the existing Congress each state still had one vote. Since there were more small states than large ones, it was not possible then or ever to carry a vote that would deprive them of the disproportionate power that voting by states gave them. The Confederation operated on that principle until the Constitutional Convention of 1787 bypassed it in a direct appeal to the people. In 1776 Franklin composed a protest calling for Pennsylvania's withdrawal from a union that would always be at the mercy of the small-state majority. But as so often when he had expressed his righteous indignation in writing, he kept the writing to himself and never presented it. Union even on iniquitous principles was better than no union. He would be there to help forge a better one in 1787.

Meanwhile, even as Congress struggled over the details of the union's future structure, Franklin was presiding at the Pennsylvania Convention over the drafting of a constitution for the state. Neither he nor any of the other members left a record of their deliberations, but it is clear that he approved of the result, which gave Pennsylvanians within the state the kind of equality he had failed to get for Americans in the Confederation. The document began with a bill of rights, asserting "That all Men are born equally free and independant." It failed to carry out that principle by abolishing slavery in the state, but it eliminated the geographical inequality that had prevailed under the proprietary government. Under the new constitution each county was to be represented in a supreme legislature (there was no upper house and no governor with a veto power) according to the size of its population. And since the population was likely to grow much more rapidly in some counties than in others, the numbers were to be recorded and delegates reapportioned through a new census every seven years.

Franklin, as presiding officer, was widely credited with the drafting of the constitution. Whatever his role, he did not repudiate the result or even deny the attribution. But the ink was not yet dry on the document when Congress found another job for him as an American. On October 22 the members chose him, along with Arthur Lee and Silas Deane, to represent the United States in France. On October 27 he set sail, accompanied by two people who would figure largely in the rest of his life. One was a young man of sixteen who went by the name of William Temple Franklin. Temple, as he was called in the family, was William's illegitimate son, who had been entrusted to his grandfather's care when his father departed England to take up the governorship of New Jersey in 1762. Temple nursed a dutiful affection for his father but cherished an unlimited devotion to his grandfather, who returned the feeling with interest. Franklin had intended a career at the Bar for him, as he had done for the father, but during his grandfather's tenure in France Temple served him in the American embassy as something more than a secretary. Franklin hoped that the experience would entitle Temple to a major diplomatic post, a wish that an ungrateful United States never fulfilled.

Franklin's other shipboard companion was a boy of six, his grandson Benjamin Franklin Bache, Sally's son. Benny was a serious child and treated by Franklin in the manner of the time as a young adult in need of constant admonition and correction. He would spend virtually all his time abroad in boarding schools, first in Paris and then in Geneva, where he did his best to please everyone but was never rewarded with the affection that Franklin lavished on Temple. It would be almost nine years before the three of them returned to the country whose place in the world Franklin had spent spent those years securing.

8 Representing a Nation of States

By the time he reached France and began a new career, Franklin had long since reached a maturity that few people of his extraordinary talents and intelligence ever attain (why do gifted people so often have trouble growing up?). Without being self-satisfied, he knew himself and was content with what he found there. In England he had enjoyed the respect of people who valued intellectual achievement and capacity. He also had the respect of people of the same kind who lived at a distance, like Giambattista Beccaria in Italy and Jan Ingenhousz in Austria. But as an American he did not have in England the general, public respect that the intellectual world accorded him. Not that he felt a pressing need for it; his self-respect did not require continual reassurance. He was content simply to enjoy the company of other human beings anywhere, of women, young and old, of men from all walks of life with whom he could exchange ideas, jokes, fun.

In France he encountered something new: a public adulation

unlike anything he had ever before experienced or expected. He had been recognized in Pennsylvania as the most important and powerful figure in the colony, but it was more a recognition of what he could do than of who he was (and he had been unable to do what Pennsylvanians sent him to England to do). In France he was appreciated at once for who he was, and the experience was a little intoxicating, or would have been for a lesser man. It was as though the whole nation, especially its social and intellectual elite, saw him as only his best friends in England had. Glamorous women could not get enough of his company. Scientists from all over Europe sought him out for advice. People vied in pouring compliments upon him, composing verses in his honor, stamping his visage on medals, dishes, and keepsakes until, as he told his sister, "my Face is now almost as well known as that of the Moon." He was addressed as "the most distinguished character in Europe," "the ornament of the New World," and (in one set of verses) the embodiment in a single man of Lycurgus, Cato, Aristotle, and Plato. It was a little embarrassing, but it meant that his mission could be carried out in negotiations with officials who treated him with the respect that English officials would never accord to a mere colonial. That in France he now represented an independent nation may have accounted for some of the difference, but not much. For the first time people of all ranks were excited and even awed by who he was.

The Pleasures of Paris

Who he was is the same man we have been getting to know, but he is now on public display as never before (as evidenced in the twenty volumes of the Papers of Benjamin Franklin that will be

BENJAMIN FRANKLIN.

Né à Boston, dans la nouvelle Angleterre le 17 Janvier 1706.

Benjamin Franklin, 1777

occupied by the papers preserved from his stay in France), and he is handicapped by what time has done to him. He was seventy years old when he landed, on December 3, 1776, and seventy-nine when he left, on July 22, 1785, an old man even by today's standards. In the course of these years he becomes increasingly plagued by the bodily ailments that come with age. They had already begun to cripple him during his mission to Canada, and his stay in France is punctuated by attacks of gout and by extremely painful kidney or bladder stones that made the jolting of travel by coach unbearable. (Queen Marie Antoinette lent him her litter, carried between mules, when he finally departed for America.) But in spite of infirmities this old man has not slowed down. He is busier in his seventies than ever before. What he has to do as principal representative abroad of the new United States, and does very successfully, is enough to have taxed the energies of a much younger and healthier man. Yet the Franklin we know is not likely to be satisfied with simply doing a job, however exacting and challenging it might be. Nor are the people of France content to let him. They cannot do without his company, and he cannot do without theirs. He cannot do without conversation. He cannot do without using his hands. He cannot do without following the trail of things that excite his curiosity. Above all, he cannot do without fun.

Before we look at him at work on the serious business of his embassy, which, however crucial to the future of the world was never much fun, we need to see him doing what he did best, the things that made life worth living for himself and for everyone around him. Shortly after his arrival he settled for the duration in Passy, at that time a separate village just outside Paris. There he rented a comfortable house on a hill, set in a large garden with

The Potager of the Château de Valentinois, Passy (Franklin's kitchen garden)

paths, where the man who liked to be outdoors could stroll. He had great good luck in his neighbors. His landlord, Jacques-Donatien Le Ray de Chaumont, who lived in an attached mansion, became a good friend, and so of course did his wife and daughters, along with the other ladies and gentlemen of Passy, who regularly stopped to visit with the great man and entice him to their homes.

Franklin liked to flirt, and here were ladies who enjoyed it as much as he did and were seasoned practitioners of the art. They did not want avuncular advice like Polly Stevenson or Georgianna Shipley or Katy Greene. Instead, they plied him with extravagant declarations of love and affection, addressing him as *mon cher Papa*. He responded in kind, insisting as eloquently as he could in an unfamiliar language that his own love for them was not just fatherly. Madame Brillon (Anne-Louise d'Hardancourt Brillon de Jouy) was perhaps his favorite. She entertained him at tea every Wednesday and Saturday for four years following his arrival. They played chess while she taught him a more idiomatic French than he had learned from schoolbooks. They dined together, walked together, talked together, and, though they lived not far apart, bombarded each other with flowery letters, each claiming an unsurpassable love for the other. He confessed to her that he could not obey the commandment not to covet his neighbor's wife. She responded that her only happiness would be "vivre toujours avec vous," that no one had ever loved him or ever would love him as much as she did, and that every day, "Il me semble que je vous aime davantage." The effusive language suggests more passion than is likely to have been present. Franklin was careful to spice his professions of devotion with witty explanations that love could be infinitely divided without diminishing, just as "the sweet Sounds of the Forte Piano produc'd by your exquisite skill" could be heard by twenty people "without lessening that which you kindly intend for me." Since she never allowed him more than kisses, there could be no lessening of his love for her if he gave some to twenty other "jolies femmes." And so he doubtless did.

Monsieur Brillon seems to have taken it all in good part, perhaps because he himself was conducting a more or less open affair with the children's governess, who lived with the Brillons. Franklin's fondness for his neighbor's wife, like hers for him, was genuine, and it was not purely platonic. But it was of a piece

Franklin surrounded by the ladies at court as imagined fifty years later by a
Belgian painter (detail)

with his fondness for all attractive women, and France seemed to have an endless supply of them. Before coach travel became hard for him, Franklin could be found regularly at the salon that the flamboyant Widow Helvétius presided over in the neighboring village of Auteuil, where French notables like Anne-Robert Turgot, the former minister of finance, were regular fixtures. For Madame Helvétius too Franklin felt a real love and affection, which she returned. Franklin loved and liked them all. They certainly made life in France worth living in a way that nothing else had quite equalled.

He did not forget more familiar pleasures. Franklin had begun his career as a printer, and he had not been long at Passy before his fingers were itching for the feel of type and paper. He bought a small press and fonts of type from the principal French typographers, the Fournier family; and despite the war ordered more fonts from his old friend Caslon in England and perhaps from Caslon's rival, Baskerville, another old friend. In 1780 he bought a printer's foundry to cast type for him; and later he corresponded with John Walter in England about casting whole words or syllables together, a process that one Ottmar Mergenthaler would perfect a hundred years later with his linotype machine. Franklin's press at Passy was not a toy. He used it to print the passports he often had to sign for Americans in Europe and the promissory notes to facilitate the many financial transactions he had to oversee. But he used it for fun too. He was fond of composing little fables and fantasies, "bagatelles," for the amusement of his friends. And since his friends were so many, why not present them with well-designed keepsakes in print? One was a letter from the flies in his house to Madame Helvétius, thanking her for seeing to the destruction of the cobwebs and spiders that

Franklin had cruelly allowed to endanger them. Another was the soliloquy of an aged "ephemera," an insect with a lifespan of less than a day, who reflected on the tribulations and triumphs of his long life of seven hours on a leaf.

These *jeux d'esprit* provided Franklin with refreshment and distraction from the daily tasks involved in enabling the United States to achieve the independence he had helped to declare. And there were more serious distractions imposed by his status as a scientist and the demands of his own scientific curiosity. The peculiarities of a lightning strike in Italy needed explaining, and only Franklin could do it. Ingenhousz needed further advice on conducting an experiment Franklin had suggested to him for determining the conductivity of heat in different metals. Another friend required a way to measure humidity, and Franklin had to design an instrument for him. Toward the end of his stay the king himself needed Franklin's help and that of other members of the Royal Academy of Sciences (Franklin had been elected to this and other European learned societies before he left England). The problem was a dispute over the cures allegedly obtained through the use of "magnetism" by one Friedrich Anton Mesmer. A commission of nine from the Royal Academy of Sciences and the Royal Medical Society (which had also made Franklin a member) concluded after careful investigation that the whole business was an elaborate fraud. The same was not true of another phenomenon that excited Parisians about the same time: Joseph-Michel Montgolfier's construction of a gas-filled balloon, twelve feet in diameter, that flew into the clouds from Paris and landed ten or twelve miles away on August 27, 1783. With the aid of the Royal Academy larger and larger balloons were quickly constructed and succeeded in carrying two passengers several miles. Franklin stood in the admiring throng that viewed the launches of most of the flights. When asked by a sour bystander at the first one what good such a contraption could be, he gave his famous reply, "What good is a newborn baby?"

Franklin was seventy-seven when he said that and was nearing completion of the task that had engaged him for so long. And it is time for us to turn from the moments of pleasure and excitement that sustained him and take the measure of what he did for his countrymen, as well as of the obstacles placed in his way.

Conflicting Loyalties

It is fair to say that Franklin was able to do what he did because the people of France knew who he was and perhaps knew it better than the people of America. What made the job difficult was that the people of America were not sure who *they* were. Neither the Continental Congress nor the states represented in it had yet decided whether the United States was one people or thirteen. Franklin had gone to France as agent of Congress, and his principal task was to get France to do what Congress had not quite done itself. He had to get France to recognize the United States as a nation with a future in the world of nations, able to make binding agreements and carry them out. Treaties were the most conspicuous form of agreement, the most public form of recognition; but a more tangible form, which occupied Franklin throughout his stay in France before and after he succeeded in making a treaty of alliance, was the recognition that the United States was a going concern, a safe bet for loans. What the United States needed and kept on needing was money to pay for the costly war in which it was already engaged. And to lend money to the United States required an act of faith, faith that America would one day be able to repay with interest the investment that Franklin had to ask the French to make. Franklin, with his belief in the American empire of the future, had no doubt that the investment would be a sound one for France, but his countrymen had not provided him with any hard evidence of the nation's future solvency. They had not given the United States in Congress assembled any power to levy taxes to pay back what he borrowed for it nor even the power to carry out the terms of any treaty he might make.

The Articles of Confederation, which for the first time prescribed the terms of the American union, were not ratified until 1781, when Franklin had been in France for more than four years, and the Articles left the union still without power to tax or even to make laws. Congress initially appointed Franklin to carry out his job in France as one of a commission of three, but when he was named sole minister plenipotentiary in 1778 what did that mean? It meant that he had the full power of the United States Congress, which itself had no power that its constituent sovereign states felt obliged to recognize.

Franklin had always believed that the American union ought to be a union of people, not just of states. With the perspective of distance, gained from so many years in England and then in France, it was probably easier for him to think that way than it was for those he represented. The members of the Continental Congress sat there as agents of particular states and had to divide their loyalties between their home states and the new nation. As the nation's envoy, Franklin could make no such division. Like Washington his loyalty had to be "continental," and like Washington he was continually frustrated by the unwillingness of the Continental Congress to make continental decisions and by the unwillingness of the states to abide by such decisions when Congress did make them.

There is a striking parallel in the roles the two men played in leading Americans to a national identity. They would both have preferred Americans to win independence on their own, without depending on foreign assistance. Franklin did not like begging from the French any more than Washington liked relying on French troops (there were more French than Americans at Yorktown). Both thought that Americans were capable of doing much more for themselves than Congress was prepared to ask of them. But in the face of congressional incompetence, corruption, and irresponsibility, both drew upon personal prestige to make the United States a national republic rather than a temporary alliance of thirteen republics. Washington's prestige enabled him to hold the Continental Army together in competition with state militias that offered more pay than Congress did. Franklin's prestige enabled him to obtain loans for the United States in competition with states that offered larger rates of interest than Congress did.

What made the competition difficult for Franklin was the fact that the states, unlike Congress, did have the power to tax and could thus borrow anywhere in the world with a seemingly more credible promise to repay than the United States could make. Anywhere in the world was likely to be France. When agents from the separate states arrived there and discovered that Franklin was the American everyone trusted, they turned to him for help against himself. Virginia, Maryland, and South Carolina were the worst. South Carolina had started its own navy in 1778 and commissioned as its commodore one Alexander Gillon, a local merchant and politician. In 1779 Gillon was in France seeking not only some warships that Franklin wanted for the Continental Navy but also the money to buy them with. For the rest of Franklin's mission, he had to fend off the discontented creditors that Gillon left in his wake. Gillon had begun by asking Franklin to help him float a loan for 1.8 million livres (roughly £75,000) in competition with Franklin's own mandate to borrow and borrow and borrow, one loan after another, for the United States. Franklin's response to Gillon's importunings was a measured rebuke which, though it did not prevent his mischief, suggests what Franklin had to contend with in the efforts of the several states to outflank the United States: "as I am charg'd to procure a Loan for the United States at a lower Interest, I can have no hand in encouraging this particular Loan [Gillon's], as it interferes with the other. And I cannot but observe, that the Agents from our different States running all over Europe begging to borrow Money at high Interest, has given such an Idea of our Poverty and Distress, as has exceedingly hurt the general Credit, and made the Loan for the United States almost Impracticable."

The need of the United States for money to buy arms, ammunition, and clothing for its troops and to pay its soldiers, sailors, and diplomats never ceased during Franklin's stay in France, nor did Congress ever cease in its expectation that Franklin would get it for them. Congress regularly made "requisitions" on its member states for funds, and they regularly failed to supply the amounts asked for and often failed to supply anything at all. When Congress sought a revenue of its own in the form of a 5 percent duty on all imports into the United States, the proposal failed to get the required unanimous consent. It was thus left to

Franklin to negotiate large loans from France for the costs of conducting the war year by year, and after the war was won, for the costs of the extended peace negotiations. Congress continually underestimated the amounts needed for a coming year; and when he obtained what they asked for, he would have to return to the Comte de Vergennes, the French foreign minister, and ask for more. When he got it, the sum would again prove inadequate. Everyone employed by Congress for whatever purpose felt free to pay bills by drafts on him, and funds destined for larger purposes would be whittled away by the unexpected arrival of demands for payment of debts he had never heard of.

In the early years the confusion was compounded by congressional management of finances through a committee that acted with the usual inconsistency and unaccountability of committees. In 1781, Congress tried to bring more order to its monetary affairs by the appointment of a single superintendant of finance, Franklin's old Philadelphia friend Robert Morris. Franklin rejoiced that now the irresponsible succession of demands on him would give way to a systematic consolidation of all the country's financial transactions. But he soon found that Morris could underestimate and miscalculate future demands as haplessly as the committee had. As unexpected drafts continued to inundate him, he was perpetually faced with the possibility of having to "protest" bills, that is, refuse to pay them for lack of funds. If that had happened, if he had been obliged to default on any payment, the credit of the United States throughout Europe would have plunged.

Franklin could not afford to let that happen, and the only reason it did not was his success in persuading the French ministry that France could not afford to let it happen either. The French ministry, being close at hand, was more susceptible to reason than the Congress in Philadelphia. The problem was not simply the divided loyalties of the members but the political divisions that always arise in a deliberative body. They had existed in Congress from the beginning, as Franklin himself had witnessed in the reluctance of a majority to move toward the independence that Franklin and a growing minority had been ready for as soon as the war began. After Congress sent him off to France, new lines of division developed, and Franklin's mission became itself a source of dispute.

A Confusion of Colleagues

The trouble came from a plausible, patriotic, and overtly paranoid Virginian in France. Arthur Lee, whom the French despised, persuaded himself and his friends in America that it was not Franklin who charmed the French but the French who charmed Franklin and bent him to their own nefarious schemes. Lee saw conspiracies everywhere. He was one of the Virginia Lees, a brother of Richard Henry Lee, who had introduced the resolution for American independence and remained a powerhouse in congressional politics. Arthur, born in 1740, had spent most of his life in England and had written numerous pamphlet and newspaper articles in defense of the American cause. He had worked with Franklin as an agent of Massachusetts and was still in London when Congress declared independence. He had been instrumental with Silas Deane in a cloak-and-dagger operation to get secret French assistance for the Americans before Franklin joined him and Deane in the official United States mission.

Despite Franklin's extraordinary skills in dealing with people, the appointment of Lee as one of his partners imperiled his mission. Deane had so much respect for Franklin that the two might have made a team, but Arthur Lee was something else. Franklin's view after three years of dealing with him was that "in sowing Suspicion and Jealousies, in creating Misunderstandings and Quarrels among Friends, in Malice, Subtility and indefatigable Industry, he has I think no Equal." Franklin was not alone in that opinion. Thomas Jefferson, who became Franklin's successor as ambassador to France, knew Lee at first hand. When Jefferson heard from his friend James Monroe in 1785 that Congress was considering Lee, now a delegate from Virginia, for two appointments, one on a Treasury Commission (to replace Robert Morris) and the other on a commission to deal with the settlers at Kaskaskia, in the Illinois country, Jefferson wrote in dismay: "he will in a short time introduce such dissentions into the Commission as to break it up. If he goes on the other appointment to Kaskaskia he will produce a revolt of that settlement from the United States." Ironically, Jefferson himself was indirectly responsible for saddling Franklin with Lee: in 1776 Jefferson had declined the appointment to serve with Franklin and Deane on the mission to France that Congress then conferred on Lee.

If Lee had simply been insane, as Franklin believed he was— and as he may indeed have been—it might have been possible to ship him, kicking and screaming, back to Virginia. But his madness grew out of the very patriotism that moved Franklin and other Americans. It was a madness that in a much milder form afflicted members of the Continental Congress and made it possible, for some of them at least, to see Lee as a kind of superpatriot. They shared with him and with most other people of that time (or any other) a belief that nations are moved only by nar-

Silas Deane, ca. 1776

row self-interest and not by any kind of altruism. In itself that was a perfectly rational belief. Washington expressed it continually. But in the midst of a young nation's birth pangs it led easily to universal distrust of other people and other countries. Lee distrusted France and distrusted Franklin for his rapport with the French. French adulation, he believed, had gone to Franklin's head and made him a mere catspaw for Vergennes.

As Lee and his supporters saw it, France had no choice but to give Americans all they could ask for, because it was only through a British defeat that France could recover its place in the European balance of power, a place it had lost in the previous war with England. Any seeming generosity toward America

Arthur Lee, 1785

must be viewed with suspicion because it would be in France's interest to keep a victorious America dependent on France. Any reluctance by the French to accede to American demands for men or money was evidence of that intent.

What Lee and others refused to admit or failed to see was that French interest might well have been served by other options. Yes, helping the Americans humble Britain was one way to recover French power. But another way might have been to forge a tripartite agreement with England and Spain to partition the North American continent. France and Spain might have helped England suppress the American rebellion in return for the restoration of Canada to France and of the Floridas to Spain.

That alternative had been seriously considered. Its rejection by France did not mean that France could afford to give Americans whatever they wanted, whenever they wanted, without weighing the consequences. France did not yet have the power, vis-à-vis England, that she was risking an American war to gain.

France could not give Americans all the naval support they wanted in the early years of the war without taking unacceptable risks. France was rebuilding a shattered navy, but had not achieved nearly enough strength to protect France, the French West Indies, *and* the Atlantic coast of North America against the still superior British navy. Until two and a half years of war had demonstrated America's staying power against the British, even an open recognition of American independence seemed too risky. And once France was committed to that course, American demands for money put a strain on the French treasury that proved in the end too great to bear. Only six years after the treaty ending the American war was signed, the emptiness of that treasury threw France into revolution.

That France chose to help the Americans was thus a calculated risk, and badly calculated at that. There can be little doubt that Franklin himself figured in the calculation. Public opinion did not operate directly on the French government through any institution. But as Franklin had reminded the British government so often and so ineffectually, all governments depend ultimately on opinion. Franklin's popularity not only in France but throughout Europe was a factor of no small weight in swinging France toward support of America instead of to some other diplomatic and military alternative.

Franklin was happy to take advantage of his fame as a diplomatic counter, but his own view of diplomatic relations, as of all human relations, did not exclude generosity. He knew that France was pursuing French interests in helping America, but he was no less grateful on that account, for he knew what a gamble France was taking both militarily and monetarily. And gratitude was in the best interests of the United States in keeping France steady on that course.

What was not in the best interests of the United States was the presence of Arthur Lee in Paris in 1777. Fortunately for Franklin, during his first months in France, Lee was haring off to Spain, Vienna, and Berlin in not surprisingly fruitless efforts to draw these powers into support of America. But by July he was back in Paris, and Franklin had him by his side, offering frivolous objections to contracts for supplies, accusing Deane of peculation, and antagonizing Vergennes in the delicate negotiations to bring France openly into alliance. To make matters worse, in July 1777 Congress appointed Lee's brother William minister to Berlin and Vienna and Ralph Izard, a former South Carolina rice planter, minister to Tuscany. These two, whose egos were soon battered by the refusal of Vienna and Tuscany to have anything to do with them, settled in Paris and convinced themselves that they should be part of the commission to France. Franklin was able to exclude them from meetings with the French ministry to draft the treaties of alliance and commerce that were signed on February 6, 1778. Lee, of course, thought that the treaties, which were incredibly generous to the United States (renouncing all French claims to Canada and Louisiana), were not generous enough because they forbade both sides to levy certain export duties (a form of taxation that Franklin opposed on principle).

Deane and Franklin finally persuaded him to sign, but then had to deal with vociferous complaints from William Lee and Izard, who took up where Arthur Lee left off.

In a letter to James Lovell in July 1778, Franklin suggested that with the treaty established, the United States had a superfluity of ambassadors to France. Three was already two too many. Izard considered himself a fourth "and is very angry that he was not consulted in making the Treaty which he could have mended in several Particulars." William Lee would gladly have made a fifth. He too was sure he could have improved the treaty. Congress recalled Izard and William Lee in 1779 and replaced Arthur Lee as minister to Spain (a post which Congress had added to his commission in 1777), but all three stayed on for another year. Izard collaborated in Alexander Gillon's shady schemes to raise money and buy ships for South Carolina, while the Lees borrowed and bargained for the state of Virginia. When they predictably quarreled with private suppliers, they asked Franklin to get what they wanted from Vergennes, in competition with what he was seeking for the United States.

The Lees' genius for making Franklin's life difficult did not end there. When Arthur finally decided to go home in June 1780, he managed to turn his departure into a comic-opera caper to defeat Franklin's most recent plans for getting supplies to the Continental Army. Crucial to those plans at the moment was the forty-gun frigate *Alliance*, built in Massachusetts and now in Lorient, a principal embarkation point of ships bound for America. In the midst of a thousand other duties, Franklin was supervising the efforts of American privateers and the infant American navy in European waters. He relied heavily on the one American naval officer who seemed able to get things done, John Paul Jones. In September 1779 Jones had shown his mettle in leading a small squadron to America's only great naval victory in the war. In the course of the Battle off Flamborough Head in the North Sea, his flagship, *Bonhomme Richard* (the namesake of Franklin's Poor Richard), was sunk by friendly fire from *Alliance*, captained in that battle by the half-mad French naval officer Pierre Landais, to whom Congress had entrusted the vessel on its maiden voyage from America. After losing *Bonhomme Richard*, Jones had taken over *Alliance* from its crazy captain. On Franklin's orders Jones had sailed the ship to Lorient, to be outfitted and loaded with the supplies that General Washington so desperately needed.

There it stood in June, nearly ready to depart, when an unsavory trio, ill met in Lorient, made other plans for it. Alexander Gillon was there trying to man another frigate he had succeeded in buying for South Carolina. Pierre Landais was there awaiting passage to America (where a court martial awaited him). And Arthur Lee was there with an order from Franklin to Jones to give him passage home in *Alliance*. Franklin had probably been happy to give any order that would get Lee out of the country. If so, he miscalculated. At Lorient, Gillon and Lee got together with Landais and easily persuaded him that he was still the rightful captain of *Alliance*. Jones should have been aboard his ship, but it would not be fully loaded for several days, and Jones had taken advantage of the wait to spend a few more nights with his favorite mistress in Paris. While he was gone, Landais, with the assistance of Lee and Gillon, concocted a spurious mutiny of the crew in his own favor. The Frenchman and Lee then went aboard, slipped the cables, and were shortly off for America with the ship half-loaded, leaving Franklin to be blamed for not sending adequate supplies.

Lee, as might have been expected, quarreled with Landais on the voyage and led a real mutiny, this time against Landais. At the court martial following their arrival in Boston, he testified that Landais was insane—one madman against another. The court found that Landais had disobeyed Franklin's orders and should be cashiered as corrupt, incompetent, and insubordinate. But the other madman could always succeed somehow in getting people to take him seriously. He arrived in Philadelphia in October 1778, to a Congress which his letters from France had already thrown into disarray. Lee's denunciation of Silas Deane had resulted in Deane's recall and return in July to account for his expenditures in the secret negotiations for French aid in 1776. Deane could not produce adequate documentation of his expenditures or of the obligations he had incurred on behalf of the United States before the mission officially began. The result was a lasting division in Congress between the advocates and opponents of Deane. In the end Deane publicly denounced the whole Congress, gave up on the Revolution, and settled in England. He thereby discredited his defenders, including Franklin. Before his defection, Congress had taken Franklin's advice about the excess of ambassadors and made Franklin sole plenipotentiary. But even as he seemed to be rid of the Lees' interference in France, Deane's course of conduct gave the Lees' adherents a handle against anyone associated with Deane. Franklin made no secret of the fact that he thought Deane, however inexcusable his later behavior, had been shabbily treated by Congress. Congress, in turn, prepared to mete out some shabby treatment to their sole remaining spokesman in France. And Arthur Lee and Ralph Izard were now on hand to testify against him as "the worst of men in the worst of times."

A Needless Hindrance

Franklin had enough friends in Congress to prevent his recall, but Arthur Lee's accusations and the shortage of supplies, resulting in part from Lee's own piratical foray with Landais, came at a critical time. The army was facing winter without enough clothing and facing the enemy without enough ammunition. On November 22, 1780, Congress voted to ask France for a new loan of 25 million livres. Franklin, after Lee's report, seemed perhaps a little too old, too feeble, and, as both Lee and Izard alleged, too partial to France. Congress therefore decided to help him out. He had been asking for a consul to take over the mercantile duties that swamped him and for a secretary to handle some of the voluminous correspondence of the embassy. Congress therefore appointed William Palfrey, a Boston merchant, as consul for all of France; but when it began to consider a possible secretary, the discussion quickly turned to a possible "Envoy Extraordinary," charged with obtaining the 25 million livre loan. Such a large sum, it seemed, might be beyond Franklin's capacity to deliver. The man appointed on December 11, 1780, to do the job was the South Carolinian John Laurens, son of the former president of Congress, Henry Laurens. At age twenty-six, Laurens was already a war hero, a colonel, an aide-de-camp to Washington, and a political favorite. Everybody liked him, and he arrived in Paris on March 14, 1781, equipped with letters of recommendation from both Washington and the Marquis de Lafayette.

Early in February Franklin had received the news of Laurens's appointment and of the desperate need behind the proposal to borrow 25 million livres. With his usual aplomb and conscientiousness, he wrote at once to Vergennes suggesting the "Danger lest the Congress should lose its Influence over the People, if it is found unable to procure the Aids that are wanted; and that the whole System of the new Government in America may thereby be shaken." He ended by warning of the dire accession to England's power in the world if the English were able to force the former colonies into submission. As a result, by the time Laurens reached Paris, Vergennes had obtained from King Louis XVI an outright gift to America of 6 million livres. The proposed 25 million loan, Vergennes told Franklin, was simply not possible, because France itself now had to borrow to pay the expenses that the war entailed.

On March 12, two days before Laurens arrived at his doorstep, Franklin reported these developments in a long letter to the president of Congress that leaves us wondering how any man could be in such control of himself. He knows that he has achieved more than anyone could have expected from France, that the gift of 6 million livres is really a testimony of French regard for him. He knows also that Congress thinks he has not done enough and that it has sent an inexperienced youngster to get the old man's job done right. Without a trace of irony, he offers corroboration of congressional doubts about him. He is seventy-five years old, crippled with gout, slowing down, finding it difficult to cope with the demands of being foreign minister, consul, and financial agent all at once (Palfrey never arrived as consul). He is "afraid therefore that your Affairs may some time or other suffer by my Deficiency." As far as he knows, his mental faculties have not suffered, but "perhaps I shall be the last to discover that." So will Congress please send someone to replace him? He does not ask it out of "any Disgust received in their Service" but simply because of his infirmities. The only favor he would ask is that Congress find a place in the foreign service for his grandson, William Temple Franklin. In the absence of the secretary that Congress had not provided, he could not have done without Temple. The young man had thus served a kind of apprenticeship in diplomacy and deserved recognition for his services.

Can Franklin have been as selfless as he seems? Was he not seething with anger at the treatment he was receiving? If so, he did not show it either in this letter or in others written at the time. Only after five months had passed and Congress had rejected his request for a replacement did he reveal something of his feelings in a letter to a friend who had told him of Lee and Izard's performance in Congress. "I fancy," he wrote, "it may have been a double Mortification to those Enemies you have mentioned to me, that I should ask as a Favour what they hop'd to vex me by taking from me; and that I should nevertheless be continued. . . . I call this Continuance an Honour, and I really esteem it to be a greater than my first Appointment, when I consider that all the Interest of my Enemies united with my own Request, were not sufficient to prevent it."

By the time he wrote these words Franklin had finished undoing the damage that Laurens left in his wake. Franklin seems to have liked Laurens, received him cordially, even suggested to him that he could be his replacement. But Laurens's mission was little short of a disaster. With Franklin's backing he was well received at the French court, but he had apparently absorbed the

John Laurens, date unknown

attitude of the Lees that France owed America whatever America needed. Vergennes found him rude. In the two and a half months he stayed in Europe he succeeded only in persuading the French to guarantee a loan of 10 million livres *if* Laurens could obtain the loan itself in Holland. He had obtained no part of it by June 1, 1781, when he embarked for home on a French frigate with 2 million, in specie, of Franklin's 6 million gift, destined to shore up American domestic credit.

Congress had given Laurens not only a commission to borrow 25 million but also a shopping list of military supplies on which to spend at least a part of it. He was more successful as a spender than as a borrower and brought back, besides the 2 million in specie, three shiploads of much-needed arms, ammunition, and uniforms. Payment for them had to come from the 6 million gift or from what was left of the other funds Franklin had previously borrowed from the French. Laurens was in such a hurry to get back that he designated his secretary, Major William Jackson, to complete his purchases. Jackson was to bring them, along with another installment of specie, to America aboard a frigate lying in Amsterdam already half loaded.

The frigate, a heavy, forty-four-gun vessel, would furnish a safe conveyance. Its commander, a fellow South Carolinian, had gladly sold Laurens what he had aboard and was prepared to work with a Dutch banker to buy and load more in Holland, indeed to load two more ships and convoy them on a nonstop voyage to Philadelphia. This convenient South Carolinian with a frigate of his own was none other than Alexander Gillon, who had brought his ship from Lorient to Amsterdam. Major Jackson, aged twenty-two, was putty in his hands. Together they were even better at spending than Laurens. By early July they had filled the three ships and had a million and a half left in specie for Jackson to bring back to America.

Franklin assumed that Laurens had successfully contracted for the 10 million loan and that Gillon and Jackson were spending a part of it on credit from the Dutch bankers. When he learned that the credit was his and that they had nothing to spend but the remainder of his 6 million, he was furious. He desperately needed all he could get to pay the stream of bills that Congress drew on him. He therefore had the remaining million and a half seized and did what he could to soothe Vergennes's irritation that Americans were expending a French gift on Dutch merchandise. Jackson, too, was indignant. Laurens had left him with the impression that he had personally raised the 6 million and could dispose of it as he saw fit: Franklin must therefore return at once the money "obtained without either your knowledge or concurrence by Colonel Laurens appointed Special Minister for that purpose."

Jackson was not mollified when Franklin attempted to disabuse him of this fancy. It took the shenanigans of Alexander Gillon to set him straight. Gillon slipped his frigate out of Amsterdam on August 12, taking an unsuspecting Jackson and several other Americans with him on what they expected to be a safe and swift voyage home. Gillon, as usual, had his own agenda. He left behind the two vessels he had promised to convoy as well as a bundle of debts. Instead of making for Philadelphia, he put in at Corunna, Spain, and refitted there for a privateering cruise to the West Indies. He did not arrive in Philadelphia until May 1782. Jackson managed to escape at Corunna (in spite of a clumsy effort by Gillon to lock him up) and wrote an abject apology to Franklin. He acknowledged that Franklin's seizure of the funds had saved him and the country from Gillon's villainy, "which would sully the blackest character on record." He did not mention Laurens's folly in trusting so obvious a swindler or Laurens's role in siphoning off the funds needed to pay American bills in Europe.

Laurens himself never offered an explanation or apology. When he reached Philadelphia on September 2, 1781, and gave an account of his mission, Congress honored him with a unanimous commendation. The members could not say enough in his praise: he had "executed his mission with admirable effect and dispatch" and "with great Reputation to himself and Advantage to his Country." In the preceding June, Congress had received Franklin's letter of resignation, written just before Laurens's arrival in Paris, with its account of how the money Laurens later took home with him had actually been obtained. The only response had been the reluctant reappointment in which Franklin took such satisfaction, requiring him to remain until the expected peace negotiations with England should be complete and appointing him to a commission of five to carry them out. There was not a word of thanks for his success in obtaining what they now credited Laurens with. Instead, when they learned, perhaps from Gillon, that Franklin had seized the funds headed for Gillon's ship, a committee of inquiry recommended in October 1782 that Franklin be censured for the "Embarrassment" he had caused in diverting a portion of what Congress still imagined Laurens had raised for it. The recommendation did not pass, no doubt to the chagrin of Arthur Lee and Ralph Izard, then serving in Congress. Laurens himself died that month in a foolish skirmish (after active hostilities had ceased), and no one in Congress seems to have realized that his mission had been a failure and that Franklin alone had rescued the country from his folly.

Franklin survived. United States credit survived. In October, General Cornwallis surrendered at Yorktown. And suddenly Franklin found himself with another job and another swollen ego to deal with.

9 A Difficult Peace

It has often been observed that civil wars tend to be bloodier than other kinds. People bring more passion to a quarrel with brothers and sisters than to one with strangers. The American Revolution was a civil war and for no one more than Franklin. He had lived in England long enough to think of staying, long enough to have close friends there (more and stronger, indeed, than he had in America), and he had directed his life toward preserving the empire as a fraternal union. British repudiation of such a union was for him a fraternal betrayal. The adherence of his only son to the Loyalist cause was a personal betrayal. He took pains to separate the insults of a Wedderburn or a Hillsborough from the larger issues of right and rights, but simply as an American he was outraged by British fratricide. As he told Jan Ingenhousz, shortly after he arrived in France, "I keep a separate Account of private Injuries, which I may forgive; and I do not think it right to mix them with publick Affairs. Indeed there is no Occasion for their Aid to sharpen my Resentment against a Nation, that has burnt our defenceless Towns in the midst of Winter, has excited the Savages to assassinate our innocent Farmers with their Wives and Children, and our Slaves to murder their Masters."

Franklin was so incensed at the barbarity of the British that he planned an illustrated book of British atrocities in America and outlined twenty-six examples, including one showing "Prisonners kill'd and Roasted for a great festival where the Canadian indians are eating American flesh, Colonel Buttler an english officer Setting at table." It could have been no surprise to him when he heard later that British privateers were loading their cannon with broken glass, deliberately inflicting wounds that were then considered fatal. There were doubtless American atrocities—every war begets them—but he heard of none to match the British. He once expressed the opinion that there had never been a good war or a bad peace, but this war exceeded others in its viciousness. "I believe in my Conscience," he told his friend Joseph Priestley, "that Mankind are wicked enough to continue slaughtring one another as long as they can find Money to pay the Butchers. But of all the Wars in my time, this on the part of England appears to me the wickedest; having no Cause but Malice against Liberty, and the Jealousy of Commerce."

Reconciliation or Huckstering?

If Franklin thought this war worse than others, it is not surprising that he also believed any peace to follow it would have to be better than others. Since it was the wickedness of the English that made the war so bad, an appropriate peace would have to embody repentance, atonement, and reparations on England's part. That, of course, was not the way the English saw it, either during the war or afterward. To them the war was a rebellion, brought on in no small part by Franklin's machinations. Peace would be a matter of restoring American subjection, perhaps with a few changes in modes of imperial control to eliminate the things that had proved so unreasonably irritating. Franklin, as a prime mover, still seemed the right person, as Barclay, Fothergill, and Howe had supposed, to speak for America, the more so when he came to France as official agent of the American Congress. He had no sooner arrived than well-meaning Englishmen began slipping across the Channel to sound him out on what would be required to bring the colonies back. To each of them, he explained, with growing anger, that the colonies were no longer colonies and would not be coming back. Moreover, peace with the people they had formerly governed was not to be bought simply by accepting American independence. That, of course, was necessary, but it would not be enough.

Franklin did not pretend to have the authority to dictate what would be enough until he was given it in a commission with four other Americans in 1781. But his views of the way two different peoples should treat each other grew from his views of the way a single people should be governed, the way England had once governed Americans. He had explained to Parliament in 1766, at the time of the Stamp Act, that Americans "were governed by this country at the expence of a little pen, ink and paper. They were led by a thread." And that was the right way to govern. Government rested on opinion, and so, in the end, did peace. It would not be merely a matter of hammering out the limits, boundaries, and privileges of each party in a treaty. There had to be trust, there had to be goodwill. Franklin knew that nations act in their own interest, but he also believed that it was in every nation's interest to cultivate goodwill, as France cultivated American goodwill by its generosity. The only way for England to live peaceably with an independent America was by generosity, by showing enough goodwill to overcome the hatred brought on by the war. A few days before signing the treaty of alliance with France, Franklin explained the need to an English friend who had asked his advice on what kind of peace would satisfy Americans:

> You have lost by this mad War, and the Barbarity with which it has been carried on, not only the Government and Commerce of America, and the publick Revenues and private Wealth arising from that Commerce; but what is more, you have lost the Esteem, Respect, Friendship and Affection of all that great and growing People, who consider you at present, and whose Posterity will consider you as the worst and wickedest Nation upon Earth.
>
> A Peace you may undoubtedly obtain, by dropping all your Pretensions to govern us. And by your superior Skill in huckstering Negotiation, you may possibly make such an apparently advantageous Treaty as shall be applauded in your Parliament. But if you do not with the Peace recover the Affections of that People, it will not be a lasting or a profitable one; nor will it afford you any Part of that Strength which you once had by your Union with them and might (if you had been wise enough to take Advice) have still retained.

The way to recover enough of the old affection to make a lasting peace would not be easy. Instead of honoring the political and military leaders of the war, England should cover them with disgrace. "This would show a national Change of Dispositon, and a Disapprobation of what had passed." Then in proposing terms for a treaty, "you should not only grant such as the Necessity of your Affairs may evidently oblige you to grant, but such additional Ones as may show your Generosity, and thereby demonstrate your Goodwill." For example, England might by treaty bargain to keep Canada, Nova Scotia, and the Floridas, all of them then and later in its possession. But a suitable show of generosity would be to grant them all freely to the United States. Retaining them would only lead to future wars.

Franklin acknowledged that this proposal would never be accepted, and the English would consider him insolent for having mentioned it. But he had been asked for his advice, and he had given the best advice that he could. It is worth considering why he should offer such advice in all seriousness, long before any kind of peace was possible. We know from the commonsense aphorisms of Poor Richard that Franklin was eminently practical in telling people how to behave. His reputation today rests on his pragmatism, his down-to-earth realism in dealing with human relations on a day-to-day basis. His activities as a peacemaker, when the time came, demanded the same kind of realism on a larger scale and for a longer term. The friend to whom he wrote was James Hutton, a founder of the pacifist Moravian Church in England, whom he could expect to listen more sympathetically than anyone who might later appear at the peace table. But he was not asking more of England than he would later, not more than he thought would be beneficial to England as well as the United States, not more than the realities of the situation seemed to him to demand.

Franklin played a major role in negotiating the treaty that ended the war, and he did not hesitate to put his name to it. But the treaty was the product of huckstering negotiations and did not fit the realities of the situation as he perceived them, precisely because it did not embody the advice he had given Hutton. The final treaty was simply the best that could be obtained from people who could not or would not recognize the larger realities. Hence the treaty itself tells us little about Franklin, but his activities, ideas, and objectives in working toward it reveal his view of the world more tellingly than anything else we have watched him do.

During his career in England, Franklin had been continually engaged in conflict, but it was conflict that he regarded as needless, brought on by the refusal of England to recognize its own best interests. Franklin did not enjoy conflict or controversy. He had learned the futility of theological controversy when he entered the lists in favor of Philadelphia's Presbyterian minister in the 1730s. In later life he met every criticism of his scientific views with silence, and he took time from his diplomatic duties in 1781 to recommend the same course to his young friend Ingenhousz. "You can always," he told him, "employ your time better than in polemics." In the many enterprises he fostered in Philadelphia—the Library Company, the hospital, the fire company—he contrived to have others take the lead so as not to appear himself as an advocate against any opposition that might occur. If people resisted doing what was right and good for them, they had to be somehow enticed, not bullied into doing it. In the long run they would see that what was good for others was good for them too. What prevented them from seeing it, what prevented statesmen and the countries they governed from seeing it, was a mistaken pursuit of present advantage over long-term benefits.

As a peacemaker Franklin could not expect to persuade others of the long view, but he hoped to eliminate as many opportunities for conflict as he could. If he had had his way he would have abolished all restrictions on trade, by England, France, or America. And since other shortsighted policies would inevitably cause more wars in the future he would have liked to establish principles of international law to hinder the participants in any war from injuring those engaged in something more productive than wholesale theft and murder. He wanted all countries to forbid privateering, impressment of seamen, and any molestation of farmers, fishermen, merchants, artists, and mechanics. "In short," he told his friend the English printer Benjamin Vaughan, as serious negotiations began in 1782, "I would have nobody fought with, but those who are paid for Fighting." In the midst of the war, without even consulting Congress, he had issued instructions "To all Captains and Commanders of American Armed Ships" requesting protection for the expedition of Captain James Cook, whose ships were returning to England from his famous last voyage of discovery. Franklin asked not merely that Cook be spared from any privateering "but that you would treat the said Captain Cook and his People with all Civility and Kindness, affording them as common Friends to Mankind, all the Assistance in your Power which they may happen to stand in need of."

The French joined him in this gesture, but to extend it to all noncombatants would have required a view of human welfare and warfare that the world was incapable of embracing then or now. Franklin nevertheless preferred to conduct negotiations as though the world were capable of doing right. His style of dealing with the French was not the suspicious, secretive, aggressive assertion of American demands that had made Arthur Lee so obnoxious but an openhanded confession of American needs and American gratitude for French help. And it had worked. When it came to dealing with the British, despite his mistrust of them, he remained free and easy. Instead of playing his cards close to his chest, bargaining this against that, his instinct was simply to say outright what he wanted, what he thought would be good for both parties. He might have been able to conduct the whole peace negotiation in that way, with what result it is hard to say. Franklin was not modest in what he wanted, namely, most of North America. He might have obtained less than he actually got if the United States Congress had left the process entirely in his open hands. Or he might conceivably have obtained a great deal more. But Congress did not leave things in his hands. In conducting the peace negotiations he had to satisfy the demands not simply of the hostile British, the friendly French, and the unpredictable Spanish but also of the impetuous colleagues that Congress saddled him with. One of them caused him more difficulty than the ministers of all the great powers combined, and it is time we had a look at this not very peaceable fellow peacemaker.

A Contentious Colleague

John Adams was never a man to be taken lightly. He never took himself lightly, and neither did Franklin. They had worked together amicably to bring the Continental Congress to independence, served together on the committee that drafted the Declaration of Independence. Trouble between them began only when Adams came to France in 1778 as a replacement for Silas Deane, after Arthur Lee's dispatches had brought about Deane's recall. Unfortunately, Adams arrived two months after Franklin, Deane, and Lee had signed the treaties with France. For a man who liked to see himself as a mover and shaker (as he had been in Congress), it galled him to find himself a little superfluous. It galled him when the French greeted him as "le fameux Adams" only because they mistook him for his namesake and cousin Samuel. And it galled him that the French treated his colleague Franklin as something between a hero and a saint. Adams's vanity was his most conspicuous quality, and his uninhibited display of it in his diary, autobiography, and letters is almost as lovable as it is laughable. It was neither of those things when it led him into paranoid delusions of persecution and treachery by people whom he thought insufficiently appreciative of his merits and achievements.

As substitute for Deane in the tripartite commission, Adams stayed on in France, consumed with jealousy at the French adulation of Franklin, listening to Arthur Lee's poisonous diatribes, and trying to occupy himself by bringing more order to Franklin's easygoing way of running the legation. As Adams later remembered those days,

> I found that the Business of our Commission would never be done unless I did it. My two Colleagues would agree in nothing. The life of Dr. Franklin was a Scene of continual Discipation. I could never obtain the Favour of his Company in a Morning before Breakfast which would have been the most convenient time to read over the Letters and papers, deliberate on their contents, and decide upon the Substance of the Answers. It was late when he breakfasted, and as soon as Breakfast was over, a crowd of Carriages came to his Levee or if you like the term better to his Lodgings, with all sorts of People . . . but by far the greater part were Women and Children, come to have the honour to see the great Franklin. . . . I should have been happy to have done all the Business or rather all the Drudgery, if I could have been favoured with a few moments in a day to receive his Advice concerning the manner in which it ought to be done. But this condescention was not attainable.

Adams confided to his cousin Samuel (le fameux) Adams that the legation would be better off in the hands of a single man, and there was not much doubt about who he thought that man should be. He bided his time for almost a year, long enough for him and Vergennes to develop a mutual distrust. When news arrived in February 1779 that Congress had indeed placed relations with France in the hands of a single envoy and that Franklin was the man, Adams prepared to return to America, deeply mortified. His departure was delayed when the ship he was to sail on, *Alliance*, was commandeered for John Paul Jones's expedition with *Bonhomme Richard*. Adams was shifted to a less imposing vessel, *Sensible*, and he immediately saw Franklin's hand behind the move. From this point on, Franklin was transformed from an indolent libertine to a conniving enemy of Adams and of the sacred cause that Adams embodied. The change of vessels "was hit upon by Franklin and Chaumont [Franklin's suspiciously French landlord] to prevent me from going home, least I should tell some dangerous Truths." The purpose of the change to a smaller vessel, notoriously a slow sailer, was obviously to increase the chances of his capture by the British. "Does the old Conjuror dread my voice in Congress? He has some Reason for he has often heard it there, a Terror to evil doers."

When Adams finally reached home, unmolested by the British, he was kept busy for the next three months drafting a constitution for the state of Massachusetts. Before it was finished Congress found him another job, as minister to negotiate peace with England, and by February 1780 he was back in Paris. Since England was not yet ready to negotiate, Adams was again left with nothing constructive to do. What he did was to exchange a series of intemperate letters with Vergennes, setting the foreign minister straight about what policies France should and must pursue. Vergennes was so incensed that he presented the letters to Franklin with a request that he forward them to Congress so that the members might reconsider whether the author was appropriate for the mission assigned him. Franklin attempted to placate Vergennes by disavowing Adams's views. In sending them to Congress as requested, he tooks pains to state his confidence that Adams "means our Welfare and Interest as much as I," but he could not entirely hide his anger at the way Adams had meddled in the relationship with France that Franklin was entrusted with: "It is true that Mr. Adams's proper Business is elsewhere, but the Time not being come for that Business, and having nothing else here wherewith to employ himself, he seems to have endeavour'd supplying what he may suppose my Negociations defective in." The defect perceived by Adams lay in Franklin's whole approach to foreign relations: "He thinks as he tells me himself, that America has been too free in Expressions of Gratitude to France; for that she is more obliged to us than we to her, and that we should shew Spirit in our Applications." Franklin's own view, the premise of his conduct in France, was that "an Expression of Gratitude is not only our Duty but our Interest."

Fortunately for Franklin, in August Adams took himself off to the Netherlands, where he remained for more than two years. There he credited himself with securing Dutch recognition of American independence, through more bull-in-a-china-shop maneuvers that actually hindered it. Meanwhile, Congress pondered his exchange with Vergennes and the recommendations Vergennes had sent via the French minister in Philadelphia. On June 14, 1781, Congress transferred future peace negotiations from Adams to a commission composed of Franklin, Jefferson, Henry Laurens, John Jay—and again, John Adams. In instructing this group Congress carried Franklin's policy of gratitude a bit further than he would probably have gone: the commissioners were "to make the most candid and confidential Communications upon all subjects to the Ministers of our generous Ally the King of France; to undertake nothing in the Negotiations for Peace or Truce without their Knowledge and Concurrence; and ultimately to govern yourselves by their Advice and Opinion."

Open Negotiations

Of the commissioners appointed only Franklin was in Paris at the time. Jefferson declined the post. Henry Laurens was captured at sea on the way and never participated actively in the negotiations after his release. Jay was detained in Spain as American minister there until the end of June 1782. Adams remained in the Netherlands seeking a loan from Dutch bankers until late in October. Thus when the time for negotiations finally arrived with the resignation of the North ministry in England, on March 20, 1782, Franklin was the only commissioner on the scene and remained so until Jay arrived (and Jay was incapacitated by influenza during most of July).

It could be said that Franklin had been singlehandedly conducting negotiations for peace throughout the war. His friend David Hartley never stopped sending him proposals, unauthorized by anyone in power, for some kind of reconciliation. Franklin had answered all of them with an unconditional rejection of any peace that failed to recognize American independence of Britain and faithfulness to France. Other unofficial emissaries and inquiries, like that from Hutton, got the same answer. In April 1782, when the British government started sending its own secret agents to test the waters, Franklin made his answer official, but he knew that spelling out the details would be a long process.

In the early months of discussions, when Franklin was on his own, British politics was in a state of flux. The two principal contenders for direction of policy were the Earl of Shelburne and Charles James Fox. Both would have liked to detach the United States from France, more with a view to harming France than helping America. Fox favored recognizing American independence at the outset in order to concentrate offensive operations against France. Shelburne, on the other hand, clung to the hope of recovering the old colonial relationship, however diluted. Franklin paradoxically threw his weight toward dealing with Shelburne, who in any case won out as, in effect, the prime minister.

We can only guess at Franklin's reasons for favoring Shelburne, but his preference may have resulted from a familiarity with the cast of Shelburne's mind. He knew that Shelburne had a reputation for deviousness, but there had been nothing devious about his opposition to the measures that had alienated the colonies. He had openly hailed the First Continental Congress as a gathering of minds more distinguished than what he found in the Houses of Parliament, and he had remained in opposition throughout the war. Franklin knew him personally. During Franklin's years in England the two had often conferred together, even dined together. Shelburne was familiar with Franklin's old friends in the Club of Honest Whigs and became a patron of one of them, a close friend of Franklin's, Joseph

Priestley, who lived for several years in Shelburne's household as his librarian. Shelburne's brother, Thomas Fitzmaurice, belonged to another of Franklin's small social groups, called the "cribbage party."

Dealing with Shelburne would mean picking up an old relationship with a kindred spirit. The fact that Shelburne was reluctant to let the colonies go was actually a continuation of his pro-American position before and during the war. He had shared with Franklin the belief that the future of the empire lay in America. Hence his current belief, endorsed by Franklin, that the loss of America would cripple the empire—a prediction that actually proved to be wrong but one that both men implicitly believed. Franklin knew what to expect from Shelburne, whereas Fox was an unknown quantity. And perhaps Franklin's conviction of America's future greatness and Britain's future weakness without America made him less concerned about the details of any treaty than he might otherwise have been. American strength was a long-term reality. Any hard bargaining resulting in agreements that failed to regain American friendship would only redound to Britain's detriment. Since Shelburne seemed more likely than Fox to recognize that reality, he would probably be more susceptible than Fox to a generous and therefore lasting peace.

In any case, Franklin's way of dealing was to lay his cards on the table, and while he conducted negotiations on his own, he was able to do that. At the outset he exchanged cordial notes with Shelburne, who assured him that he wished "to retain the same Good Faith and Simplicity, which subsisted between us in Transactions of less Importance, when we were not at so great a distance." Franklin got on well with Richard Oswald, the principal envoy Shelburne sent to deal with him. He assured Shelburne that Oswald "will be Witness of my acting with all the Simplicity and Good Faith which you do me the honour to expect from me." As a measure of that good faith he opened his mind freely to Oswald about the desirability of restoring American goodwill toward England and of what would be needed to do it. He had been thinking about this for some time, as the letter to Hutton four years earlier suggests. He had drawn up a memorandum on the subject and discussed it freely with Oswald. First he suggested reparations for the houses and towns burned by the British and their Indian allies. "I do not know," he said, "that the Americans will insist on Reparation. Perhaps they may. But would it not be better for England to offer it?" And there was the matter of Canada. American frontier settlers were "generally the most disorderly of the People" and were likely to ignite continual quarrels along the Canadian border. It might be humiliating for England to give up Canada if America demanded it. Again, "Perhaps America will not Demand it," but "would it not have an excellent Effect if Britain should voluntarily offer to give up that Province . . . ?" Franklin then made a suggestion he later regretted, that Canadian lands could be sold to indemnify both the Americans who had lost their homes to British fire and the Tories whose estates had been confiscated. In later negotiations he continued to stress reparations for American losses but opposed any recompense to Tory loyalists. He had, however, opened his mind freely and even allowed Oswald to carry his memorandum on Canada and reparations back to Shelburne.

Franklin kept Vergennes, on the one hand, and John Adams, on the other, informed of his conversations and exchanges of letters. Unfortunately, Shelburne's forlorn hope of regaining the colonies prevented him from acting with the same openness.

He never gave Oswald a full statement of his own views and objectives or any formal authority to speak for him. In spite of a number of interviews, with Oswald ferrying back and forth between Paris and London, no firm agreement on anything had been decided by the time Jay arrived from Madrid on June 23. When Shelburne finally provided Oswald with a commission and instructions early in August, he made recognition of American independence a matter for inclusion in the treaty, rather than a matter of existing fact. Franklin was willing to go ahead on that basis. "I hope we shall agree and not be long about it," he told Oswald. But Jay flatly refused to continue negotiations without prior recognition of American independence. Although Jay in his mission to Spain had depended for virtually all his expenses on the funds the French gave Franklin, he had somehow imbibed the Arthur Lee–John Adams hostility to the hands that fed him. And Adams now chimed in from Holland, with his usual charges of French duplicity and Franklin's subservience to Vergennes.

Closed Negotiations

As Jay recovered from the flu, Franklin fell ill with kidney stones and left Jay to undertake a series of dangerous undercover maneuvers designed to extract better terms from the British by suggesting a willingness to desert the French. But by the time Franklin rejoined the negotiations and Adams arrived, on October 26, Shelburne had pacified Jay with a new commission to Oswald (September 21) that implicitly recognized American independence. By early November, Jay and Oswald had worked out details of a possible treaty that would set the western boundary of the United States at the Mississippi River and the southern boundary at the St. Mary's River (the 31st parallel). These were more generous terms than France, as Spain's ally, would have accepted if Jay had followed the commissioners' instructions to be guided by the French. But the boundaries were in full accord with what Franklin had told Jay two years earlier when Jay reported from Madrid that Spain was claiming control of the Mississippi as a condition for aiding the United States. "I would rather," Franklin then wrote, "agree with them to buy at a great Price the whole of their Right on the Mississippi than sell a Drop of its Waters. A Neighbour might as well ask me to sell my Street Door."

Franklin was willing now to let Jay and Adams carry on most of the huckstering negotiation with Shelburne and his succession of envoys. He gave only token objections to their proceeding without Vergennes (who was secretly sending his own envoys to Shelburne). Nor did he continue to press for the cession of Canada. It had required such hard bargaining to get agreement on the Mississippi that Canada was out of the question. The main points of contention came over fishing rights off the Canadian coast and British demands for return of confiscated loyalist lands. The diplomats worked out compromises over these by ambiguities of wording that would satisfy their constituents and their consciences. By the last day of November 1782, Franklin was ready to place his signature beside those of Jay, Adams, and Henry Laurens (who arrived at the last minute) to a provisional treaty, one that he could not have liked but hoped to improve before it became definitive. It was left to him to explain to Vergennes what he and his colleagues had done and to offer their apologies for overriding the instructions that required them to consult the French court.

Fortunately, while Vergennes offered a perfunctory protest against the Americans' independent negotiations, he was not seriously displeased with the results. For Adams and Jay any censure of their conduct by Vergennes would merely have been proof of French treachery; for Franklin, indeed for the United States, it would have been disastrous. While his colleagues were bargaining over fishing rights, he was occupied with keeping the United States afloat, and Vergennes was his only hope. Demands for payment of debts incurred by John Laurens and Gillon continued to pour in. From Philadelphia, Robert Morris as superintendant of finance and Robert Livingston as secretary of foreign affairs instructed him to brace the foreign minister for yet another loan. Morris told Franklin that "unless a considerable Sum of Money is obtained for us in Europe we are inevitably ruined and that too whether a Peace takes Place or not." Livingston thought it his "duty to confide to you that if the war is continued in this Country it must be in a great measure at the expence of France. If peace is made a loan will be absolutely necessary to discharge an Army that will not easily separate without pay."

Franklin, reflecting on the attitude of his colleagues and of Congress, wrote in some bitterness to Livingston, "Some among you seem to have established as Maxims, the Suppositions that France has Money enough for all her Occasions and all ours besides; and that if she does not supply us, it is owing to her Want of Will or to my Negligence." But once again Vergennes came through for Franklin. In February 1783, while both sides pondered the provisional treaty, Vergennes agreed to lend another 6 million livres.

Franklin's own thoughts on the treaty went back to his hopes that through it the United States might do something for the

American Commissioners of the Preliminary Peace Negotiations with Great Britain, 1783, unfinished painting by Benjamin West. Left to right: John Jay, John Adams,

Benjamin Franklin, Henry Laurens, and William Temple Franklin (secretary).

world as well as for itself. American privateers had been extraor-
dinarily successful in the war because they could make many
short cruises to prey on British West Indies shipping, whose cargoes were worth ten times the "bulky low-priced Articles" ex-
ported from North American ports. For Americans to propose
an international prohibition of privateering must therefore, as
he told Hartley, "appear in its true Light, as having Humanity
only for its Motive." Moreover, Franklin did not wish "to see a
New Barbary rising in America, and our long extended Coast
occupied by Piratical States." In proposing a prohibition of privateering along with one exempting farmers, fishermen, and
merchants from the ravages of war, Franklin admitted that "I
rather wish than expect that it will be adopted." He did succeed
in having an article expressing his wish included in congressional instructions to him and his colleagues for making commercial treaties with England and other European countries. But
nothing of the kind was added to the provisional treaty. The final
treaty, signed September 3, 1783, was substantially the same as
the provisional one. And after briefly encouraging initial negotiations for a commercial treaty, England rebuffed all proposals.

A Long Leavetaking

Franklin did not fret over the failures. He had long since ceased
to expect the British to do right. But as he struggled to keep up
the good relations with France on which the United States continued to depend, he found himself senselessly hampered yet
again by his most obstreperous colleague. Adams had been
agreeably surprised by Franklin's unhesitating support of American territorial claims and his heated resistance to British de-

mands for restoration of loyalist lands. But the ink was scarcely dry on the provisional treaty before Adams began to think how much better it would have been if left entirely to him. That it was not left to him was, of course, part of a larger plot by Franklin. He was soon writing home about how, if he had not been "opposed, obstructed, neglected and slighted," the war would have come to an end much sooner and on better terms. Franklin was at the bottom of it all: "As if he had been conscious of the Laziness, Inactivity and real Insignificance of his advanced Age, he has considered every American Minister, who has come to Europe, as his natural Enemy. He has been afraid that some one would serve his Country, acquire a Reputation, and begin to be thought of by Congress to replace him."

Hence "the Insinuations and Prejudices against me, and the shameless abandoned Attack upon me," namely, the addition of Franklin, Jay, and Laurens to his original commission to make peace. Confident of the support of Arthur Lee and his party, Adams sent his message not only to friends in Massachusetts but officially to Congress. James Madison reported drily to Jefferson, at the very time that Vergennes was rescuing the United States from bankruptcy (February 11, 1783), that "Congress yesterday received from Mr. Adams several letters dated September not remarkable for anything unless it be a display of his vanity, his prejudice against the French Court and his venom against Doctr. Franklin." Adams's venom spread widely in France as well as America, and Franklin did his best to counteract it. "I hear frequently," he told Henry Laurens in March 1783, "of his ravings against M. de Vergennes and me whom he suspects of plots against him which have no Existence, but in his own troubled Imaginations. I take no Notice, and we are civil when we meet."

By July 1783, however, Franklin became a little alarmed that Adams's ravings at home and abroad might have an effect on Vergennes's willingness to supply further funds. He gave Livingston a summary of Adams's delusions and added, "He makes no Secret of his having these Opinions, expresses them publickly, sometimes in the presence of the English Ministers; and speaks of hundreds of Instances which he could produce in Proof of them, none however have yet appear'd to me. . . . If I were not convinced of the real Inability of this Court to furnish the farther Supplys we asked, I should suspect these Discourses of a Person in his Station, might have influenced the Refusal."

Lest these discourses nevertheless affect future relations with France, Franklin felt obliged "to caution you respecting the Insinuations of this Gentleman against this Court, and the instances he supposes of their Ill-Will to us, which I take to be as imaginary as I know his Fancies to be, that Count de V. and myself are continually plotting against him." Franklin closed his letter with the fairest and most quoted assessment anyone ever made of the character of John Adams: "I am persuaded, however, that he means well for his Country, is always an honest Man, often a Wise One, but sometimes and in some things, absolutely out of his Senses."

In these months Franklin was linked to Adams in their ineffective commission to make commercial treaties, but Adams had in view an elevation from the clutches of "the old conjuror." He wrote Congress of the need for an envoy plenipotentiary to London and a description, that everyone recognized as autobiographical, of the experience required for the job. While he waited for the appointment he traveled around England and the Netherlands, finally settling in Auteuil, where he fretted over past dishonors and present neglect until the coveted appointment finally arrived.

Neglect was something Franklin would have relished. The French assigned him credit not only for the peace but for the very creation of the United States. He must be literally a plenipotentiary, able to do everything, and soon he was deluged with requests to do it. Since the United States had come from his hand, would he please bestow its favors on the suitors who suddenly appeared from all over France and its European neighbors? Patronage was what turned the wheels of government in Europe, and people assumed that Franklin could bestow all the blessings of government office in the New World with a wave of his hand. Thirty deserving lovers of America, from Lisbon to Lübeck, sought the honor of serving as United States consuls in their cities. Franklin's "protection" would place any aspiring young professional in office as engineer or architect "in one of your provinces, of your Continent." Lest the brave Americans did not know how to organize their new governments, self-proclaimed French savants were ready to show them. "It is amazing," Franklin observed, "the Number of Legislators that kindly bring me new Plans for governing the United States." Equally amazing was the number of highly skilled, highly successful entrepreneurs who were ready to abandon their highly valued enterprises all over Europe in order to favor the United States with their presence—provided their expenses were paid, their salaries guaranteed, and suitable building locations furnished. German glassmakers seem to have been particularly eager. One from Brunswick proposed to bring a hundred workers with him and required advance payment of a mere £8,000 to get started. Another from Bremen wanted only a proper plot of land and a monopoly of all glass production in America.

Franklin's patronage could surely not be limited to his provinces in his continent. His influence must obviously extend to the French government that had stood ready for so long to do his bidding. The treaty of amity and commerce with France in 1778 had provided that the king of France would name a number of ports to which Americans could freely bring the produce of the United States. Franklin was obviously the man to tell the king which ones to name, and until four were specified (Dunkirk, Lorient, Bayonne, and Marseilles) in 1784 the officials of every port in France prepared arguments for him to name theirs. Aspiring young men looked to him for a step up in the French bureaucracy. A young lawyer hoped for a place in the French foreign office: a word from Franklin, and Vergennes would surely grant it. A young painter would like a place in one of the royal academies of design: with Franklin's support it would surely be his.

The principal American minister must himself be wealthy, and his generosity could relieve the misfortunes of the needy: an abbess needed his resources to rescue her convent from bankruptcy; a gentlewoman of Nantes whose son had run her into debt that she dared not disclose to her husband begged £12,000 to relieve her of the most cruel embarrassment. And so on and on. Franklin could not even answer most of these letters, as subsequent ones complaining of his silence attest. What bothered him most were the proposals from people "who value themselves and expect to be valued by us for their Birth or quality, tho' I tell them those Things bear no Price in our Markets." To save himself from explaining the facts of American life over and over to prospective emigrants, he wrote and printed one of his best short essays, *Information to Those Who Would Remove to America*. In it he described the disappointment awaiting people of high reputation in Europe who hoped to transport it to a country "where people do not inquire concerning a Stranger, *What is he?* but *What can he do?*" For those seeking government office, he offered what was as much his own wish as a description: "Of civil Offices, or Employments, there are few; no superfluous Ones as in Europe; and it is a Rule establish'd in some of the States, that no Office should be so profitable as to make it desirable."

The whole pamphlet was a mixture of description and prescription, of hard facts and of arguments for the policies of free trade and minimum government that Franklin favored. He drafted it at a time when he was torn between his fondness for the French and his homesickness for the totally different society he had grown up in. Temple had grown perhaps a little too French, a favorite young dandy of the Passy community. Benny Bache, who had returned there in the summer of 1783, was having the time of his life, swimming in the Seine, flying kites, and as excited by Montgolfier's balloons as his grandfather was. But he needed to experience the wholesome facts of American life. With the peace treaty concluded Franklin had repeatedly asked Congress to relieve him of office, though at the same time had started looking for a house in Versailles. "The French are an amiable People to live with," he wrote to a friend. "They love me, and I love them. Yet I do not feel my self at home, and I wish to die in my own Country." His career in France as official American beggar had made him only too familiar with things that were wrong in America, but he stopped looking for the house in Versailles. When he finally received word in May 1785 that Congress no longer required his services, he was ready to go home.

IO Going Home

Saying goodbye to France after eight years was not easy. Franklin was leaving, as he confessed to Madame Helvétius, the country he loved most in all the world. It was simply not *his* country, much as his friends there beseeched him to make it so. He made his last visit to Madame Brillon as his equipage was preparing. She could not bear to come out with the rest of Passy three days later to see him lifted aboard the queen's litter between the two large, surefooted mules who carried it. His closest neighbor, Louis Guillaume Veillard, refused to lose a minute of the great man's precious company and followed in a carriage to the port of embarkation, Le Havre. Benny Bache and Temple climbed in with Veillard. It was late afternoon, on July 12, 1785, when the procession finally got under way, leaving behind what Benny called "a very great concourse of people," standing in awesome silence, "only interrupted by sobs."

It took six days at the mules' slow pace to reach Le Havre,

with rests along the way at the homes of friends and admirers, where local notables flocked to pay court. At Le Havre they were joined by Houdon, the famous sculptor, who had already done his bust of Franklin and would accompany him to America to do Washington's. The Atlantic crossing was booked on a 400-ton vessel waiting in London, but first they all had to cross the Channel in a small boat to Southampton (Franklin alone escaped seasickness). There the Shipley family journeyed from Twyford to make their last goodbyes. Son William also appeared and took the opportunity to transfer to his son, William Temple, the title to lands he had left in New Jersey. Franklin recorded the event without comment. The ship from London arrived on July 27. The company boarded her, and Franklin invited the Shipleys to dine with him and the captain that evening. The next morning, July 28, he awoke to find his guests departed and the ship already under sail in a fair wind. On September 13 he landed at Market Street Wharf in Philadelphia.

Familiar Pursuits

As he took in the familiar sights, he knew that at age seventy-nine he could not have many years left to enjoy them, but he began in a good mood. His afflictions had diminished a little during the voyage, and the usual cheering crowd that lined the wharf lifted his spirits. Pennsylvanians at the time were bitterly divided in a contest to reconsider the state constitution that Franklin had helped write in 1776. But there was no contest over Benjamin Franklin. Both parties in the legislature joined in rare unanimity to make him president of the state. And they repeated the vote the next year and the year after that. Three years was the limit set

Madame Helvétius, date unknown

by his constitution, or he would probably have been chosen again.

It was not a burdensome office: the president had no veto power, so most of the work consisted of signing his name to documents that others presented to him. Despite his proprietary interest in the state constitution, he kept out of the party squabbles over it. Nor did he give much attention to the dangerous weakness of the national government or the divisions within it that had made life so difficult for him in France. He directed his interest in national affairs to letters disabusing his friends in England and France of the notion spread by the English press that Americans might be regretting their Revolution. Americans, he assured them, had never been so prosperous or so content.

It was a time when not all his countrymen were quite that confident. Many of his friends were already planning the great federal Constitutional Convention of 1787 in Philadelphia. Franklin would himself attend that convention faithfully, five hours a day for four months. If George Washington had not been there, he would have had to preside over it. But he took no part in the movement to bring it about and did not contribute significantly to the final result. For the most part, except during meetings he was content to do the routine work required of a president of Pennsylvania and to occupy himself with the homely jobs that went with being at home.

In the first couple of years he spent much of his time supervising the building of a sixteen-by-thirty-foot addition to his house, which gave him a spacious dining room of that size and a library of the same size above it, large enough, he calculated, for forty thousand volumes. With his usual ingenuity he devised a contraption for taking down and putting back books on shelves above an arm's reach. With the addition finished, he had three old buildings on his land pulled down and replaced with two new ones (24 by 45 feet). They would provide him rental income. He did not feel strong enough to wrestle with a printing press again, but Benny Bache had already started to learn the trade in France, and Franklin now built and furnished a printing house for him. Polly Hewson, barred from his company for so many years by the war, crossed the ocean to join him, and he found a house for her nearby. He enjoyed having his daughter, Sarah Franklin Bache, and her children at hand to play with. He enjoyed talking with friends about the scientific and "philosophical" questions that had always occupied him. The American Philosophical Society, an offshoot of the Junto, had been formally incorporated by the state in his absence and had made an annual ritual of electing him president. Now the members honored him by meeting in the new dining room of his house, and he honored his learned friends in France and England by having them elected as corresponding members, his own designation in practically every other learned society in the world.

At successive meetings of the society Franklin furnished the members with three lengthy papers he had written during his weeks at sea: one on the design of a smokeless stove, another on nine different causes and cures of smoking chimneys. The third, which we have already noticed, was his remarkable discussion of ways to improve the design of ships and their rigging, along with his observations on the course of the Gulf Stream, a piece of writing that deserves a place alongside Leonardo da Vinci's designs for aircraft. His intellectual curiosity and imagination had not diminished with age. He worked with Noah Webster to devise a more phonetic spelling of the English language, a project

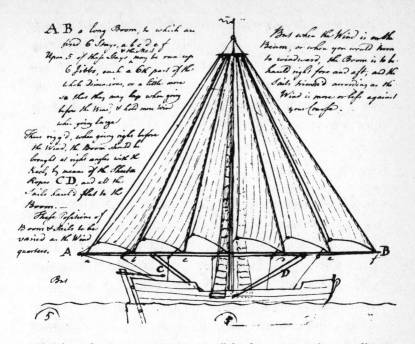

Franklin's letter showing a new way to rig a small ship for greater aerodynamic efficiency, one of Franklin's designs for improving the efficiency of navigation (detail)

he had begun long before. He gave Robert Fulton advice about designing and adapting a steam engine for ships. At the request of his friend and English publisher Benjamin Vaughan, he wrote out a proof of what he had once casually mentioned in conversation: his conclusion that lead was poisonous. After detailing his own and other printers' ailments from the continuous handling of lead type, he went on to describe his observations of the grass and plants that died from the fumes near furnaces where lead was smelted, of the effects of drinking rainwater that sluiced off lead roofs, and of his queries to sickened plumbers, painters, and glaziers in a Paris hospital. His observations of the toxic effects of lead, he noted, were nothing new; and he remarked wryly, "how long a useful Truth may be known, and exist, before it is generally receiv'd and practis'd on." Indeed it was almost another two centuries before this useful truth was generally received and practiced on.

The Responsibilities of Usefulness

In sickness and in health Franklin could never stop thinking and could never stop writing about what he thought. A bad fall down some steps in his garden in January 1788, accompanied by a fierce renewal of gout and kidney stones, kept him in pain that he could relieve only by doses of laudanum. But when he could not hold a pen, Benny would take down his thoughts for him. Although he tried to stay out of public disputes, he had earned a reputation at home and abroad that carried responsibilities he could not evade. He had become convinced that slavery was morally wrong, so when his Quaker friends started a Pennsylvania antislavery society, he was the inevitable president of it. He knew better than most Americans how badly the country needed a more effective national government. No one else except George Washington had had such direct personal experience of the existing government's incapacity. When his countrymen gathered to make improvements, he could not conscientiously stay away. He would not have much to say and neither would Washington, but they both had to *be* there. Nor could either of them withhold his approval of the result, if the new government was to win acceptance.

In his highly publicized speech closing the Constitutional

Convention, Franklin drew on the lifelong belief that had guided his political career. The success of any government, he reminded his colleagues, rests "on the general Opinion of the Goodness of that Government as well as of the Wisdom and Integrity of its Governors." Public reception of the new Constitution both at home and abroad likewise would depend on how well people thought of its makers, and the whole world thought better of him and Washington than of any other Americans. If he needed reminding, people from all over the world kept telling him. In England, Erasmus Darwin (grandfather of Charles) called him "the greatest Statesman of the present, or perhaps of any century." In Prague, François Steinsky, professor of natural philosophy at the university there, hailed him as the Solon, the Socrates, and the Seneca of that day. From France he heard that he was the first man of the universe, and that his name and Washington's would guarantee not only acceptance of the Constitution but the wisdom of its provisions.

Whether such accolades were deserved mattered less than their existence. Public opinion was what mattered in politics, and to the last Franklin was driven to use his talents and his reputation to affect public opinion. It was what political writers wrote for and printers printed for. And yet, as we try to assess the man at the end of his extraordinary life, we have to ask how much his own opinions actually did affect public opinion. His reputation, the good opinion of him throughout the world, undoubtedly helped to secure American independence and the new national government. Those were two steps toward the fulfillment of his vision of America as the scene of the world's greatest society. But as we have come to know the man, can we say that they were the steps he would have taken if he could have had his way? We have been watching what he did in the long years he spent in England and then France; and we have seen his effectiveness in getting things done. They were things he obviously wanted done, things that he did in the service of his different publics: Pennsylvanian, British American, and American. They tell us much about what public service meant to him. But we have noticed that there is generally more to Franklin than meets the eye. Before we leave him, it will be worth taking a glimpse—and a glimpse is all he allows us—at what he would personally have preferred for the publics whose bidding he served.

Franklin made it a matter of principle not to argue much for his own way. He consistently declined to answer challenges to his scientific views. After explaining his ideas, he left them to make their own way. A personal aversion to controversy may have reinforced this self-denial, but the aversion did not operate when he was engaged in a public cause, speaking not for himself but for the public he served. His career in England was one long controversy, in which he became in British eyes the embodiment of a supposed American public yearning for independence. It was a mistaken identity. The public Franklin tried to serve in the controversy was not American but British American. His objective was not to attain American independence but to prevent it, and he would have prevented it if his opponents had listened to him. Only when they failed to see that their own future lay in America did Franklin turn his energies to independence as the only way left to release America's capacity for greatness. He ceased serving a British-American public when it became clear that such a public did not exist. If it ever existed, the British part of it had opted out. The British had, in effect, declared their independence before the Americans did. Required to choose between what had become two different publics, he chose the American one. But in this and in all public controversies he engaged in, he spoke more for others than for himself. He made their cause his cause, became their instrument to achieve what they wanted to achieve, but not necessarily what he would have desired. His self-denial in scientific controversy is echoed by a more complex deference to public opinion in political controversy.

The complexity will be apparent if we consider more closely his role in the quarrel over Parliamentary taxation of the colonies. Franklin's first reaction to British taxation was to make the best of what he believed to be a Parliamentary mistake. When Americans demonstrated violently against what they believed to be a violation of their rights, he recognized the need for England and for himself to cater to that belief. But it was not a belief that he could share as long as the public he served was British American. If there was a British-American public, it had the right to levy taxes on the property of British Americans. In Franklin's view property was not a natural right. In a paper written a few months before his death, he argued that property is a "Creature of Society and is subject to the Calls of that Society whenever its Necessities shall require it, even to its last Farthing."

Was this a new view for him? Far from it. As early as 1750 we have seen him stating his conviction "that what we have above what we can use, is not properly *ours,* tho' we possess it." In 1776, presiding over the convention that drafted the Pennsylvania constitution, he gave his approval to a Declaration of Rights that did include a natural right to acquire, possess, and protect property; but he also approved a provision that the convention later dropped: "That an enormous Proportion of Property vested in a few Individuals is dangerous to the Rights, and destructive of the Common Happiness, of Mankind; and therefore every free State hath a Right by its Laws to discourage the Possession of such Property."

In 1785 he wrote Benjamin Vaughan in the same vein that "Superfluous Property is the Creature of Society." Before society came into existence, he explained, a savage could protect his own bow, hatchet, and coat of skins by himself. But when societies were formed they passed laws, and when "by virtue of the first Laws Part of the Society accumulated Wealth and grew Powerful, they enacted others more severe, and would protect their Property at the Expence of Humanity. This was abusing their Powers, and commencing a Tyranny." It would not have been an abuse of power, Franklin thought, if the Continental Congress had taken American property in taxes precisely because, he told the superintendent of finance in 1783, property is "the Creature of publick Convention." The public in this case was American, and Congress as its representative had the power to dispose of what it created "and even of limiting the Quantity and the Uses of it."

In 1764 the public that Franklin believed himself to be serving was British American and might thus be entitled to dispose of British-American property. It was a mistake for the British Parliament to devise taxes for a part of the people whose circumstances and capacities it could not understand. But Franklin did not at first think of its attempt to do so as more than a failure of judgment in need of correcting. It became a violation of rights by virtue of American opinion that it was. In his view, expressed again and again, public opinion was something no government could afford to ignore. By the same token, no servant of the public could afford to place personal opinion ahead of public opinion. Franklin thus became an advocate of American natural rights in deference to American opinion and in the default of British deference to it, a default that split the British-American public into two separate publics.

Franklin spent ten years arguing for a natural right that existed in American opinion but not quite in his own. He then spent eight years in charming the French into helping the Americans fight a war against the British, even though he believed that war was not a cost-effective way of settling differences. He told the British more than once that they could gain more from Americans by not taxing them and would lose heavily by fighting them. The objectives of war over territory, he often observed, could be achieved at a great savings by cash purchase, however high the price. When the war began, his first scheme for ending it in 1776 included the purchase from Britain of Canada, Florida, Bermuda, and the Bahamas. His confidence in American growth and strength assured him that it would be cost-effective to buy Britain out. If the United States were to pay, say, £100,000 a year for a hundred years, the amount would enable Britain to pay off its national debt instead of increasing it by an unwinnable war. The cost to Americans would be less than the cost of fighting for the territory. The independent United States, he thought, would eventually have to take that territory, one way or another, and purchase would be the easiest for everybody: "It is worth our while to offer such a sum for the countries to be ceded, since the vacant lands will in time sell for a great part of what we shall give, if not more; and if we are to obtain them by conquest, after perhaps a long war, they will probably cost us more than that sum. It is absolutely necessary for us to have them for our own security, and though the sum may seem large to the present generation, in less than half the term, it will be to the whole United States, a mere trifle."

Neither side was ready to consider so rational a proposal in 1776, and there is no record that either side ever did. With the United States under attack, Franklin was ready to serve his country in whatever way it chose to use him. The way it chose was to send him to France for help. Without hesitation he put his experience, his personal warmth, and his worldwide reputation at America's service, and he succeeded, despite the obstacles Congress unwittingly placed in his way. But again the result was not quite what he would himself have preferred. With his confidence in American strength and American growth, he would rather have had his countrymen go it alone. It might take time, but in the long run, he was sure, British armies could never achieve British dominion or ever restore a British-American public. He was grateful to France and eager to show his gratitude. But France was not the public he served and to which in the end he must return. He would have preferred to have his public do their own fighting with their own resources.

Europeans were quick to credit him with American independence and with the republican form of government they found in the state constitutions. While in France, Franklin had had all the constitutions translated into French, the lingua franca of the time, and distributed throughout Europe. When he returned to an independent America and served in the Convention of 1787, it was reasonable to attribute both its success and its provisions to him. But the government created by the Constitution contained none of the provisions that he would particularly have favored. If he had had his way, the national government would have resembled the one that he helped to make for Pennsylvania in 1776.

It would have had no senate and a plural executive or a president without veto power and without salary.

The last point was a major one for Franklin, the subject of his most extensive speech at the convention. As early as the Albany Congress of 1754 his plan of colonial union provided that representatives in the "Grand Council" should not be given "*too great* wages, lest unsuitable persons should be tempted to cabal for the employment for the sake of gain." His subsequent experiences in England convinced him that the high salaries attached to public office had corrupted the government and divided it from the public it was supposed to serve. It was his conviction, expressed in a codicil to his will in 1789, "that in a democratical state there ought to be no offices of profit, for the reasons I had given in an article of my drawing in our [state] constitution." The article was number 36, the only one which we know with certainty to have come from his hand, and it summed up much of Franklin's political philosophy:

> As every freeman to preserve his independence (if without a sufficient estate) ought to have some profession, calling, trade or farm, whereby he may honestly subsist, there can be no necessity for, nor use in establishing offices of profit, the usual effects of which are dependence and servility unbecoming freemen, in the possessors and expectants; faction, contention, corruption, and disorder among the people. But if any man is called into public service, to the prejudice of his private affairs, he has a right to a reasonable compensation: And whenever an office, through increase of fees or otherwise, becomes so profitable as to occasion many to apply for it, the profits ought to be lessened by the Legislature.

The convention had listened politely to Franklin's plea for a similar provision in the federal Constitution, treating his proposal, as James Madison reported, "with great respect, but rather for the author of it, than from any apparent conviction of its expediency or practicability." It was actually Franklin who deferred to the convention, not the convention to him. His proposal was never seriously considered. Franklin's friends in France who knew something of his political beliefs were disappointed that he had not prevailed to prevent the creation of an "upper" house in the national legislature, seemingly designed for aristocrats, that he had endorsed a presidency endowed with monarchical powers and that he had agreed to a protection of the slave trade until 1808. Franklin wrote to his friends apologies for these and other deficiencies. But the truth was that the man whom they credited with bringing the United States into being had very little influence on the form his supposed creation took. He rejoiced when the new government began operating. It was better than its predecessor under the Articles of Confederation. But he lost no time in joining others in a petition to change it by including a right that he did believe to be natural and which it failed to recognize: the right to freedom it denied to slaves. When the petition was rejected, he wrote one of his most biting satirical hoaxes, the purported speech of one Sidi Mehemet Ibrahim, mocking the southern defense of slavery as identical with an Islamic defense of enslaving Christians. Even as he wrote, Pennsylvanians were considering a new constitution to replace the one which he had valued. The new constitution provided for an upper house in the legislature and a governor with veto powers. It omitted Franklin's favorite provision about salaries.

Franklin lay dying as the people of Pennsylvania considered their new constitution. In the preceding months he had written a defense of the more democratic provisions of the old one, but it had had no effect, and he probably did not expect it to. Franklin had a more profound belief than most of his contemporaries in the ability of people to govern themselves. He had his own views of how they could best do it. What distinguished him was his willingness to submit his views to theirs. He had told his mother in 1750 that when his life was over, he would like to have it said that "he lived usefully." Being useful to the public might mean persuading people to do what he considered good for them, but it did not mean placing what he considered good above what they did. Being useful meant doing what they wanted, not what he wanted.

Franklin certainly had a private life, and the parts of it he allows us to see are full of fun, full of the personal magnetism that makes us long to sit down with him and talk about the exciting things he could always see in the world around him. His scientific discoveries were part of his private life. They might prove incidentally to be useful to mankind, as in his work with electricity and with stoves and chimneys. But the usefulness that he deliberately placed above the experiments he enjoyed so much was a usefulness that suppressed private enjoyment in favor of public service. As private property was to give way before public need, so with private preference before public policy. We are reminded again of Jefferson's view that Franklin's genius as a scientist dictated an exemption from public service. Franklin rejected not only that entitlement but any priority for his own views over those of the people he served.

In the mass of papers he left behind, Franklin has offered us the challenge to understand a man who could do that, a man who made it a maxim to "let all men know thee, but no man know thee thoroughly." Through his papers we can perhaps know him more thoroughly and comprehensively than his contemporaries could. Those who encountered him in public—in the Pennsylvania Assembly, in the Continental Congress, in the Constitutional Convention—frequently remarked on his silence. Even in private, at ease among friends he loved, he was more of a listener than a talker. He spoke to friends and enemies alike as he speaks to us, in writing. And we have more of what he wrote and of what was written to him than anyone at the time could have had.

We can know what many of his contemporaries came to recognize, that he did as much as any man ever has to shape the world he and they lived in. We can also know what they must have known, that the world was not quite what he would have liked to make it. But we may also discover a man hidden behind the affability and wit that entranced those who enjoyed his presence. We may discover a man with a wisdom about himself that comes only to the great of heart. Franklin knew how to value himself and what he did without mistaking himself for something more than one man among many. His special brand of self-respect required him to honor his fellow men and women no less than himself. His way of serving a superior God was to serve them. He did it with a recognition of their human strengths and weaknesses as well as his own, in a spirit that another wise man in another century has called "the spirit which is not too sure it is right." It is a spirit that weakens the weak but strengthens the strong. It gave Franklin the strength to do what he incredibly did, as a scientist, a statesman, and a man.

Chronology

1748	forms printing partnership with David Hall and re-tires from business
1748–50	experiments with lightning
1751	elected to Pennsylvania Assembly
1753	appointed joint deputy postmaster general of North America
1754	attends Albany Congress
1757	sails to London as agent of Pennsylvania Assembly
1762	returns to Philadelphia
1764	sails to London with petition for royal government
1765	opposes Stamp Act
1766	supports repeal of Stamp Act in examination by the British House of Commons
1772	sends Hutchinson-Oliver letters to Massachusetts
1774	denounced by Alexander Wedderburn and dismissed from Post Office, January 31; negotiates with Lord Howe against parliamentary measures; Deborah Franklin dies in Philadelphia, December 19
1775	returns to Philadelphia; elected to Second Continental Congress
1776	goes to Canada and returns; helps write Declaration of Independence; sails to France, October 27, arrives December 3
1778	signs treaties with France, February 6
1782	helps negotiate peace with England
1785	returns to Philadelphia
1787	attends Constitutional Convention
1790	petitions against slavery; dies April 17

Some of the People in Franklin's Life

Adams, John (1735–1826) Second president of the United
States; Franklin's colleague in negotiations with France and
England

Allen, William (1704–1780) Philadelphia merchant and chief
justice of Pennsylvania; a loyalist in the Revolution

Bache, Benjamin Franklin (1769–1798), "Benny" Franklin's
grandson, who accompanied him to France and was sent to
school in Geneva; later published anti-Federalist newspaper,
the *Aurora*

Bache, Richard (1737–1811) Merchant, married Franklin's
daughter, Sarah, in 1767

Bache, Sarah Franklin (1743–1808) Franklin's daughter,
mother of Benny

Barclay, David (1729–1809) English Quaker merchant and
banker, Fothergill's partner in negotiations with Franklin in
1774

Bartram, John (1699–1777) Philadelphia Quaker and distinguished self-taught botanist and plant collector

Bernard, Francis (1712–1779) Royal Governor of Massachusetts, 1760–69

Brillon de Jouy, Anne-Louise Boivin d'Hardancourt (dates unknown) Known to Franklin as Madame Brillon, his neighbor and close friend at Passy

Chaumont, Jacques-Donatien Le Ray de (1725–1803) Franklin's landlord at Passy

Colden, Cadwallader (1688–1776) Scientist and Lieutenant Governor of New York

Collinson, Peter (1694–1768) London Quaker merchant and scientist

Cushing, Thomas (1725–1788) Speaker of Massachusetts House of Representatives, 1766–74

Dartmouth, William Legge, Earl of (1731–1801) Secretary of state for the colonies, 1772–75

Deane, Silas (1737–1789) Wethersfield, Connecticut, merchant and lawyer; Franklin's associate in mission to France; replaced by John Adams in 1778

Dickinson, John (1732–1808) Pennsylvania and Delaware lawyer and statesman, principal author of the Articles of Confederation of 1781

Dumas, Charles-Guillaume-Frédéric (1721–1796) Franklin's source of European news from Leyden and The Hague

Eliot, Jared (1685–1763) Minister at Killingsworth, Connecticut, and agricultural experimenter

Fothergill, John (1712–1780) Quaker physician and scientist in London; attempted negotiation with Franklin on American affairs in 1774

Franklin, Deborah Read (1704?–1774) Wife, and mother of Franklin's two legitimate children

Franklin, James (1697–1735) Brother

Franklin, Josiah (1657–1745) Father

Franklin, William (1730–1813) Son (mother unknown)

Franklin, William Temple (1762–1823) Grandson, son of William

Galloway, Joseph (1731–1803) Philadelphia lawyer; ally of Franklin's in Pennsylvania Assembly; loyalist in the Revolution

Gillon, Alexander (1741–1794) Agent of South Carolina and pest

Greene, Catherine Ray (1731–1794) Life-long friend, wife of governor of Rhode Island

Hall, David (1714–1772) Business partner

Hartley, David (1732–1813) English friend who attempted negotiations for peace with Franklin, 1774–82

Hemphill, Samuel (dates unknown) Heretical Presbyterian minister defended by Franklin, 1735

Helvétius, Anne-Catherine de Ligniville (1719–?) Entertained Franklin regularly at her salon in Auteuil

Hillsborough, Wills Hill, Lord (1718–1793) Secretary of state for the colonies, 1768–72

Howe, Lord Richard (1726–1799) Attempted negotiation with Franklin 1775

Hutchinson, Thomas (1711–1780) Royal governor of Massachusetts, 1771–74

Ingenhousz, Jan (1730–1799) Physician to the Austrian emperor who corresponded with Franklin about electricity from 1773 to 1788

Izard, Ralph (1742–1804) South Carolina planter; appointed United States envoy to Tuscany in 1777 but remained in France until recalled in 1779

Jackson, Richard (?–1787) English lawyer and member of Parliament, close friend

Jackson, William (1759–1828) Secretary to John Laurens, later secretary to Constitutional Convention

Jay, John (1745–1829) Minister to Spain, 1779–82, peace commissioner, 1782–83, secretary of foreign affairs, 1784–90, chief justice of U.S. Supreme Court, 1790–95

Jones, John Paul (1747–1792) Naval officer; commander of *Bonhomme Richard*

Kames, Henry Home, Lord (1696–1782) Scots jurist and scholar

Landais, Pierre (1731–1820) French-born United States naval officer given command of *Alliance* in 1778

Laurens, Henry (1724–1792) Member of the peace commission but captured by the British

Laurens, John (1754–1782) Sent by Congress to seek French loan, 1780–81

Lee, Arthur (1740–1792) Commissioner with Silas Deane and Franklin to seek French aid; denounced both in Congress

Livingston, Robert R. (1746–1813) Secretary of foreign affairs, 1781–83

Logan, James (1674–1751) Secretary to William Penn; scientist, scholar, and book collector

Mecom, Jane Franklin (1712–1794) Sister, married Edward Mecom, 1727

Morris, Robert (1734–1806) Superintendent of finance, 1781–84

Oswald, Richard (1705–1784) English negotiator of peace treaty, 1782

Penn, John (1729–1785) Grandson of William Penn, Lieutenant Governor of Pennsylvania, 1763–71

Penn, Thomas (1702–1775) Son of William Penn, proprietor of Pennsylvania

Pitt, William, Earl of Chatham (1708–1778) Statesman who led British to victory in the Seven Years' War, 1756–63

Price, Richard (1723–1791) Dissenting clergyman and supporter of American cause in England, close friend

Priestley, Joseph (1733–1804) Theologian and scientist, close friend

Pringle, Sir John (1707–1782) Eminent physician, close friend, traveled with Franklin

Shelburne, Earl of (1737–1805) Friend in England and peace negotiator

Shipley, Jonathan (1714–1788) Bishop of St. Asaph, supported American cause, close friend

Stevenson, Margaret (1706–1783) Franklin's landlady and friend at 7 Craven Street

Stevenson, Mary (Polly) (1739–1794) Lifelong friend; married William Hewson, and as a widow moved to Philadelphia to be near Franklin

Strahan, William (1715–1785) London printer and close friend, but opposed American Revolution

Vaughan, Benjamin (1751–1835) Friend and editor of Franklin's writings

Vergennes, Comte de (1717–1787) French foreign minister

Wedderburn, Alexander (1733–1805) Solicitor general of England, 1771–78, denounced Franklin, January 29, 1774

Notes

Citations to documents written before March 15, 1782, are to the first thirty-six volumes of *The Papers of Benjamin Franklin*, ed. Leonard W. Labaree et al. (New Haven, 1959–2001), already in print as this book goes to press. Citations to documents written after March 15, 1782, are identified by date and can be found that way in future published volumes, in the manuscripts and copies on file in the Yale University Library, and in present or forthcoming electronic publications of them. Citations to the *Autobiography* are given by part number and apply to any published edition.

Page

ix "He missed 'the Happiness of knowing'": July 27, 1783

2 "It was probably no accident": *Autobiography*, pt. 1

4 "There was not yet a germ theory": 20:314; *Diary and Autobiography of John Adams*, ed. L. H. Butterfield et al. (Cambridge, Mass., 1961), 3:418–19.

5 "Examining them he finds": 1:93–94

6 "As the ship rocked": 10:158–60

6 "He could not drink": Dec. 31, 1782

7 "At age sixty-seven": 20:30, 463–74

7 "A Nantucket whaler": 10:94; 15:246; 22:17

7 "When he was seventy-eight": Feb. 1784

8   "We get a hint": 3:92

10   "On the evening of October 21": 3:463

10   "It soon became clear": 3:463

11   "Waterspouts": 4:358, 369, 376, 429; 9:308

11   "He tried various ways": 2:419–46; 8:455; Aug. 28, 1785

12   "In November 1749": 5:521

13   "In a volume published in London": *Experiments and Observations on Electricity* (London, 1751); *Expériences et Observations sur l'Electricité* (Paris, 1752)

13   "If a spark": 4:19

13   "French scientists": 4:367–69

14   "He later planned": 19:152–56, 424–30

14   "When another scientist": 19:424–30; 20:129–30

18   "Full of the confidence of youth": *A Dissertation on Liberty and Necessity*, 1:57–71

18   "After that admission": *Autobiography*, pt. 1 (cf. 3:88–89)

19   "His new view": *Autobiography*, pt. 1

21   "Where his Boston preachers": 2:30

21   "He ridiculed the idea": 2:114

21   "People who were brought up to do right": 2:54

25   "But Franklin had never thought of industry": 2:369

25   "Franklin was struck": 3:479

25   "Poor Richard phrased the thought for him": 2:165; 4:95

25   "And in a letter": 3:479

26   "He stated his priorities": 4:67

27   "Jefferson was fully cognizant": *The Papers of Thomas Jefferson*, ed. Julian P. Boyd et al. (Princeton, N.J., 1950–), 2:202–3

27   "Philadelphians wanted him to represent them": 3:318

28   "After his earliest electrical experiments": 3:364

28   "It was apparently a matter of principle": *Autobiography*, pt. 3

29   "In the same year he wrote his mother": 3:475

29   "'Talents and Will'": 4:254

29   "In a letter to Jared Eliot": 4:192–95

30   "Try reading Franklin's account": 18:199–202

30   "One biographer recognized": Carl Becker, "Benjamin Franklin," *The Concise Dictionary of American Biography* (New York, 1964), 313

33   "Its advice about how to behave": 3:452; 7:74; 2:370; 2:8

34   "Reputation": 1:312; 3: 6, 259; 2:252

34   "It did not follow": 3:259; 2:8, 369; 3:106, 260

87   "As Franklin told Cadwallader Colden": 5:427
87–88   "Franklin admitted to Shirley": 5:443–44
88   "On December 4": 5:444–45
88–89   "Franklin welcomed the idea": 5:449–450
89   "As he remembered it": *Autobiography*, pt. 1
90–91   "What had happened to his Albany Plan": A. G. Olson, "The British Government and Colonial Union, 1754," *William and Mary Quarterly* 17 (1960): 22–34.
94   "The wheels of government": 5:443
94   "Remember the question": 1:263
100   "In May 1755": 6:49, 163
101   "The Assembly, he said": 6:135
101   "Whatever privileges King Charles": 6:199
101   "What Franklin had stated": 6:154
101   "'To dispose of their own money'": 6:517–18
101   "Therefore 'neither the Proprietaries": 7:108
103   "The grant had empowered": 6:134
105–6   "The other members": 7:274; 9:174
106   "Deborah asked": 7:380
106   "In 1758 they traveled": 8:153
107   "They could never displace": 7:364
110   "'Can any man'": 6:216
110   "Franklin had introduced himself": 2:383
111   "'I never,' he wrote": 7:295–98
111–12   "But Strahan evidently showed": 8:92
112   "As Strahan had told Deborah": 7:297
114   "The king, he informed Franklin": *Autobiography*, pt. 4
115   "On the basis of it": 8:179–84
115   "In response to this slap": 8:232
115   "The only catch": 8:157
115–16   "Norris, a good friend": 8:101–2
116   "Jackson knew what his friend wanted": 8:21, 25–26
117   "In answer to Norris's query": 8:157
117   "In any case": 8:228
117   "In offering to resign": 8:236
118   "Jackson had added": 8:26
118   "It was they": 7:256
118–19   "Meanwhile, Franklin had secured": 7:374
122–23   "Franklin's thoughts on population": 9:6–7

165   "In a newspaper article": 14:114

165   "Franklin, rather than eliminating misunderstanding": 14:114

165–66   "The Townshend Acts": 14:228–32

166   "As he explained to his son William": 15:76

166–67   "To prevent a tax": 14:230

167   "The first rash proceedings": *A Report of the Record Commissioners . . . Boston Town Records, 1758 to 1769* (Boston, 1886), 220–30

167–68   "When news of the Boston nonimportation resolutions": 14:323; 15:52; 14:350–51; 15:52

168–69   "Franklin's first public response": 15:3–13

169   "Writing as an Englishman": 15:191–93

170   "In meetings": 16:11–12

170–71   "By the end of January": 16:31

171   "His next letter": 16:64

171   "Opening a correspondence": 16:52

171   "It would not": 16:245

172   "The members, Franklin believed": 17:111

172   "Even his son": 16:36

172   "If any of the merchants": 17:109

172   "To Charles Thomson": 17:113

172–73   "He sent the same message": 17:118

174–75   "As he told his son": 19:258–59

175–76   "That the Colonies": 17:162–63

178–79   "Hillsborough, Franklin confided": 18:122

180   "Hutchinson relied on Bernard": 16:182

180   "'The longer I live'": quoted in Bernard Bailyn, *The Ordeal of Thomas Hutchinson* (Cambridge, Mass., 1974), 22

182   "It was implied": 13:170

182–84   "In a stormy interview": 18:15–16

184   "In a long letter to Cushing": 18:120–27

186   "They painted a picture": 20:571, 576, 550, 551, 550

187   "'For my own part'": 19:412

188   "Looking back on these years, John Adams": *The Works of John Adams, Second President of the United States,* ed. Charles Francis Adams (Boston, 1850–56), 10:282

190–91   "To the Governor of Massachusetts": Thomas Hutchinson, *History of the Colony and Province of Massachusetts Bay,* ed. Lawrence Shaw Mayo (Cambridge, Mass., 1936), 3:262

191   "The Boston declaration's wholesale indictment": *The Votes and Proceed-*

ings of the Freeholders and Other Inhabitants of the Town of Boston (London, 1773), 12, 25

191 "In England the solicitor general": *Benjamin Franklin's Letters to the Press, 1758–1775,* ed. Verner W. Crane (Chapel Hill, N.C., 1950), 225

191–92 "Perhaps he waited": 20:99

192–93 "'I know of no line'": *Speeches of the Governors of Massachusetts from 1765 to 1775 and the Answers . . . ,* (Boston, 1818), 340, 364

193 "Dartmouth, Franklin reported": 20:200–202

194 "While Franklin talked with Dartmouth": 20:172–73

194–95 "Dartmouth was able": quoted in Bailyn, *Ordeal of Thomas Hutchinson,* 219, 215, 218

195 "Cushing thought it strange": 20:124

195 "The king affirmed": 20:223–24

196 "'They have no idea'": 20:228

196–97 "He betrayed his uncertainty": 19:412

197 "Franklin . . . received the petition": 20:372, 373

198 "Franklin followed them with a succession": 20:381, 389–99, 402–3, 413–18

199 "On December 25": 20:515

201 "As soon as he heard of it": 21:76

202 "That was what the petition asked": *The Writings of Benjamin Franklin,* ed. Albert Henry Smyth (New York, 1905–7), 6:280

202–3 "Wedderburn scarcely mentioned the petition": 21:60–61, 56, 66–67

203 "The councillors rejected": 21:70

203 "But when Lee departed": 21:181

204 "After reporting the incident to Cushing": 21:93–94

204–5 "He almost found reason for hope": 21:109–11

206 "In response Franklin warned": 21:135

206 "In informing Cushing": 21:153

209 "Pownall thought": *Franklin's Letters to the Press,* 266n

209 "A friend in Philadelphia": 21:218–19

209 "Franklin answered calmly": 21:233

210 "But Patrick Henry": *Diary and Autobiography of John Adams,* 2:143

211 "At the very time that Galloway": 21:334

211 "A few months later": 21:509

211 "By the time": 21:509, 522

213 "As he reported to Charles Thomson": 21:476–77

214 "Chatham's view of the Congress": 21:569

215 "Along with Pitt": 21:571

215–16   "Chatham's motion": 21:577

217   "Turning toward Franklin": 21:581, 582

218–19   "Franklin's reaction": 21:582

220   "As he wrote to his friend Priestley": 22:92

221   "To Anthony Todd": 22:393

221–22   "He could send and receive greetings": 22:349

222   "On his way to a conference": 22:218

222–23   "On the same day": 22:217

224–25   "We get a glimpse": *Letters of Delegates to Congress*, ed. Paul H. Smith (Washington, D.C., 1976–2000), 1:567, 648–49

225   "Informing an English friend": 22:95

225–26   "Members may have learned": 22:217n

226   "Congress allowed him to read the articles": 22:121n

226   "The majority of the Congress": *Letters of Delegates to Congress*, 2:123

227   "At one point": 21:584

227–28   "As he put it privately": 22:185

228   "There is no record": 23:511

228   "He quickly dispatched a letter": 22:48

229   "Would Dumas find out": 22:288

230   "Early in March": 22:373

231   "The American troops": 22:432

232   "From his flagship": 22:484

233–34   "He began the letter": 22:519–21

235   "Franklin told Howe": 22:603

236   "At its first meeting": *Diary and Autobiography of John Adams*, 1:125

236   "And John Adams": 22:603; *Papers of Thomas Jefferson*, 1:325

237   "Now Britain would be excluded": 22:125

237   "Each state": 22:122

239   "In the initial debate": *Diary and Autobiography of John Adams*, 2:245

243   "People vied": 30:583; 26:24

246–49   "Franklin liked to flirt": 26:85, 605; 27:437; 28:175; 27:164

251   "When asked by a sour bystander": Oct. 3, 1783

254   "Franklin's response to Gillon's importunings": 30:36

257   "Franklin's view after three years": 32:134

257   "When Jefferson heard": *Papers of Thomas Jefferson*, 8:230

262   "In a letter to James Lovell": 27:135–42

265   "And Arthur Lee and Ralph Izard were now on hand": quoted in Irving Brant, *James Madison the Nationalist, 1780–1787* (Indianapolis, 1948), 64

266   "With his usual aplomb": 34:373

266–67   "On March 12": 34:443–48

267   "'I fancy,' he wrote": 35:399

269–70   "Laurens had left him with the impression": 35:214, 223

270   "He acknowledged that Franklin's seizure": 35:531

270   "The members could not say enough": *Letters of Delegates to Congress,* 18:18–19, 32, 37

272–73   "As he told Jan Ingenhousz": 23:310

273   "Franklin was so incensed": 29:592

273   "'I believe in my conscience'": 23:237

275–76   "'You have lost'": 25:562

277   "'You can always'": 35:550

278   "'In short,' he told his friend": July 10, 1782

278   "In the midst of war": 29:86

280   "As Adams later remembered": *Diary and Autobiography of John Adams,* 4:118–19

281   "From this point on": *Diary and Autobiography of John Adams,* 2:369

282   "Franklin attempted to placate": 33:141, 145

282   "In sending them to Congress": 33:162

283   "In instructing this group": 35:167

285   "At the outset": Apr. 6, 1782

285–86   "He assured Shelburne": Apr. 18, 1782

286   "He had drawn up a memorandum": "Journal of Peace Negotiations," May 9, 1782

288   "'I would rather,'": 33:355

289   "From Philadelphia, Robert Morris": Sept. 27, 1782; Nov. 8, 1782

289   "Morris told Franklin": Jan. 3, 1783

289   "Livingston thought": Jan. 6, 1783

289   "Franklin, reflecting on the attitude": Dec. 5, 1782

289–92   "Franklin's own thoughts": May 8, 1783

292   "He did succeed": May 7, 1784

293   "He was soon writing home": Massachusetts Historical Society, *Collections* (Boston, 1917), 73:193, 210

293   "James Madison reported drily": *The Papers of James Madison,* vol. 6, ed. William T. Hutchinson and William M. E. Rachal (Chicago, 1969), 221

293   "'I hear frequently'": Mar. 20, 1783

294   "He gave Livingston a summary": July 22, 1783

295   "Patronage": Apr. 4, 1783; July 18, 1784; Jan. 17, 1784; July 31, 1783

296   "Franklin's patronage could surely not be limited": June 27, 1784; c. 1783; Jan. 12, 1784

296   "The principal American minister": Mar. 11, 1784

296   "What bothered him most": July 27, 1783

296–97   "One of his best short essays": see Benjamin Franklin, *Writings*, ed. J. A. Leo Lemay (New York, 1987), 975–83

297   "With the peace treaty concluded": July 1783; Jan. 21, 1784

297   "'The French are an amiable people'": July 28, 1783

298   "Franklin was leaving": July 19, 1785

298   "It was late afternoon": July 12, 1785

304   "His observations of the toxic effects": July 31, 1786

305   "The success of any government": Sept. 17, 1787

305   "In England, Erasmus Darwin": May 29, 1787

305   "In Prague, François Steinsky": June 17, 1789

305   "From France he heard": Feb. 18, 1788; Aug. 20, 1787

307   "In Franklin's view": Nov. 3, 1789

307   "As early as 1750": 3:479

307–8   "In 1776": 22:533

308   "In 1785 he wrote Benjamin Vaughan": Mar. 11, 1785

308   "It would not have been an abuse": Dec. 25, 1783

309   "The objectives of war": Oct. 10, 1786; Sept. 20, 1787; Dec. 15, 1787

309–10   "'It is worth our while'": 22:630

311   "As early as the Albany Congress": 5:397

311   "His subsequent experiences": Feb. 12, 1784; Feb. 16, 1784; Aug. 19, 1784

311   "It was his conviction": June 23, 1789

311   "The article was number 36": *The Federal and State Constitutions*, ed. Francis Newton Thorpe (Washington, D.C., 1909), 5:3090

311–12   "The convention had listened politely": *The Records of the Federal Convention of 1787*, ed. Max Farrand (New Haven, 1911), 1:85

314   "Another wise man": Justice Learned Hand

Credits

Index

Page numbers in italics indicate illustrations.

Photo: Michael Marsland, Yale University

Edmund S. Morgan is Sterling Professor of History Emeritus at Yale University. He has written more than a dozen books, including *Inventing the People: The Rise of Popular Sovereignty in England and America,* which won the Bancroft Prize, and *American Slavery, American Freedom,* which won the Francis Parkman Prize and the Albert J. Beveridge Award. Cited as "one of America's most distinguished historians," Morgan was awarded the National Humanities Medal in 2000.